OXFORD MODERN LANGUAGES
AND LITERATURE MONOGRAPHS

APRÈS L'ÉLECTION

PARIS ACCLAME GUSTAVE HERVÉ

LE BANQUET ET LA CÉRÉMONIE DU COURONNEMENT

Dimanche soir, eut lieu, dans la grande salle des fêtes du Muséum, la cérémonie du couronnement du Grand Chef de la Tribu des Bourreurs de Crâne.

Cette cérémonie fut émotionnante au possible. Tout ce que Paris compte de personnalités marquantes y assistait.

même du grand bonheur qui vous échoit aujourd'hui. Je suis un vieux routier du bourrage de crâne. J'ai inventé, sinon le mot, du moins la chose vers 1891, autant qu'il m'en souvienne, à l'époque déjà bien oubliée, hélas ! du Canal de Panama. Mon cher enfant, je me sens aujourd'hui bien petit garçon à côté de vous. Vous avez fait mieux, beaucoup mieux depuis. Les Rus-

Hormis, bien entendu, les personnalités qui sont au front et celles qui n'avaient pas cru devoir manquer la traditionnelle ouverture de la pêche à la ligne.

Après que M. Maurice Barrès, très ému, eut déposé, sur le crâne du Père La Victoire, la fameuse couronne sur-

ses à cinq étapes de Berlin ? Le thermomètre des Dardanelles ? Qu'est-ce que tout cela à côté de votre effort quotidien, mon cher Hervé ?

Cette charmante improvisation fut malheureusement interrompue par le départ précipité de M. Maurice Barrès, qui

Le Canard Enchaîné, 20 June 1917 (see p. 36).
Reproduced by kind permission of *Le Canard Enchaîné*.
Photo: Bibliothèque Nationale

DEFEATISTS AND THEIR ENEMIES

POLITICAL INVECTIVE IN FRANCE 1914-1918

CATHERINE SLATER

OXFORD UNIVERSITY PRESS

1981

Oxford University Press, Walton Street, Oxford OX2 6DP
London Glasgow New York Toronto
Delhi Bombay Calcutta Madras Karachi
Kuala Lumpur Singapore Hong Kong Tokyo
Nairobi Dar es Salaam Cape Town
Melbourne Auckland

and associate companies in
Beirut Berlin Ibadan Mexico City

Published in the United States by
Oxford University Press, New York

© Catherine Slater 1981

British Library Cataloguing in Publication Data

Slater, Catherine
    Defeatists and their enemies. – (Oxford
    modern language and literature monographs)
    1. French language – Lexicology
    2. France – Politics and government – 1914–1940
    3. France – History – 1914–1940
    I. Title
    994.081'4   D363

ISBN 0-19-815776-2

Set by DMB (Typesetting) Oxford
Printed and bound in Great Britain
by Billing and Sons Ltd.
Guildford, London, Oxford, Worcester.

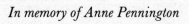

In memory of Anne Pennington

CONTENTS

CONTENTS

ACKNOWLEDGEMENTS

I have accumulated a considerable debt of gratitude over the years that this book has been in preparation. Particular thanks must go to Mrs D. R. Sutherland for early inspiration and encouragement; to the late Professor S. Ullmann for the constant support he gave me while supervising the thesis on which this study is based; to Professor R. Griffiths and Professor G. Price for their constructive criticisms of it. Professor R.-L. Wagner has been a most generous source of help throughout; I have benefited enormously from his expertise in political vocabulary, and from the backing of his team at the Centre de Lexicologie Politique de Saint-Cloud. Professor A. E. Pennington and Dr M. Slater read my manuscript at every stage and removed the worst obscurities from it: their unfailing interest and lucidity made even the most routine tasks enjoyable.

CONVENTIONS

Standard abbreviations are used to refer to the most commonly cited dictionaries. Full references are given in the Bibliography under the short title.

All italics in source material are those of the author of the quotation, unless otherwise indicated.

Translations from Russian are my own, unless otherwise indicated.

INTRODUCTION

> Durant toute la guerre, les hommes politiques français
> ont été beaucoup plus préoccupés de leurs rivalités
> féroces que des combats contre l'Allemagne. L'"Exter-
> minisme" des uns, le "Défaitisme" des autres, n'est
> qu'un masque. L'ennemi, pour eux, c'est d'abord le
> rival.
>
> ROMAIN ROLLAND[1]

The vocabulary used in 1914-18 by the various ideological factions
within France to refer to one another's activities is as hermetic at
times as trench slang, and often more insidious in that its pitfalls
are unexpected. A modern reader might well pause to wonder, for
instance, what H. Bérenger is alluding to when he writes:

> Aucun défaitisme de bavards, aucun neutralisme de videurs de crânes,
> aucun boloïsme d'embochés ne détourneront désormais nos armées de
> la tâche terrible et sacrée. (*Paris-Midi*, 26 Oct. 1917)

Some of this jargon has filtered into memoirs, histories of the war,
and literary works such as Proust's *Temps retrouvé*, and is thus in
a certain sense familiar; yet very little detail is known of how it
functioned at the time. The information that can be gleaned from
dictionaries and specialized studies about the chief neologisms of
the period—*défaitiste* and *jusqu'auboutiste* being the most note-
worthy—is fragmentary and often inaccurate.[2] Terms like *embusqué*
and *bourrage de crânes*, which originated or were popularized in the
trenches, have been extensively studied in treatises on slang,[3] but

---

[1] *Journal des années de guerre 1914-1919. Notes et documents pour servir à
l'histoire morale de l'Europe de ce temps*, Paris, 1952, p. 1395.

[2] For a useful list of First World War neologisms classified according to sources,
see G. Gaillard, "Langue et Guerre", *Revue de philologie française*, xxx 1 (1917),
19-32.

[3] See A. Dauzat, *L'Argot de la guerre*, Paris, 1918 (revised edn., 1919); F. Déchelette, *L'Argot des poilus. Dictionnaire humoristique et philologique du langage des
soldats de la Grande Guerre de 1914*, Paris, 1918; G. Esnault, *Le Poilu tel qu'il se
parle. Dictionnaire des termes populaires récents et neufs employés aux armées en
1914-1918 étudiés dans leur étymologie, leur développement et leur usage*, Paris,
1919; L. Sainéan, *L'Argot des tranchées*, Paris, 1915.

their penetration into common usage through the intermediary of journalists' polemics has never been thoroughly investigated.

The main purpose of this book is to document the early history of the neologism *défaitiste/défaitisme*. Although historians have been interested in defeatism as a political concept,[4] much confusion has arisen through lack of information about when the French words *défaitiste/défaitisme* came into circulation and how they were used initially. Statements like

> The *Action Française* had been squabbling ever since the war [i.e. since 1914] with several left-wing publications which it considered too defeatist ...[5]

may well lead one to suppose that *défaitiste* was current in French early on in the war, whereas it was not popularized until the summer of 1917. As regards the use of *défaitisme* in the following:

> Le Gouvernement s'était installé à Bordeaux [en Septembre 1914] dans une atmosphère de désordre et de défaitisme[6]

it is a doubly unfortunate anachronism: readers who are aware that this word is a First World War coinage are likely to assume not only that it was current in 1914 but also that it entered the language with its modern meaning.

Understanding who les *défaitistes* were and what the accusation of *défaitisme* conveyed to a Frenchman in 1917 involves taking a wider look at other figures from the political spectrum in France. Zealous *patriotes were* known to their enemies on the Left as *jusqu'au-boutistes* from 1915 onwards. Although only a marginal acquisition to the French language, this term—like *défaitiste*—has origins which are intriguing to anyone concerned, as F. Brunot put it, to "suivre les contrecoups des événements sur le lexique".[7] The terminology which characterizes polemical attacks on left- and right-wing extremists needs to be looked at as a whole: some of the commonest

---

[4] See in particular the work of A. Kupferman, e.g. "L'Opinion française et le défaitisme pendant la Grande Guerre", *Relations Internationales*, 1974(2), 91-100, and "Les campagnes défaitistes en France et en Italie: 1914-17", in *La France et l'Italie pendant la première guerre mondiale. Actes du colloque tenu à l'Université des Sciences Sociales de Grenoble en septembre 1973*, Grenoble, 1976, pp. 246-59.

[5] E. J. Weber, *Action Française. Royalism and Reaction in Twentieth Century France*, Stanford, 1962, p. 102.

[6] G. Bonnefous, *Histoire politique de la Troisième République*, vol. ii, *La Grande Guerre (1914-1918)*, 2nd edn., Paris, 1967, p. 54.

[7] *Histoire de la langue française des origines à 1900*, vol. ix. 2, Paris, 1943, p. xi.

tricks of journalistic rhetoric consist of juxtaposing near-synonyms
for emphasis, supplying new definitions for important words, contrasting one set of terms with another. Analysis of the connections
established by different writers between *défaitisme, pacifisme, antimilitarisme*, etc. and *jusqu'auboutisme, nationalisme, cléricalisme*,
etc. is crucial to the interpretation of First World War coinages; it
also contributes a further stage in the history of other terms which
already featured prominently in French political vocabulary.

Before *les défaitistes* and *les jusqu'auboutistes* can be introduced,
the scene needs to be set with a parade of bogeys whom all right-
thinking journalists agreed to hunt out. Part One of this book deals
with the terminology which developed at the beginning of the war
when patriotic enthusiasm was still fresh. On 4 August 1914, at
a historic session of the *Assemblée Nationale*, a truce known as
L'Union Sacrée was declared which called for an end to internal
dissension between Left and Right: all pre-war wrangling was to
cease in the interests of *la défense nationale*. Predictably, this remained a pious hope, for it soon became only too apparent that
people of different persuasions held sharply opposing views on the
aims of the war against Germany and the manner in which it should
be conducted. Old feuds were resuscitated and polemics began to
rage with as much fury as before.

Although it was inevitable that time-honoured divisions would
not remain concealed for long, *l'Union Sacrée* did survive super-
ficially in the form of a linguistic pact: by common consent, all
good *patriotes* set themselves to pursue a number of public enemies—
les embusqués, les bourreurs de crânes, etc. The identification of
these various categories of individuals became a matter of hot controversy, with agreement over terminology manifesting itself para-
doxically in squabbles over the "correct" assignment of a shared
set of evaluative labels.[8] Words such as these, which are exploited
by Left and Right in a broadly similar manner, might be called
symmetrical terms, as opposed to the strongly polarized ones like
défaitiste, jusqu'auboutiste, nationaliste, etc., which belong more
narrowly to the vocabularies of particular groups and denote some
of the specific beliefs and activities that they associate with their

[8] Cf. R. A. Waldron, *Sense and Sense Development*, London, 1967, p. 154: "The
evaluative element of meaning is ... a fixed point round which other criteria are
disposed, differently by different people, in ways which will further their own arguments."

ideological opponents.[9] These latter terms are discussed in Parts
Two and Three. It should be stressed that this division is not abso-
lute, but simply reflects the main patterns observable in usage. For
instance, *patriote* will be classed as a symmetrical term, although
one does find individuals like R. Rolland or M. Almereyda, the
editor of *Le Bonnet Rouge*, who make a show of rejecting the
accepted ideal; similarly, *nationaliste* will be treated as a key term
of abuse specific to the vocabulary of the Left, in spite of the fact
that it is also a straightforward appellation which men of the extreme
Right use to refer to themselves. What counts is not merely that a
term should be used by each side, but that it should be used sym-
metrically, fulfilling the same function for Right and Left alike—
either as a term of abuse in the language of both, or as a term of
approbation.

The vocabulary of First World War polemics cannot be examined
without constant reference to historical events. The picture of
civilian life which emerges from this study could be thought of as
complementary to the one offered by G. Guilleminault in his *France
de la Madelon, 1914-18. Le roman vrai de l'arrière.* The questions
which interest him:

> Mais comment vivaient les civils, que pensaient-ils, quelle communion les
> unissait à ceux du front, quelles répercussions avaient sur eux les vicissi-
> tudes de la guerre?[10]

can be answered in part by considering how public opinion was
manipulated through the emotive use of language[11] and how, con-
versely, the vocabulary of French adapted to meet the new demands
put upon it. Much of the unique atmosphere of a period is conjured
up in the words and clichés which everyone used or reacted against.

The importance of the press at a time when no other mass media
existed scarcely needs emphasizing. The German-run *Gazette des*

---

[9] Cf. M. Tournier, "Éléments pour l'étude quantitative d'une journée de 48",
Cahiers de Lexicologie, xiv (1969), 95: "En avril 48, des mots ont choisi leur camp,
et les phrases en grincent. Une part du lexique se trie, l'autre sert encore au jeu de
la confusion."

[10] Paris, 1965, p. 8.

[11] Cf. F. Brunot's comment on the upheavals of the French Revolution: "Combien
de déformations du jugement furent dues au cliquetis des mots, nous ne le saurons
jamais, mais il est certain que, collectives ou individuelles, elles furent extrêmement
nombreuses" (*Histoire de la langue française*, vol. ix. 2, p. 654).

Ardennes speaks of "cette grande 'faiseuse d'opinion' qu'est la presse parisienne",[12] and G. Hervé tells his readers:

> Les journaux aujourd'hui sont devenus un peu ce qu'étaient les sorciers au bon vieux temps, ce que furent plus tard les prêtres: des directeurs de consciences.
> Chacun, le matin, lit son journal de prédilection, avidement, cherchant un motif d'espérer. C'est sa nourriture spirituelle.
> (*La Guerre Sociale*, 15 Oct. 1914)

The material that was "fed" to the public each morning was far from edifying; nevertheless, the daily wrangling between journalists offers a rewarding field in which to observe the immediate repercussions of the war on the ordinary language of the time (as distinct from what ultimately filters into literary usage).

I have quoted extensively from the press in attempting to trace the fortunes of characteristic words and slogans. This material is not readily accessible, and it is essential to provide sufficient context to elucidate meanings.[13] My principal sources are newspapers with a strong ideological bias. On the whole, *la grande presse* remained faithful to the *Union Sacrée* pact and avoided the kind of polemics which gave currency to *défaitisme, jusqu'auboutisme*, etc.[14] I have also drawn on the diaries of people who lived through the war and took part in or commented upon the heated debates of the day.[15]

The study of polemical vocabulary does not call for abstruse linguistic techniques. "Soap-box political terminology", as T. D. Weldon calls it,[16] is notoriously unstable. Words from this sphere "have a descriptive function which is attended by ambiguity and vagueness, *requiring a particularly detailed study of linguistic flexibility*".[17] P. Guiraud says of them:

> ... non seulement leur valeur évolue, mais personne n'est d'accord sur leur contenu référentiel; véritables mots ivres qui ont cassé leurs amarres et dérivent à l'aventure.[18]

[12] Quoted by L. Marchand, *L'Offensive morale des Allemands en France pendant la guerre. L'assaut de l'âme française*, Paris, 1920, p. 79.
[13] Appendix II reproduces five typical articles in full.
[14] Appendix III lists all the periodical publications I have used.
[15] Memoirs written after the event do not provide reliable evidence for the lexicologist.
[16] *States and Morals*, London, 1962 reissue, p. 219.
[17] C. L. Stevenson, *Ethics and Language*, New Haven-London, 1944, p. 36 (my italics).
[18] *La Sémantique*, Paris, 1955, p. 93.

Sometimes individual journalists use the same terms in significantly different ways, resisting one another's influence; sometimes a leading figure succeeds in imposing his own personal usage on his colleagues and the public at large in the space of a few weeks as the result of a skilfully conducted press campaign. The most satisfactory way to chart these fluctuations seems to me to be chronologically, observing linguistic developments alongside events on the political front.

Words are not, of course, direct "témoins de l'histoire".[19] To treat them as such gives too much weight to their sociological significance at the expense of more strictly linguistic factors.[20] At the other extreme, there is the risk that excessive formalization will obliterate some of the most interesting nuances of usage.[21] It would be singularly unproductive to divorce the catchwords of political discourse from the specific contexts in which they functioned:

> Nous ne reconnaissons pour utiles et féconds en lexicologie comme en lexicographie que des travaux portant sur les mots *en situation* si l'on peut dire, dans un système donné, à une époque donnée, dans tous les emplois dont les textes contemporains fournissent les exemples.[22]

---

[19] Cf. F. Brunot, *Les Mots témoins de l'histoire*, Paris, 1928. The historico-lexical parallel needs interpreting with caution; see T. E. Hope, "Loan-words as Cultural and Lexical Symbols", *Archivum Linguisticum*, xiv (1962), 111-21, and xv (1963), 29-42; id., *Lexical Borrowing in the Romance Languages*, Oxford, 1971, pp. x-xii; J. Dubois, *Le Vocabulaire politique et social en France de 1869 à 1972*, Paris, 1962, p. 195.

[20] This criticism is often levelled at G. Matoré's *Méthode en lexicologie. Domaine français* (Paris, 1953); see N.C.W. Spence, "Linguistic Fields, Conceptual Systems and the *Weltbild*", *Transactions of the Philological Society*, 1961, 101 ff. R.-L. Wagner points out that the adoption of the term *coke* into French had no linguistic repercussions, whereas the new meaning acquired by *industrie* enabled it to collocate with a different set of terms, and gave rise to the derivative *industriel*; see *Les Vocabulaires français*, vol. ii, Paris, 1970, pp. 29-30.

[21] Various studies of French political vocabulary have been made using techniques of simple transformational grammar to reduce the utterances of the corpus to a number of basic types. Examples of such work can be found in *Cahiers de Lexicologie*, xv (1969); *Languages*, 23: *Le Discours politique* (1971); *Langue Française*, 9: *Linguistique et société* (1971). For the application of computer methods to the study of political vocabulary, see M. Tournier, "Le Centre de recherche de lexicologie politique de l'E.N.S. de Saint-Cloud", *Langue Française*, 2: *Le Lexique* (1969), 82-6; *Travaux de lexicométrie et de lexicologie politique. Bulletin du laboratoire d'étude des textes politiques français*, i-iii (1976-8), continued as *Mots. Mots, Ordinateurs, Textes, Sociétés*, i (1980).

[22] R.-L. Wagner, *Les Vocabulaires français*, vol. i, Paris, 1967, p. 13.

Part One

L'UNION SACRÉE

1.1 *Le patriotisme*

> Voici que s'établit un poncif nouveau, une psychologie
> conventionnelle du patriote, hors quoi il ne sera plus
> possible d'être "honnête homme".
>
> ANDRÉ GIDE[1]

In time of war, more so perhaps than at any other moment, it is to
be expected that terms like *patrie/patriote/patriotisme* will be very
freely used. But whereas most people would agree that their *amour
de la patrie* consists fundamentally in a desire to further its interests,
common ground ends there, for it is clear that there is no limit to
the ways in which these interests can be understood. Hence it is of
little help to the lexicologist to attempt to establish an exhaustive
list of definitions of the form: A, B, C ... are patriotic actions,
attitudes, etc.; these are potentially as diverse as the individuals
from whose usage they are drawn.[2] None the less, the actual role of
what C. L. Stevenson has called "persuasive definitions" is a crucial
one in polemical language: "To choose a definition is to plead a
cause, so long as the word defined is strongly emotive... Disagree-
ment in attitude may be debated over the dictionary."[3] It is because
discussion of opinions and attitudes is so often conducted as a
linguistic exercise involving explicit comments on the relationship

---

[1] *Journal 1889-1939*, Paris, 1939, p. 463 (15 Aug. 1914).

[2] The terms *patriotisme* etc. are too vague to be amenable to distributional treatment of the kind attempted by G. Provost for *socialiste/socialisme*, see "Approche
du discours politique: *socialisme* et *socialiste* chez Jaurès", *Langages*, 13: *L'Analyse
du discours* (1969), 51-68.

[3] *Ethics and Language*, p. 210. He proceeds to define the aim of a "persuasive
definition" as "to alter the descriptive meaning of the term, usually by giving it
greater precision within the boundaries of its customary vagueness; but the definition
does *not* make any substantial change in the term's emotive meaning. And the definition is used, consciously or unconsciously, in an effort to secure, by this interplay
between emotive and descriptive meaning, a redirection of people's attitudes."

between one term and another that definitions of this kind are of particular significance.

The breadth of application of *patriote* and *patriotisme* seems to have been a characteristic feature since their early days in political vocabulary. F. Brunot notes that:

> Necker, dès 1784, s'effrayait, non sans raison, de cette absorption de tout l'être moral dans une vertu mal définie, et qui pouvait s'entendre de tant de manières.[4]

Writers readily acknowledged how uninformative these terms were in 1914-18. Ch. Maurras notes:

> Le raisonnement se réduit aux termes de celui que nous avons dû tenir à tant de radicaux patriotes, de patriotes anarchistes et socialistes entre 1898 et 1900: "Votre patriotisme n'est pas douteux, nous ne doutons pas de l'attachement à la patrie commune, mais la question est de savoir si vous avez raison ou si vous vous trompez de moyens pour la maintenir."
>
> (*L'Action Française*, 15 Mar. 1916)

On the other hand, he believed that a nation at war must be united by common objectives which take precedence over long-term differences of ideology:

> Le patriotisme? Mais on peut viser très patriotiquement les objets les plus différents. La guerre exclut ce doute. Son unité est réelle, concrète, matérielle ... (*L'Action Française*, 19 Apr. 1916)

M. Barrès expresses a similar sentiment:

> On a vu au Parlement, dans les premières journées de la guerre, on voit chaque jour à l'armée un patriotisme unanime et brûlant qui se nuance des convictions de chacun, mais n'a qu'une flamme.
>
> (*L'Écho de Paris*, 7 Sept. 1917)

So does the socialist E. Vaillant:

> ... la communion patriotique et républicaine de tous les Français dans une même volonté de combattre et de vaincre, dans un même serment,

---

[4] *Histoire de la langue française*, vol. ix. 2, p. 663. *Patriote*, first attested with its modern meaning in 1562, became widespread in the eighteenth century under English influence. *Patriotisme* and *patriotique*, both English borrowings, date from 1749 and 1750 respectively; see D. Fletcher, "The Emergence of *Patriotisme*", *Semasia*, 4 (1977), 1-14; F. Mackenzie, *Les Relations de l'Angleterre et de la France d'après le vocabulaire*, vol. i, Paris, 1939, pp. 119 and 173. On the later use of these terms, see J. Dubois, *Le Vocabulaire politique et social*, pp. 65, 91, and 368-9; T. J. Field, "The Concept of La Patrie in French Writing 1898-1914", unpublished doctoral thesis submitted to the University of Wales (Aberystwyth), 1972.

à chaque fois renouvelé, de lutter jusqu'au salut, jusqu'à la victoire.
(*Le Bonnet Rouge*, 11 July 1915)

Even G. Hervé, notorious for his openly professed *antipatriotisme* before the war,[5] rallied to his country's call with proclamations like the following:

Aujourd'hui comme en 1792, aujourd'hui comme au temps des "guerres à outrance" qui firent la Commune, notre patriotisme révolutionnaire serait, le cas échéant, le grand ressort et la suprême sauvegarde de la patrie en danger. (*La Guerre Sociale*, 30 July 1914)

—or this, a month later:

Nous sommes la garde républicaine, disciplinée, fanatique, patriotique.[6]

Soon, however (as will be seen in the case of *l'Union Sacrée*), the ideal state of affairs reflected or wished for in such pronouncements gave way to one in which voices of protest were heard from the Left about "des journaux agressifs qui manient le patriotisme comme une cravache" (*La Gazette des Ardennes*, 22 Mar. 1916);[7] J. Ernest-Charles writes:

Nous penchons à croire que Barrès accapare les patriotes et le patriotisme d'une façon un peu désobligeante pour le commun des citoyens français.
(*Le Pays*, 5 Apr. 1918)

Similar reservations come from the pen of H. Barbusse:

Du patriotisme, qui est respectable, à condition de rester dans le domaine sentimental et artistique ... ils font une conception utopique et non viable, en déséquilibre dans le monde, une espèce de cancer qui absorbe toutes les forces vives ... et qui, contagieux, aboutit soit aux crises de la guerre, soit à l'épuisement et à l'asphyxie de la paix armée.[8]

R. Rolland observes with sorrow "tous les sacrifices, les violences, et l'aveuglement que [l'idéal patriotique] implique".[9] As one who believed passionately that "au-dessus des droits [de la patrie] sont ceux de l'esprit humain",[10] and declared that "je n'ai plus d'autre

[5] See Appendix I.
[6] Quoted by R. Rolland, *Journal*, p. 46 (31 Aug. 1914).
[7] Quoted by L. Marchand, *L'Offensive morale*, p. 79.
[8] *Le Feu*, Paris, 1916; 1965 edn., p. 284.
[9] *Journal*, p. 59 (24 Sept. 1914).
[10] *L'Esprit libre. Au-dessus de la mêlée*, Paris, 1953, p. 70 (Sept. 1914).

patrie que le monde",[11] his hope was to persuade people to substitute for narrow patriotism what he called "le panhumanisme"[12] and "l'Internationale de l'esprit".[13] This open rejection of the prevalent ethic was one of the chief causes of the hatred which he incurred throughout the war.

The terms *patrie* and *humanité* are frequently discussed in conjunction with one another at this period—a legacy from the squabbles of the pre-war years.[14] Men of the Left often take trouble to refute the accusation made by their adversaries that they have sacrificed patriotism in the interests of a humanitarian ideal. J. M. Renaitour is critical of

> ... ces mots d'Albert Guinon: "Pendant une guerre, tout ce qu'on donne d'amour à l'Humanité, on le vole à la Patrie." Eh bien, cela est une opinion, on peut en avoir une autre ... Il est un patriotisme plus large que celui-là. (*Le Bonnet Rouge*, 18 July 1915)

La Tranchée Républicaine expresses the desire "de servir à la fois la Patrie et l'Humanité" (31 May 1917), and P. Boulat defends a similar position:

> ### Patrie et Humanité
> On s'appliqua à calomnier cet autre idéal, à le flétrir et à le ridiculiser sous le nom d'humanitarisme ...[15] Cependant, est-ce à dire que patriotisme et humanitarisme soient contradictoires? ... Nullement. Un patriotisme sincère et clairvoyant ne suppose pas la haine de l'étranger ni l'esprit de conquêtes. (*Le Pays*, 2 Dec. 1917)

The deliberate contrasting of *le patriotisme* and *l'internationalisme* is also a well-established feature of polemics.[16] R. Rolland explains the extreme left-wing position as follows:

[11] *Journal*, p. 156 (Dec. 1914).
[12] See below, 3.5, p. 139.
[13] *L'Esprit libre. Les précurseurs*, p. 328.
[14] J. Dubois supplies evidence of the opposition *Patrie/Humanité* in socialist vocabulary in 1871; see *Le Vocabulaire politique et social*, p. 65, and quotations 3660 and 3661.
[15] Both *humanitarisme* and *humanitairerie* are found in 1871 (ibid., p. 317). Cf. G. Goyau, *L'Idée de patrie et l'humanitarisme*, Paris, 1902. The form *humanitairerie* is used by Maurras in *L'Action Française* of 24 Apr. 1916: "Petrograde, atteint d'humanitairerie aiguë ..."
[16] See Ch. Dumont, *Patrie et internationalisme*, Bourges, 1894. In 1912 Hervé wrote: "Peut-être n'était-il pas indispensable de nous affubler de l'étiquette d'antipatriotes, alors que nous avions sous la main le mot suffisamment explicite d'internationalistes" (*Mes Crimes*, Paris, 1912, p. 16). For the attitude of the French Left

Birukoff, l'ami de Tolstoï ... me fait une profession de foi internationaliste ... Il combat aussi bien l'idée de patrie que l'institution de la propriété
privée foncière ... Le patriotisme lui semble une doctrine semée et cultivée
par les dirigeants intéressés.[17]

With typical verbal dexterity, G. Clemenceau analyses the stand
taken by the French socialists at the outbreak of the war:

Un gouvernement de guerre *nationale* les appela à se *désinternationaliser*
pour prendre la direction de la lutte franco-allemande,—où se dévelop-
paient des sentiments directement contraires à tous ceux qu'ils avaient
prêchés—cela, non sans laisser la porte ouverte à la *réinternationalisation*
de l'avenir. Enfantine rouerie, où les impérieuses exigences du patriotisme
français devaient honorablement primer, chez nos révolutionnaires,
toute ritualité dogmatique à l'autel (voilé pour un temps) de la société
internationale. (*L'Homme Enchaîné*, 18 Feb. 1915)

Subsequent events were to prove him right.[18] Meanwhile, many
socialists were content to pay lip-service to the patriotic ideal. Ch.
Albert writes:

Si le prolétaire a, comme tout le monde, une patrie et, comme tout le
monde, des devoirs envers elle, il a—surtout quand il se dit socialiste et
internationaliste—un devoir plus haut encore: celui de résister de toutes
ses forces, par tous le moyens, aux gens qui, sous prétexte de patriotisme,
jettent le pays dans des entreprises de violence, d'injustice et de ruine.
(*La Bataille*, 25 Jan. 1916)

Others were sufficiently attached to this ideal, either genuinely or
for reasons of strategy, to take up arms in defence of their own
version of it. From H. Barbusse:

Ceux qui sont de l'autre côté—je ne parle pas seulement de l'autre côté
des frontières—te disputeront le droit de dire que tu aimes la France. Ils
prétendent monopoliser le patriotisme au profit de leur programme
étroit, borné, utopique et anarchique.[19]

La Gazette des Ardennes highlights the dichotomy by opposing *vrai*
to *pseudo-*:

Le *vrai* patriotisme, celui qu'incarne l'armée, la "grande muette", n'a

---

towards Germany before August 1914, see A. Kriegel and J.-J. Becker, *1914. La
Guerre et le mouvement ouvrier français*, Paris, 1964; J. Touchard, *La Gauche en
France depuis 1900*, Paris, 1977.

[17] *Journal*, pp. 112-13 (4 Nov. 1914).
[18] For discussion of the Zimmerwald movement, see below, 2.4, pp. 57-8.
[19] *Paroles d'un combattant. Articles et discours (1917-1920)*, Paris, s.a., p. 20
(June 1917).

rien de commun avec ce pseudo-patriotisme étroit, haineux et menteur
tel que le prêche la politique d'affaires ... (12 Sept. 1915)[20]

The special use made of the terms *patriote/patriotisme*, etc., in
pejorative reference to the Right—in particular, their close association with words like *chauvin* and *nationaliste*—are examined
later.[21] It is significant that excessive and distorted patriotic zeal
is not something for which the Right take their ideological opponents to task; *patriotisme*, then, is used firstly by both sides to
cover a wide spectrum of virtues having no more in common than
that they are all viewed as in some way beneficial to the nation, and
secondly, in abusive language, to imply a specific set of odious
beliefs and attitudes attributed to the Right by the Left.

1.2   *L'Union Sacrée*

This expression originated in a message from President Poincaré
to the nation, read out by Viviani in the *Assemblée Nationale* on
4 August 1914. The key passage of the proclamation was reproduced
by *Le Matin* on the following day:

> La France sera héroïquement défendue par tous ses fils, dont rien ne
> brisera devant l'ennemi l'union sacrée, et qui sont aujourd'hui frater-
> nellement assemblés dans une même indignation contre l'agresseur et
> dans une même foi patriotique.

Patriotic fervour was running high, and the pages of the press shone
with lyrical accounts of the historic *séance*. According to *L'Illustration*:

> Les pères conscrits de Rome, en des circonstances analogues, ne mon-
> trèrent pas plus de sereine dignité. Tous les cœurs battant à l'unisson
> d'un ardent amour pour la patrie, affermis par une pleine confiance dans
> ses destinées ... (15 Aug. 1914)

Under the heading, "Le jour sacré", M. Barrés writes in *L'Écho de
Paris*:

> Elle dépasse nos espérances, cette prodigieuse union de nos esprits et de
> nos cœurs. (5 Aug. 1914)

---

[20] Quoted by L. Marchand, *L'Offensive morale*, pp. 75-6. Cf. C. L. Stevenson,
Ethics and Language, p. 214: " 'True', in such contexts, is obviously not used literally.
Since people usually accept what they consider true, 'true' comes to have the persuasive force of 'to be accepted'."
[21] See below, 3.4.

Full weight is given to the adjective *sacré*; H. Lavedan describes the procession of the deputies to their seats as the beginning of a rite:

> Cette entrée lourde, ordonnée, solide, cette espèce de liturgie muette, communique à la scène un incroyable aspect de cérémonie religieuse, sous ce jour gris et austère d'église, dans cette enceinte où les colonnes sont rangées circulairement, en forme de chœur ainsi que dans un temple ... (*L'Illustration*, 15 Aug. 1914)

Ch. Maurras goes a step further, and revives the etymological link between *sacré* and the verb *sacrer*:

> On a sacré l'union afin qu'elle fasse la force qui fera la victoire.
> (*L'Action Française*, 4 Oct. 1914)

National unity manifested itself immediately in the readiness of the French socialists to vote in the necessary war budget. Although their party congress had passed a resolution in July 1914 to call a general strike in the event of war, this came to nothing when Jaurès its initiator was assassinated and the German socialists rallied round the Kaiser. Even before *l'union sacrée* was formally declared, the Minister of the Interior, Malvy, had decided not to arrest the suspects listed in the notorious *Carnet B*.[1] Two French socialists, M. Sembat and J. Guesde, entered the government on 26 August 1914. For a time, internal polemics seemed to have been silenced in this special display of patriotism; journalists praised *l'union sacrée* in a common language of admiration and respect. These lines from *Le Bonnet Rouge* would not have been out of place in *L'Illustration* or *L'Écho de Paris*:

> Quelle portée n'a donc pas ce grand fait nouveau, "l'union sacrée", ce grand acte de piété nationale scellé dans le sang des plus nobles enfants de la France! (9 Apr. 1915)

By general consent the war was presented to the public as "La guerre sainte de la civilisation contre la Barbarie" (headline in *Le Matin*, 4 Aug. 1914), or "La grande croisade des civilisés" (headline in *Le Bonnet Rouge*, 25 Nov. 1914).[2]

---

[1] See below, Appendix I, *M. Almereyda;* and A. Kriegel and J.-J. Becker, *1914*, p. 191 n. 36.

[2] The influx of Christian terminology into the vocabulary of politics dates from the Revolution; see F. Brunot, *Histoire de la langue française*, vol. ix. 2, pp. 623-9.

The phrase *union sacrée* was not merely used as a reminder of the pact that had been made on 4 August; it soon acquired vigour of its own as a slogan exhorting people to whatever forms of action a particular individual deemed necessary for the good of the country.[3] G. Clemenceau noted that there were "des ministres prêcheurs d'union sacrée à outrance" (*L'Homme Enchaîné*, 14 Sept. 1915)—a description applicable to a good many journalists. Always quick to make the most of a catch-phrase, L. Daudet writes:

> L'union sacrée, dont il est tant question, ne doit pas être seulement statique, comme elle l'est à peu près partout maintenant. L'union sacrée doit être encore dynamique, féconde en résolutions belliqueuses et immédiates, comme nous essayons de la mener ici.
> (*L'Action Française*, 28 Jan. 1915)

The expression "mener l'union sacrée" used by Daudet would seem to provide linguistic evidence of the status of *union sacrée* as a slogan, as does the variant "pratiquer l'union sacrée" exemplified in these lines from G. Hervé:

> Je crois Léon Daudet et Charles Maurras, malgré leur fanatisme royaliste, trop bons patriotes pour déchaîner une guerre civile en France alors que les Prussiens sont encore à Laon ... Leur attitude patriotique depuis le début de la guerre, malgré leur façon singulière parfois de pratiquer l'union sacrée, interdit à qui que ce soit de sensé de croire à un complot royaliste. (*La Victoire*, 29 Oct. 1917)

In the colourful language characteristic of him, H. Bérenger emphasizes a point he wishes to make by punning on the two meanings of the adjective *sacré:*

> Nous voulons une union sacrée qui ne soit plus une abstention sacrée, mais une sacrée action digne enfin de l'énergie de nos soldats dans les tranchées et de nos ouvriers dans les usines. (*Paris-Midi*, 28 Oct. 1915)

The following year a colleague of his on the same paper, A. de Monzie, was to take up Bérenger's suggestion and coin a new slogan, turning *sacrée action* into *action sacrée* to match *union sacrée:*

> L'union sacrée a fait son plein pendant deux ans. Je crois pouvoir ajouter qu'elle a fait son temps ... Il faut trouver autre chose. Autre chose? Une

---

[3] In the early months of the war, one finds a number of variants of the term *union sacrée: Le Bonnet Rouge* speaks of "l'union Nationale" [*sic*] (4 Feb. 1915), and G. Hervé mentions "le grand vent de la *Concorde nationale*" (*La Guerre Sociale*, 27 Oct. 1914). He uses this expression fairly consistently until about June 1915, when it gives way to *union sacrée*.

autre formule? C'est tout trouvé. Ne parlons pas d'union sacrée. Parlons
d'action sacrée ... Jusqu'ici il s'agissait d'abdiquer les états d'âme anciens.
Maintenant il s'agit de créer un état d'esprit nouveau.[4]

(*Paris-Midi*, 19 Nov. 1916)

Now the idea that there should be complete agreement among all
parties about the conduct of the war was clearly utopian, and left-
wing writers became increasingly suspicious of a phrase which they
thought was being flourished to silence their legitimate criticisms.
A number of them take pains to point out the danger. *L'Humanité*
notes:

Beaucoup de gens entendent par ''l'union sacrée'' qu'on pensera désormais comme eux ou qu'au moins, dans la pratique, on sera dans l'obliga-
tion d'agir comme si l'on était en tout de leur avis. Non seulement ce n'est
pas le sens de cette formule, mais c'en est même le contraire. (3 Oct. 1915)

Ch. Albert dots the *i*s and crosses the *t*s:

L'union sacrée est un contrat. Comme tout contrat, celui-ci a un objet et
une durée déterminée. Il s'agit de repousser l'envahisseur et de le battre,
mais rien de plus. (*La Bataille*, 8 Jan. 1916)

Some people regard *l'union sacrée* as mere talk, and do not scruple
to say so. G. Clemenceau, for instance, writes:

On a parlé, on parle, à tous moments de ''l'union sacrée''. Précisément
parce que nul n'y pourrait contredire, le thème est devenu trop facile aux
littérateurs du patriotisme, principalement soucieux de *phraséologiser*.

(*L'Homme Enchaîné*, 8 July 1915)

Le Bonnet Rouge strikes a more sinister note:

On peut même dire que l'union sacrée n'est que mots. Ou, plutôt, une
vaine formule à laquelle nos adversaires ne manquent jamais d'avoir
recours pour tenter de couvrir notre voix, afin de mieux faire entendre la
leur. (13 July 1916)

If one compares this with the lines quoted earlier from the same
paper, it gives some measure of how radically its ideological position
had shifted since the first months of the war.[5]

As old quarrels were revived between the Right and the Left,
accusations of violating *l'union sacrée* provided a further charge to

[4] A publication entitled *L'Action Sacrée. Organe de culture patriotique en temps
de guerre* had appeared in Marseille in the early months of 1916.

[5] For the political evolution of *Le Bonnet Rouge*, see below, 2.7, pp. 71-3.

level at the adversary. G. Hervé notes wryly that there are no limits
to the things that *l'union sacrée* can be made to justify; he comments,
for instance, on:

> L'affichage d'un manifeste burlesque où la propagande antialcoolique
> est qualifiée d'antipatriotique ... et où la suppression de l'absinthe est
> condamnée au nom de l'hygiène, de l'union sacrée et du patriotisme!
>
> (*La Victoire*, 3 Feb. 1916)

Le Bonnet Rouge makes regular use of the *union sacrée* slogan in
its important anticlerical campaign,[6] and *L'Humanité* likewise
expatiates on the misdeeds of *la calotte* under the heading "Sacrée
Union" (3 Nov. 1915)—with the pun intended in this case to convey
cynicism about the validity of the *union sacrée* pact. The message
becomes explicit when *Le Bonnet Rouge* calls Ch. Maurras "un
publiciste de sacrée désunion" (5 Apr. 1916), or *Le Pays* gives an
article vituperating *L'Action Française* the title "Désunion Sacrée
(5 Jan. 1918). In the course of the feud it was waging against *L'Action
Française* in particular, *Le Bonnet Rouge* instituted a regular column
headed "Comment on assassine l'Union Sacrée", or "Les saboteurs
de l'Union Sacrée", in which its readers were treated to material
like the following:

> Pour gagner les faveurs de la censure que faut-il? Attaquer le Parlement;
> Prêcher la guerre religieuse; Diffamer les hommes du parti républicain.
> Lisez plutôt ces textes, parus dans les feuilles de droite, pendant que le
> *B. R.* était suspendu ...

—or this:

> *Une ordure par jour*
> La censure a donné son visa, ce matin, à l'ordure quotidienne. Titre: *Les
> manœuvres des embochés.* (25 July 1916)

L. Daudet and Ch. Maurras replied in kind—so that by 1917 it was
with considerable nostalgia that G. Hervé looked back to the days
when *l'union sacrée* was

> le ciment qui tenait en France comme en Angleterre le bloc de la défense
> nationale, qui groupait sans hésitation ni murmure toutes les forces
> nationales contre l'ennemi du genre humain et de la civilisation.
>
> (*La Victoire*, 12 Aug. 1917)

The examples chosen to illustrate the use of the phrase *union*

---

[6] See below, 3.3.

sacrée are intended to show its versatility as a slogan manipulated by writers of different persuasions. Additional linguistic evidence of the degree to which it had been assimilated can be seen in the fact that it could also function adjectivally.[7] G. Hervé writes:

> Je me suis mis en tête de changer un jour le titre un peu "guerre sociale" de ce journal pour en adopter un autre plus "union sacrée".
> (*La Guerre Sociale*, 6 Aug. 1915)

Elsewhere he mentions "les socialistes les plus 'jusqu'auboutistes' et les plus 'union sacrée'" (17 Nov. 1917). H. Bérenger does likewise:

> Ce n'est pas seulement très *union-sacrée;* c'est aussi très philhellène.
> (*Paris-Midi*, 15 Nov. 1915)

Le Bonnet Rouge notes:

> Également très "union sacrée", n'est-ce pas, l'active propagande cléricale qui, depuis août 1914, se fait un peu partout … (13 July 1916)

Its antonym also occurs; R. Rolland quotes from an article on the Swiss press published in the Italian paper *L'Avanti:*

> Ils … s'unissent quand il s'agit de tomber sur les socialistes. S'entend contre le socialisme antinational, antiunion sacrée [*sic*], zimmerwaldien, kienthalien.[8]

A further indication of the popularity of the expression *union sacrée* is to be found in its comic potential. P. Renaison remarks in *Le Pays:*

> M. Charles Maurras a réalisé l'Union Sacrée sur un point: tout le monde proclame à l'envi qu'il est le plus ennuyeux des polémistes. (12 May 1918)

When *la carte de sucre* was introduced to ration supplies, V. Snell headed an article in *Le Canard Enchaîné* "L'Union Sucrée", and observed wryly of *L'Action Française:*

> La gazette du roi ne diffame plus personne comme du temps que les Français ne s'aimaient pas.[9] (28 Mar. 1917)

---

[7] With or without a hyphen.

[8] *Journal*, p. 879 (16 Aug. 1916).

[9] Maurras had published *Quand les Français ne s'aimaient pas* in 1916. It was reviewed by G. Clairet in *Le Bonnet Rouge* on 12 July 1916: "Le spectacle de M. Maurras emporté par son admiration pour M. Maurras et adorant M. Maurras, et

The final word should perhaps go to *La Tranchée Républicaine:*

> *La Sacrée Union*
> Comment Candide eut le dernier mot.
> "Cette union sacrée n'existe que dans les gazettes. Il nous faut creuser
> notre tranchée." (9 May 1917)

1.3   *Les embusqués*

The origins of this expression are much discussed in studies of
military slang. The *Larousse Mensuel illustré* for July 1915 glosses
embusqué as "soldat ayant obtenu un poste éloigné de la ligne de
feu", and notes that "il est assez piquant de comparer ce sens avec
l'ancien sens militaire: 'soldat posté dans un lieu pour surprendre
l'ennemi'."[1] G. Esnault puts the development of this new meaning
(which was to become so widely diffused in 1914) as far back as
1883,[2] and observes that before the war *embusqué* was used of
postal workers "jouissant d'un régime de faveur" and of "univer-
sitaires postés hors cadre à Paris pour le mieux de leur avance-
ment".[3]

My concern here is not with the place of the term in the language
of the *poilu*, but with its rapid penetration into common usage. It
is by its very nature a symmetrical term, and seems cut out from the
start to play an important part in polemical warfare. F. Déchelette
has this comment to offer:

> Il y a toujours une moitié du monde qui se moque de l'autre; il y a aussi
> une moitié qui traite l'autre d'embusquée. On se moque toujours de plus
> embusqué que soi. L'*embuscade* est, comme le filon, une chose très
> relative: pour le poilu qui fait une patrouille vers les fils de fer boches,
> tout le monde est embusqué.[4]

The adoption of *embusqué* by civilians took place in two stages. As
soon as it became apparent that certain individuals were finding
ways of avoiding being sent to the front, considerable indignation

---

les écrits du même, est un spectacle éminemment patriotique et moralisateur, mais
trop peu de Français se le sont offert pour qu'on puisse honnêtement attribuer à ce
spectacle la transformation de l'âme française."
    [1] The form *embuschier* (12th cent.), "to lie in wait for game", was remodelled as
embusquer in the fifteenth century under the influence of Italian *imboscare*, "to
ambush"; see T. E. Hope, *Lexical Borrowing*, p. 37.
    [2] *Dictionnaire des Argots*, Larousse, 1965.
    [3] *Le Poilu tel qu'il se parle.*
    [4] *L'Argot des poilus.*

was voiced in all quarters, and in the early months of the war journalists made a concerted effort to inform the public of the scandal. Almereyda proclaims:

> La chasse au tire-au-flanc, à l'embusqué, j'en suis! Je l'ai faite, avec un très grand nombre de mes confrères. (*Le Bonnet Rouge*, 9 Oct. 1914)

There appears to be general agreement to give *embusqué* a quasi technical meaning. The Deputy R. Angles writes:

> *Le Scandale des Embusqués*
> J'appelle embusqués ceux que leur âge et leur santé appelleraient à être au front, sur la ligne de bataille, et qui n'y sont pas.
> (*Le Bonnet Rouge*, 22 Dec. 1914)

—and G. Clemenceau, who conducted a relentless campaign against the menace, had this to say:

> La pudeur de M. le Ministre de la Guerre s'est alarmée, l'autre jour, à l'idée de prononcer ce "gros mot" d'*Embusqués* dans l'enceinte du Parlement... Et d'abord qu'est-ce exactement que ce mot représente? Tout simplement des hommes qui, aux termes de la loi, devraient être en des formations de combat, et qui n'y sont pas.
> (*L'Homme Enchaîné*, 5 Apr. 1915)

The *loi Dalbiez* was passed in August 1915 to deal with the problem,[5] and in the debate surrounding its introduction and application a number of derivatives of *embusqué* were also propagated, some of the most common being: *embusquer, embusqueur, embuscade, embuscation, débusquer* or *désembusquer*, etc., and *embuscomane* etc.[6]

Clearly, *la chasse aux embusqués* was considered by everyone to be an act of *patriotisme*, a form of cooperation worthy of *l'union sacrée*; but this being so, the meaning of the term *embusqué* was bound to be affected by the conflicting interpretations given to these two virtues. Thus high-sounding statements like the following:

> Le ministre de la Guerre, s'il veut faire son devoir envers la Patrie, doit faire une chasse impitoyable aux embusqués comme aux embusqueurs,

---

[5] The bill presented to the *Chambre* on 4 June 1915 by the Radical-Socialist Dalbiez called for "une meilleure utilisation des hommes mobilisés et mobilisables". After a minor amendment by the Senate to exempt civil servants who held key posts and could not be mobilized without serious disruption to their department, the *loi Dalbiez* was passed on 13 August. See G. Bonnefous, *La Grande Guerre*, pp. 80-1.

[6] For a list of derivatives, see G. Esnault, *Le Poilu tel qu'il se parle*.

et s'arranger pour que les mal employés soient utilement employés.
(*Le Bonnet Rouge*, 28 Feb. 1917)

are meaningless if one does not know which individuals the journalist in question regarded as shirking their duty. Opinions of course
differed about the relative importance of France's various industrial
and commercial concerns which were not linked directly to the needs
of the fighting army. The way was therefore opened for opposing
interest-groups to air their particular grievances in the form of
complaints about *embusqués*. M. Barrès warns his readers that
animosity is being fomented between workers and peasants:

> Une abominable propagande de guerre civile est poursuivie dans les
> provinces françaises ... C'est un fait que des inconnus sèment la haine
> contre les ouvriers qu'ils accusent d'être à l'abri dans les usines, où ils
> touchent de gros salaires, tandis que les paysans se font tuer pour cinq
> sous par jour, et contre les prêtres et les bourgeois, qu'ils accusent d'être
> également embusqués à l'arrière. (*L'Écho de Paris*, 6 Mar. 1916)

In this latter group, priests were a category which G. Clairet of
Le Bonnet Rouge delighted in singling out for sarcasm: he alludes
to "des embusqués en robe noire" on 15 June 1915, and to "un nid
de 'tire-au-flanc': les embusqués en soutane" on 17 August of the
same year. Anticlericalism frequently involved championing the
Jews, since so much of orthodox Catholic opinion was antisemitic:

> Pendant que les embusqués de la *Libre Parole* insultent les juifs en les
> accusant de ne pas se donner tout entiers à la cause de la France, les
> volontaires juifs continuent sur le front à faire héroïquement leur devoir.
> (*Le Bonnet Rouge*, 15 July 1916)

A somewhat lighter note is struck in an article which would doubtless have incensed Emmeline Pankhurst:

> *Embusquées*
> C'est un mot à lancer. Embusqué appelle embusquée. Les femmes qui
> parlent beaucoup et qui sont si volontiers promptes à l'invective, ont
> contribué à faire un sort au mot embusqué. Mais comme elles réfléchis-
> sent peu et qu'elles ont rarement l'esprit critique reporté sur elles-mêmes,
> aucune n'a prévu que l'épithète injurieuse pourrait bien lui être retournée.
> (*Paris-Midi*, 7 Nov. 1916)

The second stage in the propagation of the term *embusqué* is
reached when it degenerates purely and simply into a term of abuse,
and ceases to imply in any strict sense that the person designated
should be in the trenches. Thus in its column "Les Serviteurs de

l'Étranger'' *Le Bonnet Rouge* writes, punning on the two senses of
embusqué:

> Embusqué dans son journal, comme un bandit au tournant d'un chemin,
> le rédacteur de l'*Action Française*, chaque matin, tire sur la France. Il
> ne faut pas que ce louche individu poursuive sa besogne malpropre.
>
> (6 June 1915)

It is hardly L. Daudet's right to exercise his profession as a journalist that is being called into question here. Daudet, predictably, uses
the same weapons; when he announces that—

> Emil Ullmann était alors directeur de notre *Comptoir d'Escompte*, d'où
> je n'ai pu le débusquer qu'après un an d'une campagne presque quoti-
> dienne. (*L'Action Française*, 26 Aug. 1916)

—the crime he imputes to him is that of being a German agent, so
that *débusquer* cannot be interpreted as meaning ''to send off to
the front''.

Finally, the comic potential of a word is often a good gauge of
its penetration into common usage. It is understandable that journalists who regarded it as their sacred duty to write morale-boosting
articles in which they talked about the glorious exploits which others
were performing, and castigated shirkers of every description,
should themselves be very easy prey for satirists. *Le Canard Enchaîné*
supplies this definition as a humorous antidote to the ones being
furnished at the time by every serious newspaper:

> L'embusqué, c'est aussi Monsieur le Patriote patenté, grand pourfendeur
> de Boches à longue distance et grand gueulard de *Chant du Départ* qui,
> du matin au soir, hurle, à s'égosiller, la *Marseillaise*—Marchons! Mar-
> chons!—et qui marche à reculons, comme les écrevisses. (20 Sept. 1915)

It even goes so far as to advertise the following patent remedy:

> *Contre Coliques et Tranchées*
> Prenez chaque matin
> L'EMBUSKÉOL
> Le Célèbre Produit du Docteur SVELTE
> EN VENTE
> Dans toutes les Bonnes Pharmacies de l'Arrière
> (15 Nov. 1916)

Before moving on to discuss *les embuscomanes*, it is worth mentioning two ephemeral satellites of *l'embusqué*—namely *l'épilé* and
l'installé. The former is a product of trench slang; A. Dauzat notes

that "du moment que le soldat combattant était le poilu, l'embusqué devait fatalement devenir *l'épilé*".[7] The term figures sporadically in the press as a variant for *embusqué*—H. Bérenger writes, for instance:

> Les poilus de l'avant viennent de répondre aux épilés de l'arrière qui prétendaient que la révélation des "scandales" démoralisaient l'armée.
> (*Paris-Midi*, 24 Oct. 1917)

The same journalist seems to have been responsible for giving a short lease of life to the term *installé;* as was his wont, he seized on a striking expression to lend force to his campaign of the moment, and then let it slip into relative disuse when it was in danger of becoming over-worn. He warns the readers of *Paris-Midi* on 17 November 1916:

> On ne répétera jamais trop cette parole qui fut prononcée pour la première fois par Albert Thomas à notre commission de l'armée: "Il faut secouer les gens qui se sont installés dans la guerre".

There follows an elaborate descripton of the offenders in question, from which it appears that Bérenger reserves the term *embusqué* for the military, and applies *installé* to civilians who are either simply not pulling their weight, or worse still, are using the war for private profiteering. On 28 November he continues:

> Toute la nation fait partie de l'armée de la nation! S'il est quelque part des embusqués et des *installés* qui n'ont pas encore compris cela, qu'on les débusque et qu'on les désinstalle—où qu'ils soient, si haut et si bas qu'ils soient!

Installé alternates with the longer form *installé-dans-la-guerre*:[8] Bérenger speaks of "tous nos installés dans la guerre" on 9 February 1917. Typically, he reiterates his definition of the term a few months later to make sure that it is being understood:

> Les embusqués sont dans l'armée ce que sont les installés dans le civil ... L'installé, lui, se reconnaît à ce signalement qu'il ne fait rien pendant la guerre ou qu'il fait quelque chose d'absolument inutile aux besoins de la nation en guerre. (13 Mar. 1917)

Other writers take up the expression to a limited degree, often in the verbal form used originally by A. Thomas, as for instance when

[7] *L'Argot de la guerre*, p. 135.
[8] With or without hyphens.

Hansi mentions "certains bureaucrates ... merveilleusement installés dans la guerre".[9]

As I have attempted to show, public opinion in France became extremely sensitive to the *scandale des embusqués* in the early months of the war, and excesses were inevitable. G. Hervé soon saw fit to scold some of his countrymen for losing all sense of proportion in an article entitled. "L'Embuscomanie", which *Paris-Midi* commented upon in its review of the early morning press:

> M. Gustave Hervé, dans la *Guerre Sociale*, nous met en garde contre la manie de voir partout des embusqués. (24 Nov. 1914)

He continued to write regularly on the subject, and his initiative was welcomed by *L'Action Française*, which usually held him beneath contempt:

> Dans la *Guerre Sociale*, Hervé continue à dire sur cette matière des choses sensées—c'est ainsi qu'il met fort bien en relief l'absurdité malfaisante d'un des principaux articles de la fameuse proposition Dalbiez, directement inspirée par une crise d'embuscomanie démocratique.
> (5 June 1915)

Now in registers where *embusqué* was used as a loose, perjorative label, a person charged with being an *embusqué* would often reply in kind to his accuser; but an alternative defence, perhaps regarded as more subtle, consisted in countering with the term *embuscomane*. Mention has already been made of the patriotic zeal with which *Le Bonnet Rouge* had initially joined in *la chasse aux embusqués*. Later, when its ideological position began to shift, and at the same time the term *embusqué* was extended to cover individuals outside the strictly military sphere, *Le Bonnet Rouge* became increasingly subject to attack on this score: its reaction was to take a high and mighty line:

> *EMBUSCOMANES*
> Il est un fléau plus grave que les embusqués.
> Il est un péril pire que les embusqueurs.
> Ce sont les embuscomanes.
> Ceux-ci voient partout des tire-au-flanc.[10]

---

[9] Hansi (J. J. Wartz) and E. Tonnelat, *A travers les lignes ennemies. Trois années d'offensive contre le moral allemand*, Paris, 1922, p. 153.

[10] The term *tire-au-flanc* (with or without hyphens), which figures in the vocabulary of *Le Bonnet Rouge* as an alternative to *embusqué* (see above, pp. 19 and 20), comes likewise from military slang. The *F.E.W.* dates the verb *tirer au flanc*, "user

Les embuscomanes sont des pessimistes dangereux qui sèment la défiance et la haine dans tout le pays. (9 Nov. 1915)

It would appear, then, that *Le Bonnet Rouge* regarded the internal enemy as an *embusqué* of the most dangerous kind, who, in a desperate attempt to protect his own position, accused others indiscriminately of this selfsame crime and thus also qualified as an *embuscomane*.

1.4   *Les Boches et leurs embochés*

The term *Boche* is primarily a pejorative name for the Germans.[1] When applied to Frenchmen as an insult, its use tends to be more characteristic of the language of the Right, but it has nevertheless been included in the set of symmetrical terms because some of its most important derivatives function in this way.

L. Daudet's tireless campaign in *L'Action Française* to unmask enemy spies relied heavily on the appellation *boche:* corrupt individuals were "les boches de l'intérieur" (14 July 1915); to merit this label, it was sufficient for someone to fall under the slightest suspicion—Daudet's fertile imagination supplied the rest.[2] Small wonder, then, that G. Clairet of *Le Bonnet Rouge* saw fit to protest:

On est toujours le "Boche" de quelqu'un.[3]
Traiter de "boche" une personne ou une idée, c'est, dans un certain monde où l'esprit n'est pas monnaie courante, le moyen sûr de le perdre. Pour perdre votre ennemi, assurez qu'il est allemand: c'est la formule nouvelle. (23 June 1916)

La Gazette des Ardennes makes a similar point:

Ces messieurs ont l'imagination courte. Pour eux l'agent boche tient lieu de toute explication et de toute excuse; il leur épargne tout effort de pensée. Quand il y a quelque chose qui ne va pas comme ils l'ont prédit,

---

de ruses pour éviter les corvées, manquer à sa parole", as 1881, and gives 1918, Swiss military slang, for the noun *tire-au-flanc*. In fact, Sainéan had recorded it (together with its variant *tire-au-cul*) in 1915, and Déchelette in 1918, neither with any suggestion that the term had Swiss origins. Its meaning differs slightly from that of *embusqué* in that it denotes a lazy soldier who does his best to shirk unpleasant duties, rather than one who has found the means to acquire a post that is neither uncongenial nor dangerous; cf. A. Dauzat, *L'Argot de la guerre*, p. 36.

[1] For its origins see *Larousse Mensuel*, December 1914; L. Sainéan, *L'Argot des tranchées*, pp. 9-13 and 134-5; A. Dauzat, *L'Argot de la guerre*, pp. 52-9.

[2] See below, 2.7, pp. 69ff., and Appendix I, *L. Daudet*.

[3] Cf. these words from H. Barbusse: "—On est toujours, dit Bertrand, l'embusqué de quelqu'un" (*Le Feu*, p. 104).

vite ils sortent ce croquemitaine de carton, peinturluré aux couleurs de leur folle imagination ... [les prostituées dans les gares] ne sont pas ce qu'on croyait jusqu'ici, mais des *agents boches*. (10 July 1917)

Again, in an ironical article headed "Patriotisme", this paper expounds the use of

"... les épithètes accusatrices et menaçantes de mauvais Français, anti-patriote, antimilitariste, internationaliste, socialiste, pacifiste et finale-ment, immanquablement ... de sale Boche, natürlich! (27 May 1917)[4]

However, in spite of ostentatious articles like the above, *Le Bonnet Rouge* and *La Gazette des Ardennes* do at times indulge in the vice they are normally so critical of—G. Clairet, for instance, picks the titles "Boches et Royalistes" (20 Aug. 1915), and "Les Boches du Vatican" (14 Oct. 1915) for articles in *Le Bonnet Rouge* devoted to the machinations of the French royalist and clerical factions and their allies abroad.

Derivatives of the term *Boche* meaning "spy", "traitor", or "enemy agent" are also found.[5] Ch. Sancerme in his systematic analysis of *Le Bonnet Rouge* has a predilection for the form *bocherie*; he often comments: "L'article est blanchi[6]—quelle bocherie s'y étalait-il?",[7] or "Quelles bocheries avaient-ils écrites?"[8] The abstract noun summing up the general attitude of the paper is *bochisme*, as in "la preuve de l'anti-patriotisme, du bochisme et de la vénalité du *Bonnet Rouge*".[9] The form *bochisant* is used by M. Barrès, particularly in conjunction with *défaitiste*—as in "les défaitistes et bochisants", or "les journaux défaitistes et bochisants".[10] Else-where, he writes "crapules bochisantes" as a variant for "les Boches de l'intérieur" (*L'Écho de Paris*, 30 Oct. 1917).

---

[4] Quoted by L. Marchand, *L'Offensive morale*, p. 87.

[5] G. Gaillard enumerates the forms coined by L. Daudet ("Langue et guerre", p. 27); for derivatives of *Boche* in military slang, see G. Esnault, *Le Poilu tel qu'il se parle.*

[6] Newspapers were submitted to the censorship before publication, and any passages thought to be dangerous had to appear as blanks; failure to comply with official instructions led to the suspension of the offending newspaper for a matter of days or sometimes weeks. See G. Bonnefous, *La Grande Guerre*, pp. 103-6; C. Bellanger et al., *Histoire générale de la presse française*, vol. iii, Paris, 1972, pp. 412-20.

[7] *Les Serviteurs de l'ennemi*, Paris, 1917, p. 84.

[8] Ibid., p. 310.

[9] Ibid., p. 12.

[10] Preface to L. Marchand, *L'Offensive morale*, p. viii.

The most significant of these derivatives, however, is the word *emboché*—a pun of L. Daudet's indicating someone who has been engaged (*embauché*) in the service of the *Boches*. He introduces it to his readers for the first time as follows:

> ### Les Embochés
> La racaille boche continue à faire marcher, en pleine guerre, par la menace et le chantage, ses anciennes créatures. La racaille boche compte bien échapper aux mesures qui s'imposent, notamment à la confiscation, grâce à l'intervention de ces créatures, de ceux que j'appellerai les "embochés". Le gouvernement a tout intérêt à réduire au silence, à ramener à la pudeur ces embochés qui furent et demeurent aussi des embauchés de la main-d'œuvre et de la perfidie allemandes.
>
> (*L'Action Française*, 2 Feb. 1915)

Throughout February the paper carries articles headed "La rage des Embochés", "A la recherche des Embochés", "Boches et Embochés", and the like. The expression immediately becomes a key one in Daudet's idiom, and he refines the definition of it shortly afterwards:

> ### Embochés et Bochophiles
> J'appelle emboché un monsieur qui faisait, avant la guerre, des affaires avec les Boches et demeure attaché aux Boches en proportion de ces affaires. J'appelle bochophile un monsieur que de mauvaises habitudes d'esprit, universitaires ou socialistes, maintenaient en état d'admiration vis-à-vis de l'Allemagne avant la guerre et qui ne peut pas se défaire de cette admiration. On peut être à la fois emboché et bochophile, mais en général et pour la commodité de l'exposé, on peut considérer que l'emboché est un mercanti et le bochophile un idéologue.
>
> (*L'Action Française*, 9 Apr. 1915)

In addition to being a derivative of *Boche* and a pun on *embauché*, *emboché* is obviously modelled on *embusqué* (often implying that the individual concerned has found himself a safe niche by working for the Germans), and it comes to be widely used with these parent terms in pejorative registers. Ch. Sancerme describes the military correspondent of *Le Bonnet Rouge*, General N., as an "emboché de première marque", and he sees the aims of the paper as being to "prôner le pacifisme, encenser R. Rolland, couvrir les embusqués, les embochés etc."[11] *Paris-Midi* writes of "tartuferies boches ou embochées" (1 Mar. 1916), and G. Hervé in *La Victoire* applies the term to the pacifist wing of his own party: "nos socialistes em-

---

[11] *Les Serviteurs de l'ennemi,* p. 161.

bochés" (10 May 1917). *Le Bonnet Rouge* itself uses the term, albeit with precaution; one finds mention of "ce représentant du Roy [*sic*] que veut nous imposer l'Autriche et du Pape 'emboché'" (9 Aug. 1915), and discussion by G. Clairet of

> *Vlaamsche Stem*, organe que le journal officiel du gouvernement belge, le *XXe Siècle*, qualifie avec raison de "journal emboché" ... (4 Sept. 1915)

Likewise, this time with a comment on the formation of the word:

> Nous savions aussi que l'Allemagne avait embauché—ou emboché, si vous voulez, car ce détestable jeu de mots, pour une fois, n'est pas déplacé—quelques journalistes étrangers.
>
> (*Le Bonnet Rouge*, 29 Nov. 1915)

Related to *emboché* are the forms *embochement* (*L'Action Française*, 25 Feb. 1915), *embochage*,[12] and *embochade*—as in this example from H. Bérenger:

> Tout à coup, la réaction d'un jacobinisme salutaire a balayé les défaitismes trop élégants d'une politique de jouisseurs qui commençaient par l'embuscade pour finir par l'embochade. (*Paris-Midi*, 6 Dec. 1917)

L. Daudet with his medical training was responsible for the ephemeral but effective *bochectomie*, which bears something of the same relationship to *Boche* and *emboché* as does *désembuscation* to *embusqué*:

> *Émile[13] Ullmann et la Bochectomie*
> J'appelle bochectomie l'opération par laquelle une académie, une société financière, industrielle ou commerciale se débarrasse actuellement de ses membres allemands. (*L'Action Française*, 18 June 1915)

Comparison of the above with the reference to the same individual quoted earlier should make the connection with *désembuscation* clear, and confirm the close ties between *les embusqués* and *les embochés*.

The recurrent use by journalists of this family of terms centring on *Boche* was summed up by J. Longuet as "la bochophobie morbide qui sévit chez un certain nombre de 'patriotes'" (*Le Bonnet Rouge*, 2 Oct. 1916). Given that this paper had apparently decided

---

[12] One of the terms in Sancerme's list quoted below, 2.7, p. 72.

[13] The name appears here in the French form which its bearer himself used; Daudet often gives the German version *Emil* to stress the man's origins, see above, 1.3, p. 21.

on principle by this date to eschew the word *Boche*,[14] what Longuet is doing is deliberately echoing the language of his opponents, and alluding not so much to their straightforward hatred of the Germans as to their obsessive preoccupation with enemy agents.

1.5 *L'espionnite*

The obsession with spies was given a specific name in 1914-18. Discussing the popularization of suffixes from the vocabulary of medicine, J. Dubois notes: "Dès 1914 on a parlé d'espionnite".[1] On 14 August 1914 one finds G. Hervé devoting an article in *La Guerre Sociale* to "La Peur des Espions"[2] which he qualifies as "cette espèce de maladie". Later, on 26 October 1914, he heads an article on the hallucinations of L. Daudet "L'Espionnite" and asks:

> Connaissez-vous une maladie plus sotte que l'espionnite? Au début, la maladie a commencé par les énormités colportées sur la maison Maggi.[3]

The term is readily adopted by *Le Bonnet Rouge* in its feud with *L'Action Française*;[4] titles like these abound: "Le record de l'espionnite" (16 July 1916), "Espionnite et antisémitisme" (28 Nov. 1916), and definitions are supplied:

> De même que les chiens enragés éprouvent un impérieux besoin de mordre quelqu'un, les malheureux que travaille le délire de l'espionnite ont, à l'état chronique, l'irrésistible désir de dénoncer des traîtres, de découvrir des complots. (12 Oct. 1916)

The word was clearly a very powerful weapon to discredit an adversary; L. Daudet remarks in *L'Action Française* on 14 April 1917 that the authorities refuse to listen to him because they think he is suffering from *espionnite*; and L. Marchand, explaining the difficulties of attempting to uncover Germany's spy network in view of the subtlety of her propaganda, declares: "On a peur d'être accusés [*sic*] d'espionnite".[5]

---

[14] See below, 1.7, p. 35.
[1] *Étude sur la dérivation suffixale en français moderne et contemporain*, Paris, 1962, p. 68. The *Petit Robert* seems to be unaware of this, as its entry (spelt *espionite*) is dated *c*.1940, and illustrated by a quotation where S. de Beauvoir refers back to 1914-18.
[2] See below, Appendix II, text 1.
[3] This was the international dairy company accused by Daudet of spying for the Germans.
[4] See below, 2.7, p. 73.
[5] *L'Offensive morale*, p. 3.

Individuals afflicted with *l'espionnite* were termed *espionomanes*.
L. Poldès writes:

> On a raison de nous protéger contre les espions. Ne serait-il pas logique
> de nous défendre également contre les espionomanes?
>
> (*Le Bonnet Rouge*, 2 Nov. 1915)

—and J. Goldsky, in the same paper, has this to say:

> Nous demandions hier aux espionomanes de laisser leurs concitoyens
> s'occuper de choses sérieuses, nous y insistons. (27 Mar. 1916)

In the previous day's issue, the form *espionomanie* appears as an
alternative to *espionnite*. Given the readiness with which such terms
were derived, one is left wondering whether **embochomane* was
ever coined by analogy with *embuscomane* and *espionomane*; after
all, *emboché* was the name created for spies and enemy agents by
their chief denunciator in the French press, and preferred by him to
all others. I have not in fact found it attested, and the answer may
well be that *Le Bonnet Rouge* chose derivatives of the more technical, neutral *espion* in a studied attempt to make its campaign appear
dignified, and to avoid sinking to the level of its opponents.

1.6   *Kompères et Komplices*

A minor side effect of the extension of the term *Boche* and the
creation of its derivative *emboché* to cover suspected enemy agents
of all varieties is the corresponding use of the letter *k*. This is a
purely orthographic device which originated in the ironic quotation
of German terms such as *Kultur, kolossal*, etc. Doubtless the
presence of a *k* in the word *Kaiser* did much to promote this letter
to the status of a national symbol in the eyes of the French; but
other factors, including commercial ones, also played a part. The
French press contains numerous scornful descriptions of Germany's
campaign to get her population to accept the unpalatable *pain k*
made from rye and potato. In its review of the morning papers for
27 February 1915, *Paris-Midi* quotes under the heading "Contre le
K" these lines from G. Téry of *L'Œuvre*:

> Il est certain que la consonne *k* a une consonance germanique et que les
> Boches en font, avec ou sans pain, une effroyable consommation.

Of equal if not greater importance were the advertisements put
out in France by the international firm *Maggi* for its *bouillon Kub*,

which carried the slogan *"Exiger le K!"*.[6] L. Daudet's persistent denunciation of this company as being part of the German spy network had the effect of drawing the letter *k* into polemics of this sort. Without going as far as Daudet in its conclusions, *Paris-Midi* nonetheless proclaims:

> N'exigeons plus le K!
>
> Est-ce que toute cette publicité d'avant-guerre, comme dit Daudet,[7] n'aurait pas dû disparaître il y a longtemps? Qu'on chasse loin de nos esprits cette obsédante et stupide formule: "Exiger le K!" Que le souvenir même du bouillon Kub rentre dans le néant des bocheries définitivement abolies! (13 Nov. 1915)

Daudet's articles in *L'Action Française* on the subject of *les embochés* make frequent play on the letter *k*, as in "Le bouillon Kub—avis aux Konsommateurs de cette innommable Kochonnerie" (8 Mar. 1917). One of the concerns which he sought most relentlessly to unmask was the gambling-house in Monaco—"le Klaquedent de Monaco"—run by "Kamille Blanc, ses Boches et ses Kroupiers" (18 Oct. 1916). In the same vein, a suspected enemy agent becomes a "Krapule embochée" (5 Aug. 1916), while A. Dubarry, editor of the "defeatist" paper *Le Pays*,[8] is singled out as one of a band of "Kompères et Komplices" (3 July 1917). A reference to "le torchon antimilitariste qu'inspirent Ullmann et Caillaux" (i.e. *Le Bonnet Rouge*) calls it "le Kanard—exigez le K!" (26 July 1915).

This latter paper was never slow to turn an adversary's shafts against him; in a series of anticlerical articles attempting to show that the Catholic Church was a tool of the Germans, the picture of this complicity is enhanced by touches like the following:

> C'est alors qu'on se dit à Berlin: "Il faut donner un Koup de main à ces bons serviteurs ... On va les konsoler." (*Le Bonnet Rouge*, 19 Aug. 1915)

The aim of the alliance is seen as being to "placer en France sa kamelote" (3 Sept. 1915), and its chief supporters are "Karl Maurras" (19 Aug. 1915) and the Pope "Benoît Kinze" (4 Sept. 1915).

[6] During the first few days of the war the Army removed the Maggi-Kub hoardings for fear that they would guide the advancing Germans, and gangs of youths plundered the Maggi shops in Paris in a fit of xenophobia. See E. J. Weber, *Action Française*, p. 92; A. Kriegel and J.-J. Becker, *1914*, pp. 161-8.

[7] See below, 2.7, pp. 69-71.

[8] For the importance of this newspaper, see below, 2.7, p. 74.

Emotive exploitation of the letter *k* is found in newspapers differing widely in character. *Le Matin* mentions "un k de conseil de guerre, un k pendable, ou tout au moins de réforme" (27 Feb. 1915), and elsewhere refers to Russian pacifists as "les kamarades" (15 Apr. 1917); *Paris-Midi* labels "defeatist" propaganda "le Bourrage des Krânes—les nouvelles 'Made in Germany'"[9] (17 Apr. 1918). The enemies of J. Caillaux spelt him, inevitably, "Kaillaux", and his followers "kaillautistes" (*La Libre Parole*, quoted by *Le Bonnet Rouge*, 26 June 1916); L. Daudet referred to him as "le Katilina du rapprochement franco-allemand".[10] The sinister implications of the term *embusqué* in the usage of some people were aptly parodied in an early issue of *Le Canard Enchaîné*, which wrote of "les embuskés" (20 Sept. 1915). G. Hervé in *La Victoire* uses the device as a means of airing his hostility to the proposed "Konférence de Stockholm"—a German trap for weak-minded pacifists (12 May 1917); and of expressing his indignation at the succession of treasonous plots which came to light in the summer and autumn of 1917:

En plein Boloïsme[11]
Chaque jour maintenant nous apporte son scandale. C'est par tranches qu'on nous sert ce dégoûtant pain K K. (26 Oct. 1917)

The metaphor brings one back to one of the starting-points of this trick of orthography, and is a good measure of its lower limits.

1.7 *Les bourreurs de crânes*[1]

Odieux bourreurs de crânes, que nous avons tant de fois maudits, bonisseurs patentés, optimistes par ordre, menteurs patriotiques, empêcheurs de vérités, laudateurs de tous les incapables, écornifleurs du pouvoir, pervertisseurs de l'esprit public, dont vous avez assumé la garde, la fameuse "Garde Morale"! (G. Vidal, *Le Pays*, 21 Dec. 1917)

An invitation to study such individuals is proffered by G. Clairet, who predicts that a special place will be found in literary history for:

... ces écrivains spéciaux nés de la guerre et que les historiens de notre littérature étudieront à la manière de Brunetière au chapitre "les bourreurs de crânes". (*Le Bonnet Rouge*, 4 Jan. 1916)

---

[9] For further examples of this expression, see below, 2.4, p. 58, n. 6, and 3.7, p. 159.

[10] *Le Poignard dans le dos. Notes sur l'affaire Malvy*, Paris, 1918, p. 151.

[11] See below, 2.9, pp. 89-91.

[1] Both *crânes* and *crâne* are found.

—and *Le Canard Enchaîné* collects material to this end in a regular column headed:

Chez les Bourreurs de Crâne
Petite revue de la Grande Presse à l'usage des
Historiens futurs
(e.g. 6 Dec. 1916)

The importance of the term *bourrage de crâne* in journalists' polemics in 1914-18 is largely unexplored, although works on trench slang written during or immediately after the war comment extensively on the use of the expression by *les poilus*. It appears that, like so many others, it had limited currency before the war, and was rapidly propagated after 1914.[2] The impact of the term in the first months of the war was such that most people were assumed to have become familiar with it at this time; G. Hervé writes:

> Dans toutes nos villes occupées ... le moral est tellement haut que quand les Allemands annoncent un succès ... les nôtres considèrent qu'ils mentent, qu'ils veulent leur "bourrer le crâne", une expression que ne connaissent peut-être pas nos compatriotes séparés de nous depuis 1914, mais dont ils ont dû forger l'équivalent. (*La Victoire*, 10 Aug. 1917)

Bourrage de crâne was originally the name given by *les poilus* to the bombastic glorification of their exploits by men of the rear,[3] to misleading "official" versions of events[4]—to inflated rhetoric in general. It is glossed by G. Esnault as "amplification d'un rhéteur optimiste et idéologue",[5] while *bourrer le crâne* is variously ex-

---

[2] A. Dauzat notes that "il y a dix ans que je [1] 'ai ouï dire dans le peuple" (*L'Argot de la guerre*, p. 41), and the *Petit Robert* gives 1876 as its first attestation.

[3] Dorgelès illustrates this kind of exaggeration in *Les Croix de bois*: "[Sulphart] avait lu dans les journaux des récits stupéfiants qui l'avaient rendu honteux: le caporal valeureux qui, à lui seul, exterminait une compagnie avec son fusil mitrailleur et achevait le reste à la grenade; le zouave qui enfilait cinquante Boches à la pointe de sa baïonnette; un bleu qui ramenait de patrouille une ribambelle de prisonniers, dont un officier qu'il tenait en laisse; le chasseur à pied convalescent qui se sauvait de l'hôpital en apprenant que l'offensive était commencée, et allait se faire tuer avec son régiment" (Paris, 1919, pp. 414-15).

[4] D. Brogan observes: "Of course, the limitations of the freedom of the press designed to prevent the dissemination of false news were not intended to apply to false news that suited the policy of the Government. As the Government, rightly, was deeply concerned to keep up the spirits of the people, to avoid any panic, newspapers were allowed to publish any cheerful fables that they thought fit. From this arose the great campaign of 'bourrage de crâne', of patriotic 'ballyhoo'." (*The Development of Modern France*, London, 1940, pp. 513-14.)

[5] *Le Poilu tel qu'il se parle.*

plained as "tromper, mentir, exagérer, importuner",[6] or "en faire accroire, imposer une opinion toute faite à quelqu'un".[7] From the outset the extension of the term was very wide: a given speaker might label *bourrage de crânes* any pronouncements which did not coincide with his own views. From the soldiers' standpoint, the chief offenders were not unnaturally journalists—as noted by G. Hervé:

> L'optimisme des journalistes agace visiblement, dans les jours de cafard, beaucoup de nos poilus. Ils nous traitent couramment de "bourreurs de crânes". (*La Victoire*, 30 Apr. 1917)

—or by *Le Crapouillot*, a trench newspaper quoted approvingly by *Le Bonnet Rouge*:

> Ce qui déconcerte le plus les soldats, c'est de voir que l'élite des intellectuels n'a pas su s'élever au-dessus du patriotisme de cinéma et fait chorus avec les vils professionnels[8] du bourrage de crânes ... (30 June 1917)

Now these "professionals" were above all right-wing journalists like M. Barrès, and one finds their ideological enemies on the left quick to make capital out of the felicitous expression handed to them by the soldiers. Barrès himself notes:

> Cette presse vendue ... cherchait à présenter la victoire comme impossible, à traiter de "bourreurs de crânes", c'est-à-dire de menteurs, ceux qui s'emploient à maintenir la confiance et l'union.
>
> (*L'Écho de Paris*, 7 Oct. 1917)

—and Ch. Maurras observes:

> Les écrivains français assez audacieux pour déclarer ce reproche [d'impérialisme] absurde étaient couramment traités d'énergumènes ou de bourreurs de crânes dans une demi-douzaine de journaux quotidiens.
>
> (*L'Action Française*, 15 May 1918)

The kind of thing being referred to by these staunch patriots is passages like the ones quoted earlier from *Le Bonnet Rouge* and *Le Pays*, or these lines from the latter:

> Certes, on trouve encore communément, pour prophétiser quelques années de guerre, des stratèges en chambre des égoïstes ou des profiteurs, installés dans leurs pantoufles, voire une sorte de plumitifs, dont l'argot du poilu fit justice avec cet écriteau: "Bourreurs de crânes". (1 Jan. 1918)

[6] A. Dauzat, *L'Argot de la guerre*, Glossary.
[7] F. Déchelette, *L'Argot des poilus*.
[8] On the use of the term *professionnel*, see below, 3.4, pp. 133-4.

There is heavy sarcasm in the phrase "pour prophétiser quelques années de guerre": some people, it is claimed, continue (even after more than three years of fighting) to talk blithely of carrying on to the bitter end for the glory of France, until Alsace-Lorraine is regained and the Germans sufficiently humiliated, as though there were no limits to France's resources and to the endurance of her men in the trenches.

In his study of the pro-German sympathies of *Le Bonnet Rouge* and affiliated papers, L. Marchand identifies a carefully prepared campaign "contre les patriotes français",[9] the aim of which was to drag men like M. Barrès, G. Hervé, etc. into the mud, and the means of so doing consisted in calling them *embusqués, saboteurs de l'union sacrée* and *bourreurs de crânes* in particular. General N. introduces the term with an apology:

> Quelques "Bourreurs de Crânes"
> Qu'on me pardonne l'expression, elle n'est peut-être pas très journa-listique, mais elle est militaire. (*Le Bonnet Rouge*, 17 Aug. 1916)

—but uses it freely thereafter, as do other journalists on the staff. The specific accusations levelled at the right wing are discussed later;[10] suffice it to say here that all of them—*nationalisme, cléricalisme, jusqu'auboutisme*, etc.—can be subsumed under the general charge of *bourrage de crânes*. P. Brizon has this to say about the uncompromising will to fight to the bitter end:

> Philosophes de l'arrière. Le bourreur de crânes.
> Junius, intrépide, tirant non sur les Allemands mais sur les pauvres d'esprit qui avalent *l'Écho de Paris*: "Notre devoir: pousser cette guerre jusqu'au bout ... et *briser l'Empire*". Le jésuite Junius ne laboure pas la mer, il laboure les crânes, il spécule sur la bêtise.
> (*Le Bonnet Rouge*, 3 Sept. 1916)

Likewise, the same paper praises:

> ... ceux qui n'ont pas voulu s'associer aux fanfaronnades dangereuses et intéressées des annexionnistes, ni colporter les mensonges des bourreurs de crânes ... (26 June 1917)

L'espionnite is naturally a disease of *les bourreurs de crânes*:

> Les bourreurs de crânes ont tellement inoculé au public le virus de

---

[9] *L'Offensive morale*, p. 107.
[10] See below, Part Three.

l'espionnite que des faits regrettables se produisent journellement.

(*Le Bonnet Rouge*, 13 June 1917)

As the *union sacrée* pact became more and more of a dead letter, the extreme Left reacted with special virulence against the sort of chauvinistic bombast which tarred all Germans with the same brush. *La Gazette des Ardennes* is quite categorical:

> Il faut aimer sa patrie, cela est naturel, mais il ne faut pas pour cela bourrer les crânes de morale de haine et semer la médisance aux quatre coins de la tête! (17 Mar. 1917)[11]

With his keen ear ever tuned in to subversive mutterings in what he termed the revolutionary press, L. Daudet was quick to detect irritation at the indiscriminate use of the term *Boche*:

> Dès maintenant, les embochés et bochophiles ... manifestent une extrême horreur de tout écart de style vis à vis de leurs chers Allemands. Selon eux, il conviendrait de ne faire à ces incendiaires, à ces égorgeurs, à ces tueurs d'enfants, à ces souilleurs de femmes, aucune peine verbale, même légère. (*L'Action Française*, 29 Apr. 1915)

His "dès maintenant" is perhaps something of an exaggeration, since it was not until December 1915 that *Le Bonnet Rouge* (Daudet's arch-enemy) began to phase out orthodox "patriotic" articles and replace them consistently with material like the following:

> *Allemands, mais pas Boches*
> Tous ne ressemblent pas à cette brute qu'est le Kaiser.[12] (17 Dec. 1915)

Far-fetched atrocity stories constitute the quintessential *bourrage de crânes* in the eyes of many writers concerned to discredit the "official" attitude. *La Gazette des Ardennes* refers to a rumour that the Germans had set up a factory to process human flesh as:

> *Propagande civilisée*
> C'est là un échantillon particulièrement précieux de cette propagande pour la "civilisation" contre la "barbarie" allemande ... (22 Apr. 1917)

---

[11] Quoted by L. Marchand, *L'Offensive morale*, p. 86.

[12] L. Marchand comments that the Germans, in whose pay he believed this paper to be, "veulent supprimer le nom de 'Boche' de la langue française"; he identifies a campaign "contre la haine" which is built upon no less than twenty-six articles of the form "Allemands, mais pas Boches", "Il y a 'Boche' et 'Boche'", or "Un blessé allemand n'est pas un 'Boche'", spread over the period January 1916 to July 1917 when the paper was suppressed (*L'Offensive morale*, pp. 21-36).

and calls this propaganda "ce 'bourrage de crânes' vraiment trop fort" (28 Apr. 1917).[13]

Le Bourrage de crânes is one of the pet themes of *Le Canard Enchaîné*, from its first numbers onwards. Its master stroke was to organize a referendum on the subject which it announced to its readers as follows on 29 November 1916:

Sur les Sentiers de l'Arrière
Les Bourreurs de Crâne auront un Chef!
Le Canard Enchaîné ouvre un referendum à cette intention.
L'Élection du Grand Chef de la Tribu des Bourreurs de Crâne
La question est très simple:
Lequel, à votre sens, parmi les journalistes qui se mettent quotidienne-ment en vedette, mérite, à tous égards, le titre de Grand Chef?

A regular column reminded readers that their opinions were being solicited, and seven months later the results were announced:

Gustave Hervé est élu Grand Chef de la Tribu des Bourreurs de Crâne
(20 June 1917)

He gained 5,653 votes over M. Barrès who polled 5,402—a result which confirmed the preferences shown by the staff of *Le Canard Enchaîné*, to judge from the constancy with which these two journalists were satirized in articles and caricatured in cartoons.[14] The reasons suggested for Hervé's greater claim to the title are themselves significant:

A ceux de nos lecteurs qui s'étonneraient de ne pas voir M. Maurice Barrès arriver bon premier au poteau (et pour ainsi dire dans un fauteuil d'académicien), nous révélerons que grand nombre des partisans de M. Gustave Hervé paraissent savoir gré à l'éminent Président de la Ligue des Patriotes de *n'avoir pas attendu la guerre* pour bourrer le crâne de ses amis. (*Le Canard Enchaîné*, 20 June 1917)

---

[13] Quoted by L. Marchand, *L'Offensive morale*, p. 114. According to H. D. Lasswell (*Propaganda Technique in the World War*, London-New York, 1927, p. 207), the "corpse factory" rumour originated as follows: the Chief of British Army Intelligence deliberately exchanged the captions under two photographs, one of dead German soldiers on their way to be buried, and the other of dead horses destined for the soap factory.

[14] Ch. Maurras was likewise a frequent butt for this paper's wit (e.g. "O tempora, O Maurras!", 28 Mar. 1917), but his name does not appear on the list of winners of the competition.

Barrès, it is argued, at least had the virtue of being consistent in what he preached, whereas Hervé with his sudden changes of heart represented a far more insidious threat to the common reader.[15]

Typically, the interest shown by *Le Canard Enchaîné* in fashionable slogans led to puns of all kinds:

> La mode des "devises" est revenue comme on voit.
> A ce propos on demande à quel académicien appartient celle-ci:
>   Moins crâne que ceux que je bourre. (30 May 1917)

An article in the same paper on "Quelques microbes de la grippe espagnole" (6 Nov. 1918) includes discussion of "le bourrus cranus juskaboula".[16] Other instances of humorous usage can be found, for example, in *La Tranchée Républcaine*, which carried a recurrent "Ballade des bourreurs de crâne" and the motto:

> Les Imbéciles
> les "bourreurs de crânes"
> les "profiteurs"
> de tous les mondes, de toutes les religions,
> de toutes les patries, de tous les grades
>   ... ON LES AURA![17]
>   (e.g. 1 May 1917)

Language of this tone is no doubt what L. Daudet is alluding to when he writes:

> Une littérature spéciale s'était fondée, avec mission de dénoncer à la risée publique—combien amère, cette risée!—les "bourreurs de crâne", c'est-à-dire ceux qui continuaient à annoncer la victoire finale et à encourager, chacun à sa façon, le public.[18]

Discussion of the terms *patriote, embusqué*, etc. should have given a sufficiently clear picture of the way in which symmetrical terms function to make it obvious at this juncture how the Right

---

[15] See below, Appendix I, *G. Hervé*.

[16] For other puns on the theme *jusqu'au bout*, see below, 3.6, p. 149.

[17] This locution had passed into common usage from the trenches. It occurs in P. Bourget's novel *Le Sens de la mort* (Paris, 1915, p. 44): "'Et puis, je sais que cette fois on les aura.' Voilà nos hommes. Et nous les aurons, mon cousin." General Pétain was responsible for giving it wide currency; he concluded an *ordre du jour* of 9 Apr. 1916 with the words "Courage, on les aura!", and journalists took up the expression at once. M. Barrès noted: "'On les aura!' écrit Pétain, redonnant à ses troupes, dans un échange sublime, la formule que d'instinct elles lui avaient donnée" (*L'Écho de Paris*, 13 Apr. 1916).

[18] *La Guerre totale*, Paris, 1918, p. 228.

would respond when attacked for their bombast: the expression *bourrage de crânes* was a double-edged weapon, and a writer like Ch. Maurras retaliated in *L'Action Française* by accusing *Le Bonnet Rouge* of "bourrer le crâne du malheureux public" (28 Feb. 1916), or of "bourrer le crâne des nations" (15 Aug. 1916). The double use of the term is spelled out by G. Hervé:

> *Âmes neurasthéniques*
> Quel concert de lamentations.
> "On nous bourre le crâne quand on nous raconte qu'on les aura."
> Quel est donc le défaitiste, malheureux, qui vous a bourré le crâne de tous ces papillons noirs? (*La Victoire*, 20 Nov. 1917)

L. Marchand introduces his study of *Le Bonnet Rouge* with this hope:

> Puissent les documents que nous présentons éclairer le public français sur la façon dont il est travaillé et dont opèrent au cœur du pays les vrais "bourreurs de crâne", les agents du prussianisme et leurs complices.[19]

—and when quoting particularly virulent attacks by the Left, he frequently puts questions of the following form to his readers: "De quel côté sont les véritables bourreurs de crânes?"[20] The left-wing propaganda most commonly singled out by Marchand and others includes "le pacifisme libéral du peuple allemand",[21] "l'internationalisme",[22] and "le socialisme lutte-de-classes" (G. Hervé, *La Victoire*, 4 Dec. 1917). The general view is aptly summed up in these lines from *L'Éveil*:

> Les "bourreurs de crâne" du socialisme à l'allemande avaient emprunté à Karl Marx ses rêves d'internationale ouvrière qui, comme des bouffées de gaz asphyxiants, s'étaient répandus dans le peuple, paralysant les intelligences et étouffant peu à peu la notion de la patrie.
> (quoted by *Paris-Midi*, 9 Aug. 1916)

In the language of the majority *bourrage de crânes* is thus a pejorative expression designating the propaganda of the opponent, whatever that may happen to be. There are of course exceptions; G. Hervé, a man who had welcomed the label *jusqu'auboutiste*,[23]

---

[19] *L'Offensive morale*, p. xv.
[20] Ibid., p. 116.
[21] Ibid., p. 164.
[22] *La Semaine Littéraire* (3 Nov. 1917) mentions "les bourreurs de crânes internationalistes" (quoted by R. Rolland, *Journal*, p. 1338).
[23] See below, 3.6, p. 146.

did on occasion use *bourrage de crâne* as a positive term: exhorting
the troops to remain optimistic in outlook, he writes:

> Qu'ils n'aient pas peur de se faire traiter de "bourreurs de crânes".
> *La Marseillaise* n'est-elle pas le plus sublime des bourrages de crânes?
> (*La Victoire*, 24 Dec. 1917)

Given the versatility of what is perhaps the symmetrical term *par
excellence*, it comes as no surprise to find Proust writing in *Le
Temps retrouvé*:

> Le bourrage de crâne est un mot vide de sens ... Le véritable bourrage de
> crâne, on se le fait à soi-même par l'espérance, qui est une figure de
> l'instinct de conservation d'une nation, si l'on est vraiment membre
> vivant de cette nation.[24]

In addition to *bourrer le crâne, bourrage* and *bourreur de crânes*,
other derivatives of the expression are also found. Ch. Maurras
writes "débourrer les crânes" (*L'Action Française*, 21 Feb. 1917);
and *Le Canard Enchaîné* invents a "Débourreur de Crânes" whose
task is to deal with the poor souls who have read *L'Écho de Paris*,
the most dangerous contributor being none other, of course, than
"M. Maurice Bourrès (28 Mar. 1917). Of greater significance is
the form *Crâne-Bourré*, first used by General Verraux in *L'Œuvre*
on 30 September 1916:[25] it designates someone who has been taken
in by propaganda—a weak and gullible victim as opposed to the
active proponent of ideology. Under the heading "La Guerre
Longue", H. Bérenger writes:

> Ceux qui disent le contraire sont des bourreurs de crâne ou des crânes
> bourrés. (*Paris-Midi*, 3 Mar. 1917)

The term is used equally well by the Left:

> *Les Vessies dégonflées—M. M. Barrès*
> Ce bourreur de crânes est un crâne bourré, ce faux sceptique est un vrai
> naïf. (*La Tranchée Républicaine*, 31 May 1917)

In the language of the Right, *bourreur de crânes* was not the only
name given to left-wing pacifists: the form *videur de crânes* also
made its appearance around May 1917, at a time when mutinies in
the army and intensified pacifist activity were causing considerable
concern. Clearly, the inventor of the expression altered the original

[24] Pléiade edn., vol. iii, p. 773.
[25] According to G. Esnault, *Le Poilu tel qu'il se parle*.

to produce a more appropriate description of the individuals in question. G. Esnault glosses the term as "rhéteur aux idées pessimistes",[26] and illustrates it with this quotation from *L'Action Française*:

> Ces "videurs de crânes", agents évidents d'un ennemi intéressé à fomenter chez nous des troubles politiques ... (28 May 1917)

In an article in *L'Illustration* headed "Sabotage Moral" (7 July 1917) which gives an excellent analysis of the use of the slogan *bourrage de crâne*, H. Lavedan says of the "fauteur de trouble et de mésentente":

> Non, en effet, il ne bourre pas.
>   Que fait-il donc?
>   Il vide, et non seulement il vide les crânes mais aussi les os, les veines, les cœurs. Il pompe les moelles de l'énergie et suce les forces vitales.[27]

The earliest example I have found of the term *videur de crâne* comes from the pen of G. Hervé:

> Que nos femmes grévistes se méfient, par exemple, des bourreurs de crânes—ou plutôt des videurs de crâne [*sic*]—du pacifisme bêlant qui leur insinueront que des troubles à Paris feraient finir la guerre plus vite. (*La Victoire*, 27 May 1917)

He uses it regularly to attack the advocates of immediate peace, often contrasting it explicitly with the conventional *bourreur de crâne*:

> Est-ce que ces videurs de crânes ne racontaient pas aussi partout que les Américains viendraient occuper tous les postes de l'arrière? Nos pauvres poilus parlent beaucoup de leur mépris pour les "bourreurs de crânes", mais cela ne les empêche pas d'avaler les sottises les plus monumentales ... Ils verront si les gaillards qui viennent de débarquer sur la terre de France ont des têtes d'embusqués, venus pour assurer le service de l'arrière!
> (*La Victoire*, 1 July 1917)

Videur de crâne is exclusively a designation for the extreme Left, but it is discussed here for the sake of completeness. As will be shown, the set of circumstances which caused it to be coined was also responsible for the sudden introduction of the term *défaitiste* into French polemics. Comparison of dates reveals that H. Lavedan's

---

[26] *Le Poilu tel qu'il se parle.*
[27] See Appendix II, text 2.

sabotage moral had strong connections with what H. Bérenger was calling *défaitisme* at the very same period. A few months later, the latter was to associate *videur de crânes* directly with *défaitisme* in an example of multiple "linking":[28] "aucun défaitisme de bavards, aucun neutralisme de videurs de crânes, aucun boloïsme d'embochés ..." (*Paris-Midi*, 26 Oct. 1917).[29]

To end these remarks on *le bourrage de crânes*, and by way of a general conclusion to this section on symmetrical terms, it is perhaps worth spelling out what has been implicit in the discussion of individual words—namely, their interdependence. They form a stable correlation such that, in the vocabulary of any group, it is always other people who are referred to as *bourreurs de crânes, embusqués, embochés* and the like, whereas the speaker claims to be a genuine *patriote* and faithful observer of the *Union Sacrée* pact. Furthermore, this speaker will note that one of the chief forms taken by his opponents' *bourrage de crânes* is an attempt to make out that they themselves are the *patriotes* and he and his kind the *embusqués* and *saboteurs de l'Union Sacrée*. Far from causing difficulties, the inherent vagueness of such terms is a positive asset: it enables the holders of conflicting opinions to present them within a common framework of accepted values calculated to appeal to the general public in a time of crisis.

[28] For discussion of this stylistic device, see below, 3.7.
[29] See below, 2.9, p. 90.

Part Two

LE DÉFAITISME

2.1 The Problem

> L'ennemi qui, à l'avant, combat nos enfants et nos frères
> avec tous les engins de mort, nous savons qui il est. Celui
> qui, à l'arrière, par la parole et par la plume, dissocie les
> forces, verse le poison, détruit l'idéal, châtre les haines,
> les saintes haines, borne l'effort, raille la vigilance,
> excuse l'agresseur, sème le découragement, réclame
> chaque jour la Paix, bave sur les patriotes ardents, veut
> entretenir des intelligences avec l'ennemi, combat les
> hommes d'État chargés des lourdes responsabilités du
> pouvoir, donne asile à toute la lie de l'humanité, aux
> criminels, aux voleurs, aux escrocs, aux étrangers louches,
> aux anarchistes, cet ennemi-là, *pour le démasquer, il
> fallait faire ce que j'ai fait.*
>
> > CHARLES SANCERME[1]

The most noticeable effect on the French language of the campaign
against left-wing agitators during the First World War was the
creation of the terms *défaitiste/défaitisme.* Anyone who glances
now at the French daily press for the month of July 1917 is likely to
take for granted headlines of the type: "Riposte au défaitisme", or
"La presse défaitiste à Paris", which are regular features of certain
newspapers. Yet during those critical weeks, many members of the
public would have been seeing the words *défaitiste* and *défaitisme*
for the very first time. These terms are so well established in the
French language that one does not normally pause to wonder how
long they have featured there, unless one has a special interest in
the question.

A second error which an unwary modern reader is liable to make
when faced with these headlines consists in assuming that the terms
défaitiste/défaitisme meant the same thing to people in 1917 as they

---

[1] *Les Serviteurs de l'ennemi,* p. 2.

do to him now. Taking this to run roughly along the lines of the definition supplied by the *Lexis*:[2]

> *défaitisme* État d'esprit de ceux qui s'attendent à être vaincus, qui n'espèrent pas la victoire et qui préconisent l'arrêt du combat

one has to conclude after analysing usage in 1917 and 1918, that it does not really fall within the scope of the modern definition, in spite of deceptive superficial similarities. Besides, even this statement is an oversimplification: talk of usage in 1917, for instance, is only meaningful if one specifies which journalists are involved and what particular weeks are being considered. A Frenchman who had followed events in Russia rather closely in the press and in books dealing with the subject might have heard before July 1917 of a handful of revolutionaries known as *les défaitistes*, but until this time he would not have seen this word applied systematically to his own countrymen.[3]

Judged as a lasting acquisition to the French language, the terms *défaitiste/défaitisme* are undoubtedly one of the most important coinages produced by the First World War; they also occupy an extremely significant position in the polemics of the day, and serve to characterize them in relation to comparable writings belonging to other periods. Whereas in the Franco-Prussian War, the opposing camps within France had labelled each other *capitulards* and *outranciers*,[4] from mid 1917 onwards it was *les défaitistes* who were pitted against *les jusqu'auboutistes* in the conflict of attitudes towards the war. Proust observes in *Le Temps retrouvé*:

> [M. de Charlus] gardait tout son respect et toute son affection à de grandes dames accusées de défaitisme, comme jadis à celles qui avaient été accusées de dreyfusisme. Il regrettait seulement qu'en s'abaissant à faire de la politique elles eussent donné prise "aux polémiques des journalistes".[5]

Proper understanding of First World War press campaigns hinges on the correct interpretation of the neologism *défaitiste/*

---

[2] Larousse, 1975.

[3] A. Kupferman is mistaken in claiming that the term *défaitisme* "devient d'usage courant vers 1915" and that "[il] s'impose avec la guerre d'attente" ("L'Opinion française et le défaitisme pendant la Grande Guerre", p. 92).

[4] See J. Dubois, *Le Vocabulaire politique et social*, p. 135, and example quoted below, 3.6, p. 146.

[5] Pléiade edn., vol. iii. p. 800.

défaitisme. It cannot be fruitfully or even adequately discussed without a detailed examination of the complex chain of events which brought it into being in 1915 and determined its subsequent evolution in 1917 and 1918. This is only to be expected of words belonging to polemical registers: the pairs of terms *capitulard/ outrancier* and *défaitiste/jusqu'auboutiste* are not equivalent except in a very broad sense, for each bears the distinctive mark of the circumstances in which it arose, and to discount these differences is to neglect the most interesting features of the individual expressions.

2.2   Lexicographical preliminaries

Although it is generally known that the terms *défaitiste/défaitisme* were borrowed into French from Russian, the information supplied by standard dictionaries is far from satisfactory: there is no agreement about dates and no hint that the terms may not always have had the meaning which is now associated with them. A more striking illustration could scarcely be given of how little notice lexicographers appear to take of one another's findings.

The *F.E.W.* (vol. iii, 1934) gives 1916 as an approximate date for both terms, and supplies the following glosses:

> *défaitisme* "pendant la Grande Guerre, opinion et politique de ceux qui
> ne croyaient pas à la victoire"
> *défaitiste* "partisan du défaitisme"

The terms do not appear in the first three editions of the *Bloch-Wartburg* (1932, 1949, 1960), but the fourth edition (1964) contains an entry which adds a considerable degree of precision to the general indications of the *F.E.W.*:

> *défaitisme*, 1915 (créé par l'écrivain russe Alexinsky pour traduire le mot
> synonyme russe *porajentchestvo* formé aussi par lui).

This information forms the basis of the entry in the *Petit Robert* (1967), and stands unaltered in the fifth and sixth editions of the *Bloch-Wartburg* (1968 and 1975).

A much earlier date is proposed by A. Dauzat in his etymological dictionary (1st edn. 1938—10th edn. 1954). He claims that the terms *défaitiste/défaitisme* were first applied to the Russians in 1904, and became widespread in 1915. The six-volume *Robert* (1951) repeats this information, citing Dauzat as its source. However, in the *Dauzat-Dubois-Mitterand* (which appeared in 1964, the same year as the fourth edition of the *Bloch-Wartburg*) Dauzat's original dates are abandoned in favour of a single date: 1918. Since the reference turns out to be to a lexicographical article in the *Larousse Mensuel illustré*, it is clear that this date cannot mark the moment when the neologism first entered the French language.[1] Further confusion is engendered by the comment "appliqué aux Russes", which one assumes to be derived from the article in question; in fact there is no mention of Russians in the illustrative quotation— the term *défaitisme* is used of Frenchmen.[2] This unsatisfactory entry is drastically revised in the second edition of the *Dauzat-Dubois-Mitterand* (1971) to read: "1916, Alexinsky, appliqué aux Russes", where the source proposed by the *Bloch-Wartburg* is accepted, but curiously combined with the *F.E.W.*'s date.

The most recent etymological information to hand is contained in the *T.L.F.* (vol. vi, 1978), which gives 1918 for the first attestations of both *défaitiste* and *défaitisme*, based on M. Barrès's use of the terms in *Cahiers*. This date is somewhat surprising, since the bibliographical notes refer to an article published by G. Alexinsky in *Vie et Langage*, entitled "'Défaitisme'. Naissance et vie d'un néologisme".[3] Here Alexinsky explains how in 1915 he came to coin the Russian terms *porazhenets/porazhenchestvo/porazhencheskiĭ*[4] and their French equivalents. His article is undoubtedly the source of the strikingly specific entry in the 1964 *Bloch-Wartburg*. At first sight it would appear to provide a definitive answer to the questions surrounding the early history of *défaitiste/défaitisme*, yet its repercussions among lexicographers seem to have been rather limited.

As for the Russian word *porazhenchestvo*, the Soviet Academy Dictionary[5] gives a quotation from Lenin in January 1918, but no information about the origin of the expression. The Soviet Encyclopædia[6] is exclusively concerned with the history of the doctrine (as

[1] The information is no doubt taken from J. Dubois's *Étude sur la dérivation suffixale*, p. 35.

[2] See below, 2.12, p. 111.

[3] Dec. 1957, 538-47.

[4] I have transliterated Russian material according to the modified ISO system, except for the final syllable of personal names which is rendered uniformly as *-y*. The practice of other authors has been respected in quotations from their works, and Alexinsky's own name has been left as he himself wrote it.

[5] *Akademiya Nauk SSSR. Slovar' sovremennogo russkogo literaturnogo yazyka*, vol. 10, Moscow-Leningrad, 1960.

[6] *Bol'shaya sovetskaya entsiklopedia,* vol. 46, Moscow, 1940.

distinct from the word), suggesting that it began during the Russo-Japanese War (1904-5).[7] In fact, according to A. Kizevetter, patriotic Russians had a similar belief in the cathartic effect of defeat right at the beginning of the Crimean War:

> The Sevastopol tragedy appeared to them as a redeeming sacrifice for the sins of the past and an appeal for regeneration. The sincerest patriots put their hopes in the defeat of Russia by the external enemy.[8]

It seems, however, that the term *porazhenchestvo* and its cognates were not coined until after the outbreak of war in 1914. A. Mazon mentions them in his *Lexique de la guerre et de la révolution en Russie*:

> Ainsi ... dès longtemps avant la révolution de février, la guerre ... obligeait les socialistes russes à prendre position suivant qu'ils étaient *oborontsy* "défensistes", d'après le substantif abstrait *oborona*, ou bien *porajentsy* "défaitistes", d'après le substantif abstrait *porajenie*.[9]

He does not attribute any of the neologisms he discusses to individuals.

2.3 Grigory Alexinsky[1]

It is a rare privilege for the lexicologist to discover that the author of a neologism has provided a detailed account of the circumstances of its creation. However, people are notoriously unreliable about their own linguistic usage, and even such authoritative testimony must be subjected to close scrutiny.

Alexinsky first had occasion to publicize the origins of *porazhenchestvo* and *défaitisme* in an article entitled "Le 'défaitisme'. L'origine d'un néologisme", in *La Renaissance politique, littéraire, artistique* of 5 August 1922. He asserts there that the Russian neologism made its appearance in print in his weekly *Rossiya i Svoboda* (*Russia and Freedom*) in August 1915, and the French calque in his

---

[7] The date 1904 which Dauzat initially proposed for *défaitiste/défaitisme* may well have been inspired by writings like an article in *La Revue des Deux Mondes*, where P.-G. La Chesnais uses the term *défaitiste* ambiguously: "En 1905 l'opinion russe était contre la guerre japonaise, et, dans les milieux libéraux aussi bien que dans les milieux socialistes, les 'défaitistes' étaient nombreux" (16 June 1917, p. 3). On "retrospective" usage, see below, 2.12, pp. 110-111.

[8] *Istoricheskie otkliki*, Moscow, 1915, p. 191 (translated by G. Katkov, *Russia 1917*, Fontana edn., 1969, p. 46).

[9] Paris, 1920, p. 22.

[1] See Appendix I.

book *La Russie et la Guerre* published in the same year. He sub-
stantiates this claim with dates, page references and further corro-
borating evidence in the article already mentioned which he wrote
for *Vie et Langage* in 1957, forty-two years after the event. Unfortunately, his account is riddled with errors and inconsistencies, not
all of which can be blamed on his advanced years, since the main
facts he alleges are outlined in the 1922 version.[2]

To begin with what there is no cause to question: Alexinsky
coined the Russian words *porazhenets/porazhenchestvo/porazhen-
cheskiĭ* (regular derivatives of the noun *porazhenie* "defeat") to
designate his ideological opponents and their doctrine:

> Je cherchai une expression simple, brève et "collante" pour résumer
> d'une façon lapidaire la position de Lénine devant la guerre et le sens de
> sa propagande.[3]

Lenin openly urged Russian social-democrats to work for the defeat
of the tsarist government in the imperialist war. Soon after arriving
in Switzerland he revived his paper *Sotsial-Demokrat* (no. 33,
1 Nov. 1914), and in the articles which appeared there he made
much play with slogans centring on the word *porazhenie*.[4] His
pronouncements were eagerly picked up and commented upon by
his critics in Russia and abroad, prominent among whom were
Plekhanov in Italy and Alexinsky in France.

What Alexinsky had forgotten by 1922, however, was that the
direct target of the polemical attack which produced the term *porazhenchestvo* was not Lenin himself but the heterogeneous group
of émigré revolutionaries who contributed to the Paris daily *Nashe
Slovo* (*Our Word*)—Trotsky and Martov being the most notable
among them. Their publication presented a far more immediate
threat to the cause of national defence as championed by Alexinsky
and other Russian patriots in Paris than did the sporadic output of
Lenin in Geneva. On 13 April 1915[5] Alexinsky sent an article headed
"Sham Internationalists" ("Mnimye internatsionalisty") to the
Paris daily *Novosti* (*News*), explaining his desire to join forces with

---

[2] For detailed discussion see C. Slater, "Note critique sur l'origine de *défaitisme*
et *défaitiste*", *Mots*, i (1980), 213-17.

[3] *Vie et Langage,* Dec. 1957, 542.

[4] See in particular no. 35, 12 Dec. 1914, and no. 40, 29 Mar. 1915, reproduced
in V. Lenin, *Polnoe Sobranie Sochineniĭ,* 5th edn., vol. 26, Moscow, 1961, pp. 108-
9 and 166.

[5] Well before the first number of *Rossiya i Svoboda* appeared on 29 Aug.

like-minded socialists who were adopting a point of view which he
proposed to describe as "anti-defeatist for short" ("... nasha
tochka zreniya, kotoruyu ya nazovu dlya kratkosti—anti-pora-
zhencheskoĭ"). That this is the first time he uses his neologism in
print seems clear from the immediate storm of protest which it
aroused. *Nashe Slovo* took strong exception to the term on 16 April
in an article headed "Defeatism and Misrepresentationism"
("Porazhenchestvo i Iskazhenchestvo"); the author, who signs
himself Alpha, apologizes for using this jargon, and blames Alexinsky for "introducing the word 'defeatism' into common parlance—
specially to define the position of *Nashe Slovo*". Alexinsky replies
on 20 April (again in *Novosti*), this time putting the form *pora-
zhentsy* "defeatists" in his title; he accepts the charge laid against
him by Alpha of having given the name *porazhenchestvo* to his
opponents' attitude.

What emerges very strikingly from this significant exchange is
that neither journalist is in the least concerned with which particular
variant of the neologism in question occurs on a given occasion. It
so happens that Alexinsky uses *anti-porazhencheskiĭ* first (in print
if not in speech); but by so doing he establishes a model for the
morphological family *in toto*, which can be deemed to have come
into existence at the same moment.[6] Individuals of course vary in
their sensitivity to linguistic form. By contrast, S. Volzhsky, writing
in the Paris daily *Zhizn'* (*Life*) on 4 May, shows meticulous accuracy
over the terminology used by Alexinsky in *Novosti* of 13 April;
according to the latter, he argues, Russian socialists have taken up
two conflicting standpoints with regard to the war: "one is 'anti-
defeatist', the other must then be 'defeatist'" ("drugaya—oche-
vidno—'porazhencheskaya'"). Volzhsky is well aware that in his
first article Alexinsky does not actually use the term "defeatist"
to refer to his opponents, but calls them "our internationalists"
with heavy scorn throughout.

From the Russian press in Paris Alexinsky's neologism rapidly
travelled to Petrograd, where it appeared on 27 May (9 June, New
Style) in a letter he sent to the daily *Rech'* (*Speech*) to complain
about the way people had been distorting what he said in an article

---

[6] Many apparent instances of long delay separating first attestations of related
forms as e.g. in -*iste*/-*isme* can be put down to inadequate documentation. See
below, 2.9, p. 91, n. 14, and 3.5, p. 137, n. 12.

"On Provocation" ("O Provokatsii") published in March by the review *Sovremennyĭ Mir* (*The Contemporary World*). The word is still used very consciously: "so-called 'defeatist' leanings (tak nazyvaemye 'porazhencheskie' tendentsii) ... in a small number of Russian émigré circles". Soon, however, it ceases to be treated as a neologism. The forms *porazhenets/porazhenchestvo/porazhencheskiĭ* all occur in an important collection of articles *Voĭna* (*The War*) published privately[7] by Alexinsky, Plekhanov and others. Alexinsky's contribution "Who has the Majority?" ("S kem bol'-shinstvo?")[8] contains numerous examples, as does an article by Mark Z...r (A. Lyubimov) "Defence or Defeat" ("Oborona ili Porazhenie?"),[9] both writers use the terms without defining them, or even putting them in quotation marks.[10] Mark Z...r must have composed his article in May 1915 since he mentions that the War is in its tenth month. One can assume, then, that a month after its first appearance in print, Alexinsky's coinage was well assimilated into the vocabulary of his immediate political circle.

The stir caused by *Voĭna* served to publicize the neologism further. The collection came out some time between the end of June and the middle of July: it received savage reviews from Trotsky in *Nashe Slovo* on the 18th, and Lenin in *Sotsial-Demokrat* on the 26th. Alexinsky himself called the attention of his Petrograd readers to it in the number of *Sovremennyĭ Mir* dated end of June (Old Style, hence thirteen days behind the West). This latter article of his, "Austrian Agents and Russian Muddleheads" ("Avstriĭskie provo-katory i rossiĭskie putaniki") is a sequel to his earlier contribution "On Provocation"; it differs from it linguistically in that the terms *porazhenets* etc., not yet in print in March, are put to good polemi-cal use in June.

The French calque *défaitiste* made its appearance a few months later. Interestingly enough, the first texts in which Alexinsky uses it are revised editions of earlier works, where its introduction marks a noticeable improvement in his style.

The first edition of *La Russie et la guerre*, the preface to which is dated April 1915, came out in Paris in June. Alexinsky devotes a chapter to the activities of Lenin and his followers, describing

[7] At the Imprimerie des Langues Étrangères "Idéal", 14 rue Vavin.
[8] pp. 97-106.
[9] pp. 62-75.
[10] See below, 2.12, pp. 106-7.

their attitude by means of cumbersome periphrases reminiscent of
the Russian slogans:

> Au point de vue psychologique, le désir de la défaite de la Russie est
> compréhensible et presque plausible.[11]

—or again:

> La propagande en faveur de la défaite de la Russie fut bientôt discréditée
> parmi les révolutionnaires russes.[12]

He also uses expressions like "les représentants du désespoir révolutionnaire"[13] and "la propagande de la 'peur de la victoire'",[14]
but these, which constitute a hostile interpretation of Lenin's doctrine, are not as common as the "defeat" phrases which reflect
Lenin's own pronouncements directly.[15]

Later in the same year, Alexinsky brought out a new edition of
La Russie moderne[16] containing, as he explains in a preface dated
September 1915, "un chapitre additionnel consacré à un bilan de
l'évolution de la vie russe de 1911 à 1915". This is in essence a brief
outline of *La Russie et la guerre*, but with one significant modifi-
cation: the word *défaitiste* is introduced—once in the summary
and five times in the text. The first occurrence in the chapter is
accompanied by a brief explanation:

> Quant aux vrais démocrates et révolutionnaires de Russie, ils méprisent
> les menées des "défaitistes" (c'est ainsi qu'on appelle les partisans de la
> défaite russe) ... [17]

The neologism is next attested in the second (revised) edition of
La Russie et la guerre which appeared in December 1915. It does
not feature where one might have expected it—in a redrafting of
the chapter on Lenin. The text of the first edition is reprinted un-
changed, the only revision consisting in the addition of a short
chapter on the situation in Russia at the beginning of the second

[11] p. 220.
[12] pp. 239-40.
[13] e.g. p. 222.
[14] e.g. p. 220.
[15] In the space of twenty-nine pages, there are nineteen expressions based on "la
défaite de la Russie", eight on "la peur de la victoire", and three on "le désespoir
révolutionnaire".
[16] First published Paris, 1912.
[17] *La Russie moderne*, 2nd edn., p. 395.

year of fighting. Here Alexinsky uses the form *défaitiste* without comment:

> Quant aux ouvriers, les défaitistes ont tenté de les détourner de travailler au salut commun.[18]

Now it was clearly for reasons of "semantic economy" and "comparative efficiency"[19] that Alexinsky replaced locutions like *partisan de la défaite de la Russie* by the single word *défaitiste*. Given his desire to find a French equivalent for his felicitous Russian coinage, the theoretical choice before him was between straight borrowing and calque. In the case of names of foreign political groups, the former solution might have seemed the more appropriate; and had the source language not been Russian but one having closer affinities with French, it could well have presented no difficulty. However, the Russian terms *porazhenets* etc. convey nothing to a French speaker, whereas they are transparent and motivated to a Russian.[20] This being so, Alexinsky was bound to resort to the process of loan translation:[21]

> Je fis donc avec le mot français *défaite* la même opération morphologique qu'avec le mot russe *porajenié*; en ajoutant à la racine *défait* les suffixes *iste* et *isme*, je fabriquai les mots *défaitiste* et *défaitisme* qui s'adaptaient parfaitement à la "nature" du vocabulaire français et à l'"esprit" de la langue française.[22]

Strictly speaking the parallel is not exact in that where Russian disposes of two suffixes, one nominal, indicating an animate agent as in *porazhenets—un/le défaitiste*, and the other adjectival: *porazhencheskiĭ*, the French suffix *-iste* usually does duty for both.[23]

---

[18] *La Russie et la guerre*, 2nd edn., p. 297.

[19] These terms are taken from T. E. Hope, "The Process of Neologism Reconsidered with Reference to Lexical Borrowing in Romance", *Transactions of the Philological Society*, 1964, 58 and 72 respectively.

[20] What facilitates the borrowing into French of e.g. *fasciste/fascisme* or even *bolchevik/bolchevique/bolcheviste/bolchevisme* is their suffixation according to a "standard European" pattern. Note, however, that in 1917 the calque *maximaliste* was more widely used than the borrowing *bolchevik*. For the development in Russian of the suffixes *-izm* and *-ik*, see V. Kiparsky, *Russische historische Grammatik*, vol. iii, Heidelberg, 1975, pp. 210-11 and 213-14.

[21] See L. Deroy, *L'Emprunt linguistique*, Paris, 1956, p. 216; T.E. Hope, *Lexical Borrowing*, pp. 618-19; L. Guilbert, *La Créativité lexicale*, Paris, 1975, pp. 100-1.

[22] *Vie et Langage*, Dec. 1957, 543.

[23] But note that these are cases of double suffixation in *-iste/-ique*, e.g. *bolcheviste/bolchevique, bouddhiste/bouddhique*.

A calque, however, can only be the nearest equivalent form given the morphological and semantic structures of the source and target languages. Unless detailed research is carried out, the foreign inspiration behind a neologism may never come to light, and it will be classified as a purely native coinage; in some cases it may prove difficult to establish whether cognate terms which appear in different languages around the same time are independent formations, or whether one has influenced the other.[24] With suffixes as productive in modern French political vocabulary as -iste/-isme, the same derivative may well be coined afresh on more than one occasion.

Nothing has been said in the preceding pages of the French form *défaitisme* for the simple reason that no trace of it is to be found in any of the books published by Alexinsky in 1915—contrary to what he implies in his two articles on the coinage. There can be no doubt at all that it must have been in his vocabulary at the time, since pairs of words in -iste/-isme form a unit by this period;[25] and furthermore, he used the Russian abstract noun *porazhenchestvo* from the outset. He was a prolific writer, and *défaitisme* may yet turn up in an article of his in the French press in 1915-16.[26]

Fascinating though the search for first attestations may be, it forms only the prelude to a proper study of a neologism. As soon as one begins to examine how a new term is assimilated into a language, one moves from the domain of the arbitrary onto somewhat firmer ground. Indeed, when datings are revised, one's view of the subsequent stages in the adoption of a term often remains unaffected.[27] In the case of a word like *défaitiste*, which was borrowed into French with a highly specific, even technical meaning, the important questions to ask are how quickly it became widespread, who used it, and how long it remained exclusively associated with the doctrine of a few Russian revolutionaries.

[24] See E. Benveniste, "*Civilisation*. Contribution à l'histoire du mot", in *Problèmes de linguistique générale*, Paris, 1966, pp. 336-45; and below, 2.9, p. 90, n. 11, for the case of *boloïsme*.

[25] See J. Dubois, *Étude sur la dérivation suffixale*, pp. 45-6.

[26] In 1916 he contributed to *L'Événement* (e.g. 10 May) and to *Le Temps* (e.g. 7 Nov.).

[27] Cf. F. Brunot, *Histoire de la langue française*, vol. ix. 2, p. xii; M. Riffaterre, "La Durée de la valeur stylistique du néologisme". *Romanic Review*, xliv (1953), 283; L. Guilbert, *La Créativité lexicale*, pp. 44-54.

The diary of the French ambassador to St. Petersburg, Maurice Paléologue, provides a useful commentary on Russian affairs during the War. His first reference to Lenin's ideology occurs in October 1914—without any echoes of the latter's jargon:

> Un de mes informateurs, B..., qui a ses entrées dans les milieux avancés, me rapporte qu'on y discute actuellement une thèse étrange, dont l'auteur est l'anarchiste Lénine, réfugié en Suisse.
>
> Disciple fervent de Karl Marx, chef des "sozial-démocrates maxima-listes", Lénine proclame que la défaite militaire de la Russie est le prélude nécessaire de la révolution russe et la condition même de son succès. Il exhorte donc le prolétariat russe à faciliter, par tous les moyens, la victoire des Allemands.[28]

In September 1915, Paléologue uses language similar to Alexinsky's to describe this doctrine:

> Il ajoute que les idées de Lénine et sa propagande "pour la défaite" font de grands progrès parmi les éléments instruits de la classe ouvrière.[29]

Likewise in November:

> Chez les ouvriers, le virus révolutionnaire suffirait à expliquer le dégoût de la guerre et cette oblitération du sentiment patriotique qui va jusqu'au souhait de la défaite.[30]

It is not until March 1916 that the term *défaitiste* appears; there are no quotation marks or comment—the meaning is obvious from the context:

> Leur arrestation remontait au mois de novembre 1914, à l'époque où Lénine, réfugié en Suisse, inaugurait sa campagne défaitiste par cette profession de foi: "Les socialistes russes doivent souhaiter la victoire de l'Allemagne, parce que la défaite de la Russie entraînera la ruine du tsarisme ...[31]

Paléologue's memoirs were not published until 1922; they cannot therefore be held responsible in themselves for the introduction of the term *défaitiste* into French. However, it is probable that the Ambassador would have mentioned the Russian revolutionaries in private letters sent to France, and in diplomatic exchanges.

[28] *La Russie des Tsars pendant la Grande Guerre,* vol. i, Paris 1922, p. 174 (17 Oct. 1914).

[29] Ibid., vol. ii, p. 75 (17 Sept. 1915).

[30] Ibid., vol. ii, p. 106 (21 Nov. 1915).

[31] Ibid., vol. ii, p. 232 (30 Mar. 1916).

On 15 September 1916 the Paris daily *Nashe Slovo* was banned and Trotsky was promptly expelled from France for subversive propaganda. In the debate following this incident, the neologism *défaitiste* made its appearance in the French socialist press.[32] The Government's action was deplored by papers like *Le Populaire* which represented the extreme, internationalist fraction of the French Socialist Party (*les minoritaires*). Their pleas on Trotsky's behalf evoked a hostile reaction from *L'Action Socialiste*[33] on 22 November:

> Les minoritaires ont ... oublié de nous dire que le "vaillant journal" en question se recommandait des idées de certains Russes qui proclamaient la défaite de la Russie comme nécessaire et qu'on appelle pour cette raison les défaitistes.

It is clear from the phrasing of this criticism that the neologism *défaitiste* is still presumed to be unfamiliar to the general public.

From the evidence available it seems plausible to suggest that the term *défaitiste* (and doubtless *défaitisme* too) must have been current well before the revolution of February 1917 among people who took a particular interest in Russian affairs. Alexinsky's book *La Russie et la guerre* had sold so well that he felt the need to produce a revised edition in December 1915, only six months after the first. This and other writings by Alexinsky were known to E. Laskine, the author of a book entitled *L'Internationale et le pangermanisme*[34] which shows the hand of the German government in a great many pacifist and revolutionary manifestations. Laskine discusses the collection of articles *Voĭna* in some detail here,[35] so it is certain that by 1916 he knew the Russian words *porazhenets*, etc. He himself uses the term *défaitiste* in the French press just before the revolution; writing in *Le Matin* on 17 February 1917 he singles out certain Russian socialists for praise:

> ... les Plekhanow, les Alexinsky, dont l'effort s'est courageusement opposé à l'intrigue zimmerwaldienne, à la propagande de trahison des "défaitistes" ...

---

[32] See J. Maxe, *De Zimmerwald au bolchevisme, ou le triomphe du marxisme pangermaniste*, Paris, 1920, pp. 58-60.

[33] A new paper founded on 27 Sept. 1916 with the expressed aim of promoting unity among socialists.

[34] Paris, 1916. It was listed by the *Mercure de France* as a new publication on 16 June 1916.

[35] p.389.

No explanation is offered—Laskine's whole article assumes a fair degree of specialized knowledge about the Zimmerwald movement and left-wing activities in general.

2.4   The February Revolution[1]

The revolution naturally brought events in Russia to the forefront of the news abroad. Articles in the French press contain frequent references to the pre-revolutionary activities of different political groups, and it is in this context that the doctrine of the *défaitistes* is explained to the general public. This is not the place to discuss the accuracy of the beliefs circulating in France at that time about the internal politics of Russia. The picture given is doubtless grossly over-simplified, but since it is opinions put across to the public by journalists that account largely for the development and subsequent fate of the term *défaitiste*, these are all that need concern us here.

Three examples will suffice to give an idea of a commonly recurring type of explanation that appears in the press in the weeks immediately following the revolution. One is taken from an article entitled "Les Chefs extrémistes de Petrograd", written by a recent refugee from Russia and published in *Le Matin* on 23 March 1917:

Soukhanov est nettement zimmerwaldien. Il était même "défaitiste", c'est-à-dire qu'il exprimait l'opinion que seule une défaite pouvait libérer la Russie de l'absolutisme.

Another example appears in a leader in *La Victoire* on 19 April. With characteristic verve, G. Hervé proclaims:

Il y a une bévue qu'on peut être sûr, archi-sûr que [la Russie] ne commettra pas, c'est de suivre ceux qu'on appelle là-bas les "défaitistes". Non, ceux-là, vraiment, sont trop bêtes pour être dangereux. On les appelle ainsi parce qu'avant la Révolution, ils vous disaient froidement que seule une bonne défaite de leur pays délivrerait la Russie du tsarisme, et que, dans ces conditions-là, un bon révolutionnaire devait souhaiter la défaite de la Russie.

The third definition comes from the pen of the Belgian socialist

---

[1] Strikes began in Petrograd on 23 Feb., Old Style. The double abdication of Tsar Nicolas II and his brother, the Grand Duke Michael, was announced in Petrograd on 3 Mar., and news of it appeared in the French press on the following day—17 Mar., New Style.

minister E. Vandervelde, president of the Second International. He uses not only the form *défaitiste* but also *défaitisme*:[2]

> Il y avait en Russie, et surtout parmi les exilés russes, des "défaitistes" qui préféraient la défaite au maintien de l'autocratie, qui attendaient de la défaite la chute d'un régime d'arbitraire et de corruption. Ce régime n'est plus. Le "défaitisme" n'a même plus l'apparence d'une raison d'être ... (*L'Action Socialiste*, 4 Apr. 1917)

As presented in these definitions, the doctrine of the *défaitistes* is extremely specific, and the word would seem to be of limited application. One might even be led to suppose that it would only survive as a retrospective historical label, rendered obsolete by the very events which brought it to the notice of foreigners. This is certainly the conclusion one is tempted to draw from the passages quoted from *Le Matin* and *L'Action Socialiste*. Soukhanov is described as *having been* a *défaitiste*—in other words *formerly*; and *le défaitisme* is claimed to be an ideological position that is no longer relevant.

In fact, however, in the months following the overthrow of the Tsar, the term *défaitiste* is applied with growing frequency to members of extremist parties in Russia in connection with current, not past activities. It may seem something of a quibble to regard this as paradoxical: after all, logical considerations do little to explain how a word or expression becomes fashionable. Once the label *défaitiste* had become attached to certain individuals, it was likely to stick even if no longer fully appropriate. There would be no need to labour the point, were it not for the fact that a number of extreme left-wing journalists, sensing this apparent contradiction, were quick to make political capital out of it by pointing out the ignorance of their opponents. The writer of an article which appeared in *Les Nations* on 2 July seizes upon what he considers to be improper use of words in a rather clumsy attempt to defend the so-called *défaitistes* against their right-wing critics in the French press:

> Ce fut d'abord un concert d'imprécations pour discréditer les "défaitistes", alors que ceux-ci n'étaient plus défaitistes puisqu'ils attendaient d'un échec militaire la chute du tsarisme et que, leur prévision étant réalisée, ils reprennent leur formule: "Ni vainqueurs ni vaincus".[3]

---

[2] This is the earliest occurrence of *défaitisme* that I have found, although it was almost certainly in use before 1917. It appears in Paléologue's diary later in April ("l'outrance de son défaitisme", *La Russie des Tsars*, vol. iii, p. 307, 21 Apr. 1917).

[3] Quoted by L. Marchand, *L'Offensive morale*, p. 224.

Writing in *Le Bonnet Rouge* on 7 July G. Clairet also protests against the indiscriminate flourishing of the label *défaitiste* as a term of abuse:

> Il n'y a pas une semaine, je signalais ici même un article de M. René d'Aral du *Gaulois*, représentant Lénine comme un "défaitiste" et un "agent de Bethmann-Hollweg" ... Défaitistes, aussi, suivant M. Saint-Brice du *Journal*, les révolutionnaires Tchernof et Tcheïdzé, qui ne sont d'ailleurs pas des amis politiques de Lénine. Défaitiste aussi, dans son ensemble, cet admirable conseil des ouvriers et des soldats, le *Soviet* de Pétrograd.

Nevertheless, this strictly literal interpretation is something of an exception: it is, after all, exploited as a deliberate device in protest against what was rapidly becoming the established usage, and as such, it merely serves to provide confirmation of the latter. It should be noted in this connection that contrary to what is implied by the journalist of *Les Nations*, Lenin and his followers did not switch tactics when Kerensky came to power: they continued to reject "defencism" as premature, refusing to support the war effort of any but a truly proletarian government fighting for survival against the forces of imperialism.[4]

However, the continuing use of the term *défaitiste* cannot be justified by reference to the constancy of Lenin's ideological position. It occurs more and more in contexts where the doctrine of the overthrow of the Russian government via military defeat is quite clearly not the direct target of the attack in question, even if it is in some way related to the issues that are.

The current activities and beliefs alluded to earlier which earned certain individuals the name of *défaitistes* were chiefly connected with the Zimmerwald movement. This took its name from a conference of socialists held in Zimmerwald, Switzerland, in September 1915, and organized with a view to promoting international socialist cooperation. The resolutions adopted were phrased in terms of slogans such as *pas de responsables, ni vainqueurs ni vaincus, la paix immédiate sans annexions ni indemnités.*[5] The overriding aim

[4] See the pronouncements made by Lenin in March and April 1917 (*Polnoe Sobranie Sochineniĭ*, 5th edn., vol. 31, pp. 11-22 and 103-12).

[5] See E. Laskine, *L'Internationale et le pangermanisme*, p. 366; and M. de Roux, *Le Défaitisme et les manœuvres pro-allemandes*, Paris, 1918. The latter explains (p. 49): "Comme conclusion, la conférence de Zimmerwald adoptait la formule de paix sans indemnité ni annexion, qui paraît là pour la première fois."

was rapid peace, and this became variously known to the French patriots who opposed it as *la paix blanche, la paix boiteuse*, or simply *la paix boche*.[6]

In spite of its portentous resolutions, the conference did not produce a united front.[7] Its leftmost fraction was dominated by Lenin, who proclaimed that the imperialist war must be stopped and transformed into civil war in each of the participating countries. Now this was a far cry from the humanitarian-inspired pacifism of some of the adherents of the movement.[8] Lenin must have regarded many of their preoccupations as pitifully irrelevant: with the advent of world revolution there would be no place for capitalist squabbles over payment of war indemnities or possession of Alsace-Lorraine.

Patriotic French journalists are not to be blamed for failing or refusing to unravel the ideological intricacies of the Zimmerwald movement. As far as they were concerned, talk of worldwide proletarian revolution and talk of making peace before Germany was brought to her knees were equally loathsome, and—what is more to the point—equally certain to play straight into the hands of the enemy. Lenin was regarded by his detractors as a German agent, and the fact that he may have accepted Germany's aid while despising her aims and indeed hoping one day to destroy her (along with the rest), was a subtlety his opponents had no time for. These same people believed—not without reason—that the Zimmerwald conference (and its successor, the Kienthal conference, which took place in April 1916) was infiltrated by German spies. It is no secret that when fighting settled down to a state of deadlock on the Western Front, Germany was quick to turn to subversive tactics

[6] One even finds the epithet *Made in Germany*: "Les extrémistes russes ... reprennent donc à nouveau la formule: *Made in Germany* sur la paix rapide sans annexions ni indemnités" (*Le Matin*, 16 May 1917). L. Daudet speaks of "la paix K. K. de ces voleurs, incendiaires, esclavagistes et tueurs de femmes" (*L'Action Française*, 15 Dec. 1916).

[7] According to G. Katkov, "the movement had no ideological or political cohesion" (*Russia 1917*, p. 600). For the involvement of French socialists, see A. Kriegel, *Aux Origines du communisme français (1914-1920)*, Paris, 1964, pp. 109-12.

[8] Lenin had nothing but scorn for "bourgeois humanitarianism", so readily exploited in an imperialist war by the secret services of the enemy. He stressed his hostility to pacifism in a pamphlet *Socialism and the War* put out in August 1915: "We Marxists stand apart from pacifists on the one hand and anarchists on the other" (*Polnoe Sobranie Sochinenii*, 5th edn., vol. 26, p. 311).

in order to defeat the Entente, or at least to bring about a rapid peace before too much had been lost.[9]

In view of the violent feelings of hostility which every aspect of the complex Zimmerwald movement aroused, it is not surprising to find that in the months following the February Revolution the term *défaitiste*, a technical, yet abusive and highly expressive name for a minority of its members, came to be applied indiscriminately to people professing all shades of Zimmerwald opinion, or anything believed to be such, since the issues were so confused. Its transparent affiliation to the word *défaite* (itself highly charged in time of war) made it eminently fitted to bear the full weight of odium that was thrust upon it.

Once the strict ties with Lenin were broken, the term was used with increasing frequency. Again, this is to be expected, for discussions about immediate peace were a matter of far greater and more direct concern to France than Russia's purely internal quarrels: if Russia contracted a separate peace with the Kaiser, what would happen to the Allies? It is easy to see why the French press at this time is so full of articles attacking the Russian extremists: although Kerensky's government had affirmed its will to fight to the bitter end by the side of the Allies, the situation in Russia was highly precarious, and the extremist groups were viewed abroad as a very real threat. Hence a new spate of definitions of their ignominious aims. *L'Action Française* explains to its readers on 19 July 1917 that a number of Russian revolutionaries are in fact German born:

Leurs noms: les noms des défaitistes russes
Nous trouvons dans le *Journal des Débats* un bien intéressant renseignement sur l'identité de ceux qu'on a baptisés d'un nom barbare, les maximalistes, c'est-à-dire les révolutionnaires extrêmes qui, en Russie, sont partisans de Lénine et de la paix allemande.

It mattered little for the purposes in hand that the *maximalistes* (Bolsheviks) were in reality by no means all *défaitistes*.

---

[9] For Germany's intervention in Russian affairs and her subversive tactics in general, see Katkov, *Russia 1917*, ch. 5 and bibliographical notes; Z. A. B. Zeman (ed.), *Germany and the Revolution in Russia 1915-1918. Documents from the Archives of the German Foreign Ministry,* London, 1958; A. Scherer and J. Grunewald (eds.), *L'Allemagne et les problèmes de la paix. Documents extraits des archives de l'Office allemand des Affaires Étrangères,* 4 vols., Paris, 1962-78; A. Kupferman, "Les Débuts de l'offensive morale allemande contre la France (déc. 1914-déc. 1915)'', *Revue Historique,* 505, 1973, 91-114.

This example provides a good illustration of a much favoured stylistic device which establishes a rough and ready equivalence between terms like *défaitiste, extrémiste, anarchiste, maximaliste, zimmerwaldien* (and *kienthalien*):[10] individuals given one label in a newspaper headline are commonly referred to by a different one in the body of the article. Another instance of this occurs in *La Victoire* on 17 June:

> *LÉNINE EN DÉCONFITURE*
> *À l'occasion des élections municipales, le Suffrage universel se prononce contre les défaitistes*
> ... la troisième place revient aux extrémistes et anarchistes du groupe Lénine.

It is impossible to determine from such examples what the relationship is, in the usage of a given writer, between words which function as "alternatives" in this way.

Of the terms most closely associated with *défaitiste* at this time, *anarchiste* dates from the French Revolution,[11] whereas *extrémiste* was a recent acquisition to the language.[12] Maurras refers in 1913 to a handful of "anarchistes et libertaires" as "ces extrémistes, comme on dirait en Italie" (*L'Action Française*, 17 Aug. 1913), and *Le Canard Enchaîné* also uses *extrémiste* to denote a type of *anarchiste* —or rather, someone who does not quite qualify as such:

> [Gustave Hervé] fut un pamphlétaire vigoureux, acerbe, presque un anarchiste (on dirait aujourd'hui un extrémiste).[13] (16 May 1917)

To conclude discussion of the treatment given by the French press and writers to the *défaitistes russes*, it is worth alluding briefly to the analogical extension of the term *défaitiste* to cover two other closely related varieties of extremists. The first consists of individuals in countries other than Russia who held views similar to those of Lenin. In October 1915, Romain Rolland describes the attitude

[10] Sometimes spelled *kientalien*. The variants *zimmerwaldiste* and *kient(h)aliste* are also found (e.g. *La Victoire*, 18 Dec. 1916 and *Le Rappel*, 3 Oct. 1916).
[11] See F. Brunot, *Histoire de la langue française*, vol. ix. 2, pp. 828 and 847, n. 4.
[12] Not attested in the *F.E.W.* or *Bloch-Wartburg*. The *Petit Robert* gives 1911, and the *Larousse Mensuel illustré* includes the term (spelt *extrêmiste*) in April 1918. According to J. Dubois (*Le Vocabulaire politique et social*, p. 301), *extrémiste* had also been noted by the *Larousse Mensuel* in 1907.
[13] Anarchists and their activities in the years leading up to the First World War are discussed by J.-J. Becker, *Le Carnet B. Les pouvoirs publics et l'antimilitarisme avant la guerre de 1914*, Paris, 1973, pp. 61-8.

of certain German intellectuals to the war, using terms reminiscent
of the examples quoted earlier from Alexinsky and Paléologue:

> Bref, tous les vœux des intellectuels libres ... sont pour une défaite du
> militarisme prussien qui convainque la nation de son inutilité.[14]

In December 1917 he applies the word *défaitiste* to Leonhard Frank:

> Leonhard Frank est le type du "défaitiste" allemand fanatique. Jouve
> dit: "... C'est un ancien ouvrier et (je crois, je n'en suis pas sûr), le seul
> qui ne soit pas Juif parmi tous ces révoltés ou frondeurs allemands. Il
> veut la défaite de son pays, il veut son écrasement, pour que vienne la
> révolution allemande."

He continues:

> Écoutez-le: "Jusqu'à ce que la révolution ait éclaté en Allemagne, je
> suis, dit-il, avec les ennemis de l'Allemagne contre l'Allemagne! Mais
> dès que la révolution sera là-bas, je serai avec l'Allemagne contre le reste
> du monde. Le monde entier est pourri. L'Allemagne l'est plus que tout
> le reste: elle doit donc être la première châtiée et épurée. Mais ensuite, le
> reste du monde doit être châtié et épuré!" Voilà qui promet du plaisir,
> pour quelques générations! C'est le *jusqu'auboutisme défaitiste*, qui
> n'est pas moins implacable que l'autre.[15]

The term is given its strictly technical meaning, and is not intended
to be abusive, although Rolland has little sympathy for the doctrine
in question. The coupling of *défaitiste* with *jusqu'auboutisme*,
extremely apt in the context, is particularly piquant because the
terms had come to symbolize two diametrically opposed attitudes.[16]
   The second type of parallel development concerns the use of the
term *défaitiste* to refer more generally to all kinds of *internationalistes* in countries other than Russia. Indeed, it is hardly surprising
to find that once *défaitiste* came to be identified or confused with
zimmerwaldien and *kienthalien*, it began to lose its connections
with Russia—after all, the Zimmerwald movement deliberately put
international solidarity before national identity.[17] Examples of the
kind:

---

[14] *Journal*, p. 563 (29 Oct. 1915).
[15] Ibid., pp. 1378-9 (15 Dec. 1917).
[16] See below, 3.6, pp. 150-2.
[17] In view of the common misapprehensions on the subject, it should be stressed
that the term *défaitiste* was not applied by the press *in 1915-16* to the French
socialists who attended the Zimmerwald and Kienthal conferences.

LE DÉFAITISME

;eries de quelques défaitistes de Pétrograd ou d'ailleurs ...
(Paris-Midi, 9 June 1917)

all for comment. A bolder step in the same direction
ɪɪau already been taken by a journalist writing in *La Victoire* on
7 May:

Branting contre les Défaitistes
Le leader de la social-démocratie suédoise regrette notamment que le
député socialiste hollandais ait, dans différentes interviews, répété les
mots de "paix séparée".

This occurrence points unambiguously forward to the next phase
in the history of the neologism.

2.5 The Mutinies

As far as the French were concerned, the Russian revolution was
only the first of a long series of upheavals which were to shake
them in quick succession throughout 1917. It was a year aptly
described by Poincaré in the title of a volume of his memoirs as
"l'année trouble".[1] Mutinies in the army followed close upon the
threat of an international socialist conference meeting in Stockholm
to discuss immediate peace; shortly afterwards, a number of scan-
dalous affairs involving foreign agents came to light, culminating
eventually in the trial of the Minister of the Interior, Malvy, on
a charge of treason. The reactions of different journalists to the
various disasters of 1917 and early 1918 mark important stages in
the permanent adoption of the terms *défaitiste/défaitisme* into
French. In the space of a few weeks, owing to a particular com-
bination of circumstances, a label that had been applied to Lenin
and his followers came to be used to castigate Frenchmen—but in
connection with activities which carried their own specifically
internal stamp, and were no longer direct derivatives of the Bolshevik Party platform.

The mutinies which disrupted the French army in the early
summer of 1917 have been described by the very man who was
called upon to deal with the situation: General Pétain. His account
of the events,[2] written some time before 1925, was not published
at the time, largely for reasons of political expediency, although it

[1] *Au Service de la France*, vol. ix, *L'Année trouble 1917*, Paris, 1932.
[2] *La Crise morale et militaire de 1917*, Paris, 1966.

was in circulation before 1966.[3] Another testimony from someone immediately concerned with the mutinies is provided by the memoirs of J. de Pierrefeu.[4] Pétain's role in handling the crisis need not be discussed here;[5] on the other hand, his diagnosis of the cause of the troubles in the army has direct bearing on the history of the terms *défaitiste/défaitisme*.

Both Pétain and Pierrefeu stress the fact that morale among the French troops had reached a very low ebb in the winter of 1916-17. The soldiers were not only physically exhausted after the long-drawn-out fighting at Verdun, but were also profoundly discouraged by the apparent futility of the sacrifices they were called upon to make. Moreover, conditions in the army were a legitimate subject of discontent, and though this had doubtless been the case all along, the cumulative effects were beginning to show. The troops were thus an ideal target for pacifist and revolutionary propaganda. General Nivelle complained to the Ministry of the Interior on 29 December 1916 about "l'envoi aux armées de tracts à tendance antimilitariste et anarchiste",[6] and on 25 January 1917 to the Ministry of War about strikes and disturbances in military factories etc., news of which was having the most adverse effect on morale at the front, and constituted a serious threat to discipline.

When the disastrous failure of the Nivelle offensive in April 1917 brought matters to a head, and mutinies began to spread through the army,[7] Pétain noted that the men were always *"entraînés par quelques meneurs très habiles—qui semblent, d'après les témoignages recueillis, faire vraiment figure de chefs d'émeute"*;[8] he identified these revolutionary agitators as members of various internationalist organizations acting—whether naïvely or deliberately—in line with the interests of the Berlin Government. Accordingly, he advocated strong measures on the part of the

[3] General Laure makes ample use of this document in his book *Pétain*, Paris, 1941.
[4] *G.Q.G. Secteur 1. Trois ans au Grand Quartier Général par le rédacteur du "communiqué"*, vol. ii, Paris, 1920, pp. 15-38.
[5] For a full account, see A. Horne, *The Price of Glory. Verdun 1916,* London, 1962, pp. 322-5; R. Griffiths, *Marshal Pétain,* London, 1970, pp. 42-9; J. Williams, *Mutiny 1917*, London, 1962.
[6] Pétain, *La Crise morale et militaire,* p.33.
[7] They started on 29 April among units due to go into action at the Chemin-des-Dames; trouble continued throughout May, reaching its climax in the first few days of June.
[8] *La Crise morale et militaire,* p. 75.

French authorities to curb pacifist tracts and newspapers, especially *Le Bonnet Rouge* and *La Gazette des Ardennes*. On 31 May he warned the *Comité de Guerre* that he would be unable to answer for the army if passports were granted to the French Socialist delegates who wished to attend the Stockholm peace conference.[9] The question of the conference was being ardently discussed in public during the weeks in which the mutinies occurred, and Pétain regarded this as one of the major factors contributing to the widespread demoralization in the army. He believed that in a time of crisis, more harm than good is done to democracy if the press enjoys too much freedom, and he frequently advised the Government in strong terms to see to the correct "orientation de la grande presse".[10]

Now in this particular case, press comments on the various sources of tension which helped to trigger off the mutinies had an interesting linguistic result: a certain number of activities carried out in the pursuit of a specific aim became so closely associated that a single label was found for them—*le défaitisme*. Looking back after the event, Pétain laid the blame squarely on the press for its part in this development:

> Certains journaux, bien que mal renseignés sur les questions russes, en entretiennent quotidiennement leurs lecteurs. Ils exposent, parfois en y applaudissant, des mesures prises par les révolutionnaires telles que les créations de comités d'ouvriers et de soldats, l'abolition du salut et des appellations réglementaires. Ils font la plus large publicité aux tentatives des socialistes pour la reprise des relations internationales, pour l'organisation des réunions où les adhérents du parti,—alliés, russes, neutres et ennemis,—se proposent de discuter de la paix. Ils soulignent la gravité de la crise économique, l'importance des grèves, etc...
> *Tant et si bien que les voix du Pays lancent l'idée et le mot de "défaitisme" à l'heure même où le Gouvernement, qui eût dû les contrôler, cherche à forcer la Victoire.*[11]

Pétain suggests here that to name an evil in this way often merely serves to attract an unwanted amount of attention to it.[12] This was

---

[9] For the stand taken by the French Socialist Party over Stockholm, see A. Kriegel, *Aux Origines du communisme français*, pp. 148-50 and 167-70.

[10] *La Crise morale et militaire*, p. 135.

[11] Ibid., pp. 37-8.

[12] In his own correspondence with the Ministry of the Interior (through the intermediary of the Ministry of War), he complains about "la propagande *pacifiste*" (my italics) even after the term *défaitiste* was in use. See his letter of 28 July 1917 and the official reply of 20 Aug. 1917 (*La Crise morale et militaire*, pp. 130-2).

clearly not the opinion of the journalists concerned, for without any doubt their intentions were to use a new and striking label as an effective polemical weapon against a dangerous enemy.

2.6 Henry Bérenger

A day-to-day account of the way in which this new weapon was forged can be pieced together from close reading of the relevant newspapers. After what has been said about the connection between the internationalist movement and the mutinies, it may not seem particularly surprising that the term *défaitiste*, associated in the mind of the French public first with *léniniste* and then with *zimmerwaldien*, should come to be used of the agitators who disrupted the army—they were, after all, individuals of a similar brand. However, granted that this basic analogy facilitated the extension in the use of the term *défaitiste*, it cannot be proposed as a sufficient condition for its acceptance. Other words whose associations might seem to render them equally apt to fulfil the need in question did not catch on with anything remotely resembling the same success. If the terms *défaitiste/défaitisme* were promoted to the status of a slogan in a very short space of time, it was due almost exclusively to the action of a single journalist—Henry Bérenger.[1]

As vice-president of the *Commission sénatoriale de l'Armée*, Bérenger compiled an important dossier on the mutinies, which included a document entitled *Agents provocateurs dans les milieux militaires de mai-juin 1917.*[2] He also seems to have been well informed about affairs in Russia. The first use of the term *défaitiste* by Bérenger that I have been able to trace in the press occurs on 24 May 1917:

> Je le répète: est-ce bien à nous ... qu'il convient de proclamer "le droit au libre développement" de nos envahisseurs et de nos mutilateurs? .... Nous n'avons à faire plaisir à aucun "défaitiste" par aucune défaillance.
> (*Paris-Midi*)

The term is not explained, but it refers by implication to those who preach "la paix sans annexions ni indemnités". A similar type of example, this time with the word *défaitisme*, appears on 5 June. The *Chambre* had just passed a vote specifying that the return of

[1] See Appendix I.
[2] Mentioned by L. Daudet, *L'Hécatombe. Récits et souvenirs politiques 1914-1918*, Paris, 1923, p. 17.

Alsace-Lorraine to France was an essential precondition for peace. This was a snub to the would-be Stockholm delegates—hence the title of Bérenger's article:

> *Strasbourg et non Stockholm*
> Après le vote de la Chambre, l'heure est passée du "défaitisme". Celle de la *discipline* a sonné. (*Paris-Midi*, 5 June 1917)

In neither case are the terms defined, and taken in context, they do not receive any striking emphasis apart from the quotation marks.[3] The turning point comes on the following day with an article published in *Le Matin* entitled "Au tournant des démocraties—défaitisme ou organisation?" It is essential to remember that of course no direct reference to the mutinies was allowed to get into the press at the time. "Anastasie"—as the French affectionately called the censorship—did her work thoroughly. Hence there was an imperative need to find some way of conveying the danger that hung over France without specifying what it was. Bérenger's answer was to launch a full-scale scare about a new and sinister form of threat, taking an existing word as a name for it and defining it to suit his own purposes. His article is of the utmost significance;[4] nothing like it had appeared before, and it was undoubtedly responsible for giving the term *défaitisme* its great "send-off".[5] The key passage runs as follows:

> Les démocraties ont aujourd'hui à combattre un ennemi plus dangereux que le Kaiser, et *cet ennemi est en elles*. On l'affuble, depuis quelque temps, d'un nom nouveau: le "Défaitisme". Mais c'est une vieille connaissance. Elle s'appelle l'Anarchie. (*Le Matin*, 6 June 1917)

A different version of this article occurs in *Paris-Midi* on the same day, entitled "Occident et Orient". Its theme is similar, and there are very strong verbal echoes ("L'Occident ne s'agenouillera pas ...", "le *Nitchevo*[6] oriental", etc.) but the word *défaitisme* does not appear. The article in *Le Matin* is an isolated contribution to this paper; Bérenger continues his campaign in *Paris-Midi* in the ensuing days. On 8 June the leader is headed:

---

[3] On the use of quotation marks and italics, see below, 2.12, pp. 106-7.

[4] It is reproduced in full in Appendix II, text 3.

[5] *Le Matin* had a circulation of almost 1,500,000 copies on 1 July 1917, as compared with 28,500 for *Paris-Midi*. See Appendix III.

[6] The Russian word meaning "nothing".

La Victoire des Armes

Voilà la meilleure réponse des démocraties occidentales aux propa-
gandes imbéciles et infâmes de *défaitisme* qui leur parviennent depuis
quelque temps de sources corrompues et empestées ... le meilleur antidote contre tous les poisons de nihilisme et tous les commencements de
désordre qui peuvent naître à la fois de la durée de la guerre et de la
faiblesse des gouvernements.... Le peuple français a trop louché du côté
de l'anarchie pétrogradienne.

The term *défaitisme* is thus equated by Bérenger at this stage with
anarchie, and linked with such words as *désordre* and *nihilisme*; it
is contrasted with *organisation, discipline, patriotisme*, and *démocratie*. Both articles are strikingly barren of factual information:
the semi-mystical panegyric of the Western democracies at the
expense of the equivocal East relies on highflown rhetoric to boost
morale and strengthen the desired loyalties.

In this rather theoretical context, it is not surprising to find that
Bérenger favours the abstract noun *défaitisme*: he studiedly avoids
precise mention of any particular *défaitistes*. Later, the form *défaitiste* does appear—"les défaitistes du Kaiser" (3 July 1917), "l'abo-
minable propagande *défaitiste*" (26 June 1917), but it seems to be
secondary in Bérenger's usage, and does not bear the weight of
repeated definitions—as was to be the fate of the term *défaitisme*.
As a result of Bérenger's efforts, the latter ceases to denote exclusively a political ideology or doctrine. It comes to refer more generally to an attitude or mode of behaviour which may spring from
a rigidly definable set of beliefs, but which is considered from the
point of view of its practical effects and consequences. Hence the
shift in emphasis which enables the word *défaitisme* to become
associated with wider terms like *anarchie* and *désordre*, and which
makes it available for all kinds of further polemical exploitation.

Bérenger must have sensed that the word he had thrown into the
political arena was provoking the desired response. He continues to
make skilful and conscious use of it, gradually building up a composite picture of what he understands *le défaitisme* to be. Headlines
of the type "Sus au défaitisme" (26 June 1917), "Riposte au
défaitisme" (3 July 1917), or "La fin du défaitisme" (7 July 1917)
become regular features of *Paris-Midi*. That the mutinies were
uppermost in Bérenger's mind is abundantly clear from an article
written on 12 June, where the allusions scarcely qualify as veiled:
he mentions "une entreprise de démoralisation" which makes use

of tracts and is dependent on "argent suspect", and he describes this as "une pourriture de l'arrière". He concludes:

Ainsi, un certain "défaitisme" a fini par naître puis grouiller dans les corruptions de la tolérance. C'est parmi les embusqués, les filles, les permis de séjour, les installés de toute catégorie, que se recrute l'équipe honteuse et ignoble de pacifisme qui s'attaque en ce moment à la discipline de nos troupes et au labeur de nos usines.

Here, Bérenger refers to the individuals who engage in subversive activity as "l'équipe honteuse et ignoble de pacifisme", but it is not clear from this example what he considers the relationship between le défaitisme and le pacifisme to be.[7]

The evolution in Bérenger's use of the term défaitisme in these early weeks closely reflects the way in which he was looking at the problem of the mutinies. Emphasis on their visible results explains the association of défaitisme with anarchie; later, when Bérenger had access to more facts about the causes of the uprisings, one finds that treason is the aspect which tends to receive greatest prominence:

Le défaitisme .... traître, ... essaya de tourner la victoire en échec, la résistance en reculade, l'offensive ailée en paix boiteuse.... Les démocraties, qui se battent pour un idéal, ont déjà démasqué le défaitisme, qui trahit pour de l'argent. (Paris-Midi, 12 July 1917)

This association between défaitisme and trahison was soon to become firmly established.

2.7 Les Serviteurs de l'ennemi

Some two weeks elapsed during which Bérenger appears to have had the monopoly of his slogan. It was then adopted, quite suddenly, by a number of other polemical journalists who were quick to realize its possibilities as a weapon of attack, and, according to their affiliations, either included it in their arsenal, or devised a means to parry it. At this stage, the terms défaitiste/défaitisme, used in connection with the troubles inside France, did not find their way into the ordinary run of journaux de grande information which aimed to avoid polemics—papers like L'Illustration, Le Petit Journal, or Le Matin[1]—although they were used quite freely there

[7] This is further discussed below, 2.8, pp. 75ff.
[1] Bérenger's influential article in this paper was an exception, as has been pointed out. Troublemakers were usually labelled extrémistes and pacifistes. H. Lavedan does not use the term défaitiste in his article "Sabotage moral" in L'Illustration (see Appendix II, text 2).

as pejorative labels for Russian extremists and their activities. They remained almost exclusively within a very limited polemical sphere, the prerogative of a few individuals who had already established a reputation for themselves as lexical innovators.

One of the most striking features of the neologism at this time is its versatility: in each case, it is fitted by a given journalist into the set of words which he has already evolved to deal with the particular *bêtes noires* which are the object of his attacks. The newly acquired term is then coloured by surrounding terms, and takes on fresh overtones as a result. This is of course characteristic of words which have recently entered a language, but is especially applicable to a term like *défaitiste* which is so closely bound up with personal fears, hatreds, and prejudices.[2]

One of the first people to follow Bérenger's example was Léon Daudet. Writing in *L'Action Française* on 21 June 1917 about the unpatriotic sentiments expressed by *Le Bonnet Rouge*, Daudet remarks (without comment on the term *défaitisme*, although this appears to be the first time he uses it in *L'Action Française*):

> Chaque jour, sous une forme quelconque, le défaitisme y était prôné, chaque jour y était prise ouvertement la défense des agents allemands.

To understand what Daudet meant by *le défaitisme*, one must take a look at some of his chief preoccupations dating from the outbreak of the war and even earlier. Though a staunch royalist by conviction, Daudet boasted that since August 1914 he had faithfully observed the *Union Sacrée* pact, and had therefore done all he could to further the interests of France's Republican government, in spite of fundamental lack of sympathy with it. He had directed all his energies to unmasking his country's enemies, in whatever guise he found them. Before the war, he had become aware of what he considered to be an alarming amount of German infiltration into all areas of French life, but particularly commercial and

---

[2] T. E. Hope's remarks on the assimilation of loan-words apply equally to neologisms in general: he observes that there is generally an "*interim period* between the moment of borrowing and full integration into the language. During this interval semantic change is rapid. The process by means of which semantic adjustment takes place is in great measure a stylistic one. The borrowed term, divested of its habitual semantic accompaniment, enters upon a period of fluidity, of comparative semantic autonomy. Appearing in a host of different contexts it provides great material for figurative expressions and evocative *tournures*" ("Loan-words as Cultural and Lexical Symbols" (1963), 41).

financial undertakings. He coined the expression *l'Avant-Guerre*, defined as "l'espionenvahissement juif-allemand", to denote the intense subversive activity carried on by Germany preparatory to declaring war, and he made it the title of a book which he published on the subject in March 1913.[3] His contemporaries rapidly took up the expression. J. Bainville notes:

> Une des opérations d' "avant-guerre" (selon le mot si admirablement créé par Léon Daudet et qui restera dans la langue française), une des opérations d'avant-guerre les mieux réussies de l'Allemagne a été le coup porté à la Bourse de Paris.[4]

The vigorous campaign conducted by Daudet against German infiltrators and agents centred, as has been shown, on the person of the *emboché*;[5] these *embochés* in their turn had their own appendages, as Daudet explained to his readers:

> Ce petit groupe de coquins ou de dupes a lui-même une clientèle, qui subit l'influence des patrons. C'est ce que j'ai appelé le Clan des Ya.[6]
>
> (*L'Action Française*, 2 Dec. 1916)

Throughout the war, Daudet worked with tireless energy to uncover the hand of the enemy at work. Scandals swelled and subsided with a certain regularity around enterprises as diverse as the Maggi-Kub firm and the gambling houses at Monaco, both of them accused of being German concerns.[7] In every case, Daudet's readers were treated to a rich account of the activities of the *embochés* and the *clan des Ya—la pègre de l'Antifrance* as he also called them (e.g.

---

[3] The work had sold 11,000 copies by the outbreak of war, and 25,000 by Jan. 1915. See E. J. Weber, *Action Française*, p. 89. Daudet makes no secret of his antisemitism—he writes in the preface: "L'Avant-Guerre, s'il en était besoin, justifierait l'antisémitisme comme une nécessité de la Défense Nationale."

[4] *Journal inédit* (1914), Paris, 1953, p. 188 (24 Nov. 1914). Bainville was right in his prediction: the expression reappears in the title of R. Brasillach's memoirs *Une Génération dans l'orage. Mémoires: notre avant-guerre. Journal d'un homme occupé* (Paris, 1968).

[5] See above, 1.4, p. 26.

[6] From the German word *ja* meaning "yes". The expression antedates *emboché* since it appears in *L'Avant-Guerre*, e.g. p. 217: "Partout en France il y a, embusqué, un agent électif français ou juif du clan des Ya, que manœuvre l'Allemagne, qui vend à l'Allemand la clé de son pathelin..."

[7] See Appendix II, text 4, and above, 1.6, pp. 29-30. See also E. J. Weber, *Action Française*, pp. 89 ff.; A. Kupferman, "Le Rôle de Léon Daudet et de *L'Action Française* dans la contre-offensive morale: 1915-1918", *Études Maurrassiennes*, vol. ii, Aix-en-Provence, 1973, pp. 121-44.

L'Action Française, 16 Oct. 1916).[8] His overall strategy can be summed up in another of his coinages—the phrase *la guerre totale*. He makes constant references to it in *L'Action Française*, and he published a book under this title in 1918 from which the following definition is taken:

> Qu'est-ce que la guerre *totale*? C'est l'extension de la lutte, dans ses phases aiguës comme dans ses phases chroniques, aux domaines politique, économique, commercial, industriel, intellectuel, juridique et financier. Ce ne sont pas seulement les armées qui se battent, ce sont aussi les traditions, les institutions, les coutumes, les codes, les esprits et surtout les banques.[9]

Thus by the summer of 1917, Daudet had already developed an elaborate terminology to sustain his campaigns; when he adopted *défaitiste* into his vocabulary, it joined the ranks alongside *embochê* etc. as a name for enemy agents and traitors—here no longer referring exclusively to troublemakers in the military sphere (as had been the case with the mutinies) but in all areas of civilian life as well. It so happened that just at this time a quarrel which had been smouldering between Daudet and some of his arch enemies flared up into a new blaze, fanned no doubt by the mutinies in the army. This was the longstanding feud which set *L'Action Française* against *Le Bonnet Rouge*.

The *Bonnet Rouge* affair is notorious; it received considerable publicity when it occurred and immediately afterwards. In June 1917, shortly before the dramatic *dénouement*, Charles Sancerme completed *Les Serviteurs de l'ennemi*[10]—an analysis of *Le Bonnet*

---

[8] *Les Cahiers de l'Anti-France* was the title given by J. Maxe to a periodical he launched in 1922. It was published in book form as *L'Anthologie des défaitistes*, 2 vols., Paris, 1925.

[9] *La Guerre totale*, p. 8. H. Bérenger comments on the expression in *Paris-Midi* (1 May 1918): "*Guerre totale*, a dit justement un jour Léon Daudet." The first occurrence in *L'Action Française* dates from 11 Mar. 1916.

[10] The title is a deliberate echo of a regular column-heading in *Le Bonnet Rouge*: "Les serviteurs de l'étranger". The latter was explained as follows: "Voilà pourquoi nous disons que Léon Daudet et les siens sont les serviteurs de l'étranger: par leurs propos et leurs écrits, ils tendent à ruiner l'autorité du gouvernement et la confiance du pays dans ses chefs—autorité et confiance également indispensables" (*Le Bonnet Rouge*, 19 Oct. 1915). Daudet and Maurras were constantly insulted and accused of being German agents themselves, and of using the war to try to restore the monarchy in France (see Daudet, *L'Hécatombe*, p. 128). There is a certain inconsistency in the accusations of the Left: *L'Action Française* is sometimes portrayed as supporting the pro-German Catholic Church (see above, 1.6, p. 30, and below, 3.3, pp. 124-5), and sometimes blamed for its *bochophobie* (see above, 1.4, p. 27).

Rouge from the outbreak of war to the end of April 1917 (with some June texts included in an appendix just before publication), consisting mainly of direct quotations followed by brief comments. The author shows that from 1915 onwards *Le Bonnet Rouge* began increasingly to express pro-German sentiments, to defend German points of view, and in general to follow a line calculated to undermine the morale of a fighting nation.[11] *Les Serviteurs de l'ennemi* was written before Bérenger and Daudet began to use the term *défaitisme* to denounce the activities of enemy agents in France. Sancerme is of course dealing with the same phenomenon, but he does not call it *défaitisme*. His comments frequently take the form of a list of names for the behaviour he is unmasking which punctuates the text at intervals like a refrain:

> Désertion, anarchie, jeu, pacifisme, kientalisme, chantage, espionnage, réformes frauduleuses, tripotage, escroquerie, surinage, embochage, trahison.[12]

If he had published only a short while later, the odds are very strong that the word *défaitisme* would have figured in this list.[13]

Sancerme's conclusion that *Le Bonnet Rouge* was a German newspaper is endorsed by Louis Marchand in his book *L'Offensive morale des Allemands en France pendant la guerre*.[14] Marchand was a teacher of German who, when war broke out, was seconded as an interpreter to the *Bureau d'étude de la presse étrangère*. In the course of his work there, his attention was drawn to certain similarities between *Le Bonnet Rouge* and *La Gazette des Ardennes*, a German newspaper published in French at Charleville (seat of the German H.Q.), and aimed at the French population of occupied areas. On his own initiative Marchand undertook a systematic comparison of the two papers concerned; painstaking collation of articles led him to the strong conviction that *Le Bonnet Rouge* was

[11] Sancerme's indictment of *Le Bonnet Rouge* is all the more damning since it comes from the pen of someone who admits that he was a pacifist before the war, and had little in common with men of the extreme Right such as Daudet and Maurras.

[12] *Les Serviteurs de l'ennemi,* p. 14 *et passim.*

[13] In February 1918 he founded *La Voix Nationale*—a paper which soon lapsed through lack of funds. He published a selection of articles from it under the title *Les Batailles de l'arrière. Cinq mois sur la brèche* (Paris, 1918). The first number of *La Voix Nationale* warns readers that "il y a encore en France des pacifistes défaitistes" (p. 44, 5 Feb. 1918). By this time Sancerme was using the neologism quite freely.

[14] This did not appear until April 1920, although it was the result of work carried out during the war, and was completed approximately a year before publication.

a satellite of *La Gazette des Ardennes*, financed with German subsidies.[15]

Before Marchand's study was made public, however, Léon Daudet had already got his claws into *Le Bonnet Rouge*. He does not refer to it by name in *L'Action Française*, but calls it *Le Torchon* or *Le Torchon à Vigo*,[16] persistently ignoring its editor's pseudonym Almereyda except for facetious purposes.[17] The detail of the various accusations made by Daudet against Almereyda and his associates at one time or another, and the lawsuits which these produced, is not pertinent to the present discussion. Suffice it to say that he made easy capital out of Almereyda's criminal record (particularly the connections with drug trafficking, illegal abortions, blackmail, and trade in fraudulent *réformes médicales*), evidence of which he detected in *Le Bonnet Rouge*'s campaigns in favour of absinth and alcohol (in the name of Liberty), and in articles by a so-called Dr Lombard opposing the suggestion that all *réformés* should undergo further medical inspections.[18] More serious complaints were that *Le Bonnet Rouge* preached the doctrine of Franco-German co-operation, greeted peace proposals with undisguised sympathy, openly defended writers like Romain Rolland and Henri Barbusse who were dragged in the mud elsewhere, and did its best to whitewash the German character, reacting vigorously against such epithets as *sale Boche*.[19]

[15] As evidence of this collusion Marchand suggests, *inter alia*, that *Le Bonnet Rouge* picked up the term *rouleau compresseur* from the German-run paper. He quotes an example from *Le Bonnet Rouge*: "Le rouleau compresseur qui devait en cinq étapes broyer les défenses de Berlin à la Noël, faisait-il machine en arrière?" (9 May 1916), and notes: "Soulignons enfin ce 'rouleau compresseur' qui fait partie du vocabulaire de la pseudo-gazette, mais non de celui du *Bonnet Rouge*, puisque, les 2 et 5 septembre 1914, le journal d'Almereyda parlait non de rouleau compresseur, mais de rouleau à vapeur" (*L'Offensive morale*, pp. 253-5). Both terms were current in 1914, as designations for the Russian army, although *rouleau compresseur* was more widely used. For the origin of this latter term, see R.-L. Wagner, *Les Vocabulaires français*, vol. ii. p. 28.

[16] Cf. Ch. Maurras, *Les Conditions de la Victoire*, vol. iv, *La Blessure intérieure*, Paris, 1918, p. viii: "Ce journal infect s'appelait le *Bonnet Rouge*. C'est la première fois que j'écris son nom. Il nous paraît usurpé. Nous éprouvions une indicible répugnance à confondre avec l'insigne historique d'un parti révolutionnaire, *mais français*, le chiffre ignoble d'un agent provocateur allemand. Nous ne l'avons nommé pendant trois ans que le *Torchon*." *Le Bonnet Rouge* complains that *L'Action Française* refers to it as "Le Papier hygiénique" (20 Aug. 1915), "une feuille stercoraire" and "une issue d'égout" (15 June 1915).

[17] See Appendix I, *M. Almereyda*.
[18] See Appendix II, text 4.
[19] See above, 1.7, p. 35.

The situation towards the end of June was critical. Although the press kept silent about the mutinies, people in high places were perfectly aware of what was happening, and were beginning to realize the part that had been played by certain pacifist newspapers in stirring up trouble. Investigations revealed that uncensored copies of *Le Bonnet Rouge* had been distributed in large numbers at the front, along with supplies of free wine to intoxicate the troops; the soldiers, believing quite naturally that "Anastasie" had done her work, assumed that the articles they read talking of immediate peace and an end to all fighting had received official sanction and could therefore be trusted.

Le Bonnet Rouge was not the only newspaper to be regarded with deep suspicion. In its pacifist campaigns it had long been backed by *La Tranchée Républicaine* whose editor, a certain Goldschild, preferred to be known as Goldsky; and it was joined on 1 June by a new paper—*Le Pays*. [20] The first numbers created a furore in the press, and from the end of June onwards one finds large headlines in *L'Action Française* of the type: *"LA PRESSE DÉFAITISTE A PARIS"* (1 July 1917), or *"UN JOURNAL DÉFAITISTE A PARIS"* (2 July 1917). In the ensuing days Daudet's leaders contain repeated references to the new paper, with *défaitiste* as an epithet *de rigueur*: "le ténébreux directeur du défaitiste *Pays*" (3 July 1917), "Albert Dubarry, directeur du *Carnet de la Semaine* et du *Pays*—organes de propagande défaitiste" (4 July 1917), etc. Examples of this kind very quickly become too numerous to quote. [21] At this stage, *défaitiste* collocates readily with the term *allemand*, or is coupled with it by implication. On 5 July Daudet declares:

> Les défaitistes en sont pour leurs frais, et la propagande allemande a fait fiasco.

[20] L. Daudet describes how on 27 June 1917 he went to see Maginot, then Minister for the Colonies and a member of the *Commission de l'Armée*, to discuss the subversive activities of the men who directed and backed *Le Bonnet Rouge*; he was ushered to a seat "devant une table couverte de numéros du *Bonnet Rouge* et du *Pays* de Dubarry. C'était le moment de la grande propagande défaitiste" (*Le Poignard dans le dos*, p. 14).

[21] The immediate success of *Le Pays* made it an adversary to be reckoned with: on 1 July 1917 it printed 78,000 copies, as compared with only 24,000 for *Le Bonnet Rouge*, 16,000 for *La Tranchée Républicaine* (weekly), and 42,500 for *L'Action Française* itself. See Appendix III.

Likewise, on the 8th, he speaks of "la propagande défaitiste et allemande", and again, on the 20th, he claims that:

> Une méthode scientifique rigoureuse ... m'a permis de dresser la carte de la propagande défaitiste allemande en France.

The apparent ease and the speed with which this new word slips into Daudet's vocabulary is remarkable. Comparison of his use of it with Bérenger's reveals at once that there is nothing of the deliberate emphasis which the latter is careful to give it. No aura of novelty surrounds it—in fact, Daudet handles it quite unselfconsciously, never pausing to supply any definition or explanation.[22]

2.8 *Les pacifistes bêlants*

If one has a strict regard for the chronology of usage as it is reflected in the daily press, Léon Daudet was not the first person to take up the terms *défaitiste/défaitisme* after Henry Bérenger. The first occurrence in *L'Action Française* dates from 21 June 1917. Three days earlier Gustave Hervé had mentioned French *défaitistes* in *La Victoire*. He, it will be remembered, had supplied a good definition of the *défaitistes russes* in April of that year;[1] he was deeply alarmed by their activities and by those of the Zimmerwald movement in general, and he might have been expected to have had quite as much use for the terms *défaitiste/défaitisme* in June 1917 as Bérenger or Daudet did. In fact, what one has to explain in Hervé's case is why he was slower than other journalists to adopt them into his vocabulary. The answer is probably that he had already found an extremely expressive label for the individuals he wished to attack, and saw every reason to be satisfied with it. When one looks at the leader he wrote in *La Victoire* on 18 June, one finds him talking about "le troupeau de nos pacifistes bêlants"—who are then further qualified as "les capitulards et les défaitistes de chez nous". This early example of the term *défaitiste* remains an isolated instance in Hervé's usage at this time, whereas the expressions *pacifiste bêlant/ pacifisme bêlant* occur in almost every article he writes.

Now *défaitiste/défaitisme* were developing close links with *pacifiste/pacifisme*, well established terms in French by the time

---

[22] Remarks made by Daudet a few months later show that he was in fact interested in the origin of the expression. See below, 2.12, pp. 107-8.

[1] See above, 2.4, p. 55.

of the war.[2] The neologism quite frequently comes to denote
activities and attitudes that had previously fallen under the heading
of *pacifisme*, and this is a marked departure from what was understood by *le défaitisme de Lénine*.[3] Hervé was a renegade pacifist
himself,[4] and as is so often the case with people who change their
allegiance, the opinions he was least able to tolerate were those
which he had once held himself. Of course, he did not regard his
own behaviour in quite this light: on the many occasions when he
felt called upon to justify his dramatic about-face, he claimed that
circumstances had changed, not his personal convictions:

> J'appelle propagande infâme, moi qui suis un pacifiste et qui ai attrapé
> onze ans de prison pour avoir essayé d'empêcher la guerre quand on
> pouvait l'empêcher, j'appelle propagande infâme à l'heure actuelle
> toute propagande pacifiste. (*La Victoire*, 27 June 1917)

Hervé still regarded himself as a pacifist in one sense, i.e. as a man
to whom the idea and the facts of war were totally repugnant;[5] but
at the same time he particularly wished to attack pacifists of another
brand—men who refused to lay any guilt at Germany's door, and
were anxious to conclude immediate peace on terms most disadvan-
tageous to France. This duality implicit in the term *pacifiste* may
explain why Hervé preferred to avoid possible ambiguity by quali-
fying it with an adjective when he intended it in the second of the
two meanings alluded to. The choice of *bêlant* was a stroke of
genius for which Hervé was widely held responsible in view of the
key position that this expression occupied in his vocabulary; in
fact, however, as the socialist J. Longuet pointed out, it was
Clemenceau who made this addition to the French language:[6]

---

[2] The *Petit Robert* gives 1845 for *pacifisme* and 1907 for *pacifiste*, while the
F.E.W. gives 1907 for both terms, and the *Bloch-Wartburg* puts their appearance
at the end of the nineteenth century. J. Dubois does not mention them in *Le
Vocabulaire politique et social*.

[3] See above, 2.4, p. 58, n. 8.

[4] See Appendix I.

[5] It should be noted that to define *pacifiste* in this way was the classic defence of
men accused of pacifism. One reads in *Le Bonnet Rouge* (7 July 1917): "Il n'est pas
un homme digne de ce nom qui ne soit au fond pacifiste... Mais ceci dit, ce serait
une malhonnêteté que de prêter aux pacifistes des pensées et des intentions qu'ils
n'ont pas, que de calomnier leurs sentiments en les représentant comme les partisans
d'une paix à tout prix."

[6] The term still survives: "Une lettre de réconfort provenait de l'Union Pacifiste
de France ... Je suppose que c'est ces gars-là qu'on appelle les pacifistes bêlants?

Georges Clemenceau et la Démocratie

... ses railleries violentes, ses sarcasmes contre les "pacifistes bêlants"—
car l'expresssion n'a pas été, comme on le croit à tort, inventée par M.
Gustave Hervé, mais par lui—il les a jetés jadis en pleine paix.

(*Le Pays*, 16 Nov. 1917)

If pacifism was anathema to Hervé, the individuals he felt most
strongly about were the members of the French Left who were
guilty of it. He shows a rather parochial interest in the internal
divisions of the French Socialist Party, and hence the term *pacifistes
bêlants* is applied primarily to his own countrymen who proclaim
Zimmerwald ideology. He uses it first when looking back to the
stand taken by his party at the time the German socialists decided
to mobilize:

Certes, Jaurès et nous tous, les républicains de gauche et d'extrême-
gauche, nous aurions été des aveugles et des malfaiteurs publics si nous
avions été des pacifistes bêlants. (*La Guerre Sociale*, 21 Dec. 1914)

Later, referring to the Zimmerwald peace conference, he warns
certain French socialists as follows:

Supposons que la majorité parlementaire nous suive et bâcle cette paix
allemande "sans annexion"; savez-vous ce qui arriverait, ô pacifistes
bêlants? (*La Guerre Sociale*, 12 Dec. 1915)

Elsewhere, he speaks of "le zimmerwaldisme, qui n'est autre chose
que la forme socialiste du pacifisme bêlant" (*La Victoire*, 28 June
1916), and he links the term *pacifisme* with *extrémisme*: "des
propos d'un extrémisme et d'un pacifisme inquiétants" (*La Victoire*, 11 May 1917).[7]

After the February Revolution, when the French press begins
to take an interest in Russian extremists who had been to Zimmerwald, the term *défaitiste* comes to be used in conjunction with
zimmerwaldien and *extrémiste* to describe them; Hervé does on
occasion refer to them as *pacifistes bêlants* (a variant in his vocabulary for *zimmerwaldien* and *extrémiste*) to stress the affinities
between them and their French counterparts: they are "les mauvais
bergers du pacifisme bêlant" who can only "épeler le b-a ba du

---

Merci, pacifistes bêlants!" (*Charlie Hebdo*, 7 Aug. 1972). The same paper refers
again ironically to "des emmerdeurs anti-militaristes et autres pacifistes bêlants"
(9 Oct. 1972).

[7] The adjective *bêlant* would not fit in here.

socialisme allemand'' (*La Victoire*, 26 Mar. 1917). More often, however, he reserves the term *pacifistes bêlants* for the French:

> Les extrémistes de Pétrograde et de Cronstadt, frères des pacifistes bêlants et des capitulards de chez nous ... (*La Victoire*, 21 June 1917)

The historian in Hervé was always eager to draw parallels between events of the moment and those belonging to France's past. Thus he had already explained to his readers that the terms *pacifiste bêlant* and *capitulard* are equivalent:

> Le père Vaillant, en qualité de vieux blanquiste, d'ancien communard guerre-à-outrance, était un jusqu'auboutiste enragé qui n'aimait pas les capitulards: c'est ainsi qu'il appelait les pacifistes bêlants.
>
> (*La Victoire*, 29 Dec. 1916)

As will be seen, when he does adopt the term *défaitiste* to refer to Frenchmen, he makes exactly the same comparison with *capitulard*.

Before this happens, one finds Hervé using two ephemeral terms as occasional variants for his standard *pacifiste bêlant*. The first, *paix-à-outrance*,[8] is modelled on the form *guerre-à-outrance* just illustrated.[9] R. Rolland makes the following note in his diary:

> Article injurieux d'Hervé, le 9 novembre [1915], sous le titre: *Vilaine besogne*; il y dénonce, dans la Conférence de Zimmerwald, "les manœuvres du gouvernement de Berlin pour obtenir une paix honorable", et invite les socialistes à "rentrer dans la gorge à ces paix-à-outrance leur colossale niaiserie".[10]

Some weeks later, Hervé again speaks slightingly of "nos socialistes de Zimmerwald, nos 'paix à outrance'" (*La Guerre Sociale*, 26 Dec. 1915). The second term, *père la défaite*,[11] was applied by Ch. Maurras to Hervé when he announced his intention of altering the name of his newspaper to *La Victoire*,[12] and was taken up by Hervé to refer to some of his fellow socialists on the occasion of the Party Congress held at the end of December 1915:

> J'ai été salué de quelques "bonjour, père la Victoire!" Ah! puissions-nous dans ce congrès n'entendre la voix d'aucun "père la défaite" .... Nous en avons recontré, hélas, dans notre parti, depuis le début de la guerre, des pères "la défaite". (*La Guerre Sociale*, 27 Dec. 1915)

[8] Spelt with or without hyphens.
[9] See also below, 3.6, pp. 146-7.
[10] *Journal*, p. 680.
[11] Sometimes written with hyphens.
[12] See Appendix I.

He singles out for criticism "leur belle besogne de démoralisation" and "leurs jérimiades sur nos insuccès militaires"; continuing to exploit the theme, he proclaims:

> Que la peste soit des Pères-la-Défaite et des Pères-la-Panique!
>
> (*La Victoire*, 2 Jan. 1916)

and again, three days later:

> Et les Pères-la-Défaite de nous inviter à ... bâcler une paix boiteuse.

J. Bainville had commented on a similar mood of pessimism and panic right at the start of the war, using the term *grand-père Panique*:

> Ce sont les vieillards, les témoins de 1870, qui sont dans l'état d'esprit nihiliste de la défaite sans espoir, du désastre inévitable, de la chute dans le noir et le néant voulue par une aveugle destinée. [On leur a déjà donné] ce surnom: grand-père Panique.[13]

Now this attitude was to become known as *défaitisme* at the end of 1917, but not until then, when the term had undergone considerable semantic change.[14] However, it is interesting to note in anticipation that *défaitiste* in the sense of "pessimist" had an early parallel in the form of *père la défaite*.

To return to the upheavals of summer 1917, it is instructive to compare Hervé's use of the term *pacifiste bêlant* with Bérenger or Daudet's use of *défaitiste*, and to consider the response which these attacks called forth from the Left; one can then see how Hervé came to adopt *défaitiste* into his daily vocabulary. In many cases, Hervé's *pacifistes bêlants* are clearly the same troublemakers as the other journalists' *défaitistes*. Writing about the strikes in Paris factories, Hervé issues the following warning:

> Que nos femmes grévistes ... se méfient, par exemple, des bourreurs de crânes—ou plutôt des videurs de crâne [*sic*]—du pacifisme bêlant qui leur insinueront que des troubles à Paris feraient finir la guerre plus vite.
>
> (*La Victoire*, 27 May 1917)

He speaks again of German infiltration on 16 June, this time with a barely disguised reference to the mutinies:

> Les Allemands se figurent que notre gouvernement ... laissera, par une criminelle complicité, ou par lâcheté politicienne, la propagande des

[13] *Journal*, p. 62 (30 Aug. 1914).
[14] As will be shown, it is in fact more accurate to speak of *acquisition* of meaning, rather than *change*. See below, 2.11, p. 102, and 2.12, pp. 112-13.

pacifistes bêlants se faire impunément à l'intérieur et dans la zone des
armées, et dégénérer en propagande de révolte et d'anarchie.

On 24 June he uses the word *trahison*:

> Il est incroyable que le gouvernement, en pleine guerre ... laisse se faire,
> ouvertement ou jésuitiquement, une propagande pacifiste qui, en pareil
> moment, constitue une véritable trahison au profit du Kaiser.

Hervé draws his conclusions in a virulent article on 28 June: these
pacifists may be sincere, but they are acting in the interests of the
enemy:

> Nous accusons les pacifistes bêlants d'être des agents inconscients de
> l'Allemagne impériale et kaiseriste, de se laisser sottement manœuvrer
> par elle, de travailler, sans le savoir, pour elle ...
> C'est l'Allemagne qui nous a envoyé ce choléra, le pacifisme bêlant.
> Elle nous l'a inoculé à Zimmerwald, par l'intermédiaire du socialiste
> suisse Grimm ...
> Complices inconscients, si l'on veut, mais complices quand-même ...

This passage sheds useful light on the difference between *pacifiste
bêlant* and *défaitiste* as used by Hervé and Daudet. Faced with the
same phenomenon, Hervé judges it to be the work of fools whose
activities amount in effect to treason, whereas Daudet believes
that his country is at the mercy of deliberate, cold-blooded traitors.
At this stage each has his special word to refer to a set of actions
which both would agree to single out for censure—the difference
in terminology reflecting the divergent assessments of the matter
in question.

As long as one confines oneself to the personal usage of individuals, these subtle distinctions remain of prime importance. The
situation becomes more complicated when one goes on to consider
how, in this rather specialized sphere, one journalist interprets the
jargon of another. The scandal created by the early numbers of
Le Pays provides a good opportunity to observe this interpenetra-
tion of jargons. On 1 July, Daudet rather patronizingly congratu-
lates Hervé for spotting the danger:

> Ce brave Hervé vient de découvrir l'existence à Paris d'un clan des Ya
> et d'une presse défaitiste. (*L'Action Française*)

The significant point is that the subject of Hervé's article is in fact
"le nouveau journal *pacifiste*" (my italics). How closely Daudet
perused *La Victoire*, and how far this is simply a case of seizing any

excuse to hammer away at a pet theme, is a matter for debate. At any rate, this sort of equivalence is very likely to be felt when two terms overlap to such a considerable extent.

It is worth mentioning in connection with *les pacifistes bêlants* that Daudet himself had at one time singled out from among the motley crowd of *embochés* the proponents of pacifist theories, and had christened them *paciboches*:

> *Les Paciboches et l'Allemand Ullmann*
> J'appelle "paciboches"—de *pax*, paix, et de boche—ceux qui, appartenant avant la guerre au clan des Ya, voudraient conclure aujourd'hui avec l'Allemagne une paix prématurée, une paix bâtarde, une paix boche en un mot, qui serait la fin de la France financièrement, économiquement et militairement ... Les paciboches, qu'ils agissent ainsi par intérêt ou par stupidité—sont donc un véritable danger pour le pays.
> (*L'Action Française*, 12 Nov. 1915)

He explains further to his readers that

> l'Allemagne, mauvaise psychologue, ... a eu tort de compter sur ces "paciboches", sur la détestable troupe des embochés qui vont répétant que "nous n'en viendrons jamais à bout" ..... Le travail paciboche [consiste à] démoraliser les faibles et inquiéter la fermeté nationale, gêner le gouvernement et semer la méfiance entre alliés ... (15 Dec. 1916)

This looks very much like what Daudet was later to call *défaitisme*. Did he adopt the new word in preference to his own coinage because it was more specifically associated with the events of early 1917? He no doubt sensed that *paciboche* was an ephemeral creation belonging to a limited stylistic register,[15] whereas *défaitiste* had the advantage of being regularly derived by suffixation from a common French word, and of fitting into a well-established category of political terms.

To continue the discussion of how polemicists react to each other's jargon, and what this reveals of the relationship between the terms *défaitiste* and *pacifiste* during the months under consideration, it can be examined practically through an analysis of the way in which the journalists of *Le Bonnet Rouge* and similar papers behaved under fire.

---

[15] The formation can be viewed both as an expansion of *Boche* (cf. *Sur-Boche*—as applied to Nietsche), and as a remodelling of *pacifiste* with the slang suffix -*boche* (cf. *fantaboche* for *fantassin*, *rigolboche* for *rigolo*). For the development of this suffix, see *Larousse Mensuel illustré,* Dec. 1914.

They must have realized immediately that the new accusation of *défaitisme* was a very real threat, and could seriously discredit them in the eyes of the public. They tried ingeniously to counter it by pretending to have discovered a right-wing plot aimed at republicans of the extreme Left. At the end of June 1917 the *Chambre* introduced a bill to curb pacifist propaganda: *Le Bonnet Rouge* retorted that most dangerous foreign agents of the kind being referred to were by now in prison, that the press was already heavily censored, and hence this uncalled-for severity was merely a pretext enabling the Right to lay hands on its political opponents. G. Clairet, political editor of *Le Bonnet Rouge*, devoted an important article to the subject on 28 June:

> Quand ils réclament du gouvernement des mesures sévères, ce n'est pas aux apôtres de la paix immédiate qu'ils pensent: ces apôtres, ils le savent, sont pourchassés, quand ils ne sont pas déjà en prison.
> A qui donc en ont-ils?
> Il faut bien se décider à le dire.
> Ces appels pseudo-patriotiques, ces déclamations contre un "léninisme" qui n'existe probablement pas en Russie, et certainement pas en France, ces cris indignés contre la liberté qui est laissée aux "défaitistes" alors que personne, même parmi les propagandistes arrêtés ne souhaite la défaite de nos armées, toute cette littérature, toute cette rhétorique, visent les républicains d'extrême gauche, ceux qui sont restés fidèles à l'idéal démocratique.... La réaction essaie maintenant de perdre tous les républicains d'extrême gauche, en les confondant avec une poignée de libertaires exaltés, dans une accusation aussi imprécise que mensongère de "pacifisme", de "défaitisme",—quelques-uns lâchent le mot de trahison.

And again, on 10 July:

> Nationalistes et partisans d'un gouvernement a poigne auraient traqué la presse indépendante et, sous prétexte de combattre le défaitisme, supprimé la liberté de penser et d'écrire,—ce qu'il en reste.

An essential part of Clairet's thesis is that the reactionaires hurl ill-defined, inappropriate epithets at their enemies in a desperate and clumsy attempt to persuade the public that they are guilty of the most heinous offences; words like *pacifisme, défaitisme*, and *léninisme* are bandied about in a most irresponsible fashion by *Paris-Midi, L'Action Française* and *La Victoire*. Clairet speaks scornfully of a debate in the Senate where the only evidence brought

forward to show that subversive activities were being carried on
was a few quotations from *La Victoire* and

> un article tout aussi imprécis de M. Henry Bérenger contre des "défait-
> istes" et des "léninistes" que le sénateur de la Guadeloupe se gardait
> bien de désigner,—et pour cause. (*Le Bonnet Rouge*, 1 July 1917)

This accusation of imprecision is a piece of calculated policy on
the part of Almereyda and his associates: they claim that the Right
misuses words, but by making this claim—by lumping together
the terms in question when they quote what their opponents are
supposed to be saying—they themselves deliberately add to the
existing confusion, or even *create* it if it is not there already. This
is very obvious when Clairet notes with satisfaction in an article of
9 July headed *"Le Défaitisme"* that the *Chambre* does not share
Bérenger's hysteria:

> M. Henry Bérenger déclarait samedi, dans un article de *Paris-Midi*
> intitulé "la fin du défaitisme":
> > Si la Chambre sait, par un ordre du jour, fixer le sentiment national,
> > elle se prononcera fortement pour la fin du défaitisme.
> Or la Chambre ... n'a pas estimé que la propagande "pacifiste" ou
> > "défaitiste" était assez importante et surtout assez peu surveillée par
> le gouvernement pour qu'il valût la peine d'en parler dans l'ordre du
> jour... Pas un mot sur le fameux "péril pacifiste".

Clairet is quoting the terms used by Bérenger and his like when he
writes "la propagande 'pacifiste' ou 'défaitiste'": one is meant to
take this as implying "pacifist propaganda etc.—or whatever else
they care to call it". The effect of labelling it "'pacifiste' ou
'défaitiste'" is to pour scorn on something that is so indeterminate
that it can hardly be thought to constitute a threat.

Le Bonnet Rouge did not fight alone. *La Tranchée Républicaine*
supported it, with fervent diatribes against the base wretches who
were insulting the French nation. On 17 July Goldsky writes:

> On a parlé de défaitistes, comme si pareil mot ne devait pas être le dernier
> à jaillir de la plume ou de la bouche d'un Français. On a osé prétendre
> qu'une partie de la presse française pouvait—crime ou légèreté—s'être
> laissé soudoyer par l'ennemi.... *Il n'y a pas de défaitistes chez nous.*
> Tous nous voulons que cette guerre voit [*sic*] le triomphe de la France.

Here, the tactics are different: Goldsky defines certain precise
charges which he then denies, instead of pretending that *défaitisme*
is a meaningless accusation.

The odium attaching to the label *défaitiste* was such that people did not seem prepared to apply it to themsleves in a bid to remove the stigma from it.[16] Towards the end of the war, one does come across an exception in Stefan Zweig; as R. Rolland explains:

> ... il a la malencontreuse idée de chercher un mot de ralliement pour les ennemis de la guerre, et, par une sorte de paradoxe passionné, il prétend n'en pouvoir trouver de meilleur que le titre de *"Défaitiste"*. Il se pare de cette injure, comme d'un honneur.[17]

Admittedly, Zweig makes this proposal in an article in German: "Bekenntnis zum Defaitismus". More significant in regard to French usage is the way in which Rolland, called by one of his detractors "le père du défaitisme intellectuel",[18] refuses categorically to accept the term as Zweig urges him to do. He replies to Zweig:

> ... je ne puis vous suivre dans votre revendication du "Défaitisme". Non, je ne verrai jamais en cette injure un titre d'honneur, et je le repousse, quant à moi, de toutes mes forces.[19]

Whatever form the particular defence strategy takes, it is always word-oriented as is to be expected in a polemical war: imprecision, inappropriateness—the purpose of these accusations is to render the lexical weapons of the adversary harmless. Ridicule is also a classic method. Not surprisingly, perhaps Hervé came in for a good deal of this with his heavy-handed attacks on the *pacifistes bêlants.* His opponents were given a heaven-sent opportunity to get their own back when the Pope expressed the desire to see a rapid end to hostilities. *Le Pays* takes obvious delight in proclaiming on 16 August:

> On n'éprouvera aucune surprise à voir l'Agneau Pascal prendre place parmi les "pacifistes bêlants", encore qu'il y vienne un peu tard ...
> Quant aux catholiques français, l'acte du Saint-Siège ne manque pas de leur occasionner un trouble de conscience. Ils ont tant médit des "pacifistes bêlants" ...

[16] Cf. Hervé's acceptance of the appellation *jusqu'auboutiste* (below, 3.6, p. 146). Although Lenin does not appear to describe his own doctrine as *porazhenchestvo* in the ideological debates of 1915-17, after the Bolshevik Revolution of October 1917 he seems happy to adopt the term in retrospective appraisal of his earlier position: "We only recognized defeatism with regard to *our own* imperialist bourgeoisie" (*Pravda*, 24 Feb. 1918, reproduced in *Polnoe Sobranie Sochineniĭ*, 5th edn., vol. 35, p. 247).

[17] *Journal,* p. 1533 (14 July 1918).

[18] Ibid., p. 1502 (25 May 1918).

[19] Ibid., p. 1533 (14 July 1918).

How were people at large affected by these journalists' quarrels? The new terms *défaitiste/défaitisme* were given sudden publicity by prolonged polemical exchanges: they were lifted from the narrow sphere of Russian political theory and made available for wide-ranging discussions on the national security of France. Even if initially they were not used by more than a few journalists, they must have come to the notice of a fairly extensive public.[20] At the same time, readers of the daily press would have seen the individuals labelled as *défaitistes* by one writer, called *pacifistes bêlants* by another and plain *pacifistes* by others still. As mentioned earlier, certain equivalences can be set up which cut across the jargons of two journalists. How much more likely these identifications are to occur where the general public is concerned. At this level, the fact that on the whole each polemicist remained faithful to his own favourite term is relatively unimportant. Members of the public can scarcely have failed to regard them as synonymous, although they were not interchangeable in the vocabulary of any one individual. As a result, the term *défaitisme* develops even closer associations with *pacifisme*. These were always latent, ever since the early ties with the Zimmerwald movement via Lenin; but Hervé's contribution to the polemical war was necessary for the connection to become firmly established and popularized.

Towards the end of August 1917, one finds Hervé himself beginning to use *défaitiste* quite freely of French offenders:

> Pour que je croie que Duval a touché de l'argent de l'Allemagne pour faire la campagne défaitiste qu'il faisait dans le *Bonnet Rouge* sous le nom de Monsieur Badin, il faudrait que l'on me le prouve cent fois.
>
> (*La Victoire*, 26 Aug. 1917)

Significantly, he shows a marked tendency to put it with *pacifiste* in the same sentence:

> Le ministre de l'intérieur paye la faiblesse qu'il a eue pour la propagande pacifiste et défaitiste ... (*La Victoire*, 1 Sept. 1917)

Or again:

> Je connais ceux qui mènent la campagne pacifiste et défaitiste dans le parti socialiste: ce sont des illuminés, des aveugles et des ignorants. Mais ce ne sont ni des traîtres ni des canailles. (*La Victoire*, 18 Dec. 1917)

---

[20] Figures for the circulation of the papers concerned are given in Appendix III.

If *pacifiste* is not qualified by *bêlant* in the above examples, this is of course because the compound expression cannot function adjectivally; Hervé does however couple *les défaitistes* with *les pacifistes bêlants*, or use the two abstract nouns in conjunction, as here:

> Caillaux ... se défendait ... de toute complaisance envers le pacifisme bêlant et le défaitisme. (*La Victoire*, 18 Dec. 1917)

One also finds the form *antidéfaitiste* in Hervé's idiom:

> Je considère comme un sabotage de toute notre campagne *antidéfaitiste* l'exagération tintamarresque de Léon Daudet...
> Mais j'avoue que je préfère encore les hurlements de Daudet au silence prudent de tous les journaux qui, depuis six mois, se gardent de prendre parti dans la lutte contre le défaitisme. (*La Victoire*, 30 Nov. 1917)

Hervé's readers are given formal notification that the term *défaitiste* has acquired recognized status in his vocabulary when he makes the same comparison between it and *capitulard* as he had previously done for *pacifiste bêlant*:[21]

> ### Les Défaitistes
> Pendant la guerre de 70, les républicains rouges de Paris avaient trouvé un mot énergique pour désigner ceux qui ne croyaient pas à la victoire, et qui, dès les premiers jours du siège, n'avaient qu'un désir: la paix, la paix à tout prix. Ils les appelaient les capitulards.
> Les capitulards de 70 ont des héritiers. Ce sont les défaitistes de nos jours ... (*La Victoire*, 24 Sept. 1917)

It must be stressed that a chronological presentation of the adoption of the terms *défaitiste/défaitisme* into French, necessary in the interests of clarity, may tend to falsify the picture slightly. What appear to be successive phases in the history of the terms are in fact parallel developments, taking place within a very short space of time. Anarchy, treason, and pacifism are in this case three facets of one problem, and the flexibility of the new terms *défaitiste/ défaitisme* reflects the different ways in which it can be viewed. If one wishes to single out the features which remain constant throughout these various personal usages, one can only say that the neologism is a strongly pejorative term used in connection with specific activities deemed to constitute a threat to the security of France; beyond this, it is sufficiently broad in meaning to accommodate

---

[21] See above, p. 78.

a wide range of individual beliefs and attitudes, and to collocate with a variety of other terms.

2.9   En regardant au fond des crevasses[1]

Public discussion of the scandals which came to light in the summer and autumn of 1917 provided a continuing opportunity for the use of the new terms *défaitiste/défaitisme*, thereby increasing their chances of becoming permanent fixtures in the language. Brief mention of the events which caused the greatest stir in the press will help to consolidate the picture of the kind of activities that qualified as *défaitisme*.

On 14 May 1917, Duval, financial director of *Le Bonnet Rouge* and author of articles signed M. Badin, was arrested at Bellegarde with a cheque in his possession worth 158,000 Swiss francs, ultimately traceable to a bank in Mannheim. An official inquiry was opened on 2 July, and a few days later, during a debate in the *Chambre*, Maurice Barrès made his famous challenge to the Minister of the Interior, Malvy:

> De toute ma force, je lançai dans le creux de l'estomac du ministre: "Quand donc arrêtez-vous la canaille du *Bonnet Rouge*?"
> Ah! quel remous dans la vase, quel clapotis! quel émoi! Et comme M. Malvy devint verdâtre! Il refusa obstinément de me répondre.
>
> (*L'Écho de Paris*, 7 July 1917)

The warning did not go unheeded: from 13 July *Le Bonnet Rouge* was suspended for good. Military documents were discovered in the offices of the paper, and Almereyda was arrested. He was found mysteriously strangled in prison on 14 August, and it was rumoured that he had been *suicidé*[2] by his accomplices.

A question which must have perturbed anyone who read *Le Bonnet Rouge* with a critical eye was how it had succeeded in remaining immune for so long, when much of what it preached ran counter to the wartime interests of France. The indefatigable Léon Daudet, with his flair for probing the real and imaginary

---

[1] The title of a work by M. Barrès on the mutinies and related cases of treason (Paris, 1917).

[2] L. Daudet uses this expression: "On a suicidé Vigo" (*L'Action Française*, 20 Aug. 1917). D.W. Brogan observes: "He killed himself because his drug supply was cut off, said the Government; he was murdered, said Léon Daudet" (*The Development of Modern France*, p. 537). On the arrest of Duval and Almereyda, see also R. Poincaré, *L'Année trouble 1917*, pp. 227 ff.

scandals which lurked beneath the surface of public life, had by this
time amassed impressive files on all the *défaitistes* implicated in the
Bonnet Rouge affair, and concluded that they were carrying out
their nefarious work with the connivance and financial support[3] of
Malvy, himself a tool of Caillaux. From January 1915 onwards,
Daudet had denounced the "agissements de Malvy et de Caillaux",
referring to them in *L'Action Française* as "l'Inexplicable" because
of the censorship. After the dramatic end of *Le Bonnet Rouge*,
attacks on Malvy began to multiply in other quarters too. On
22 July 1917 Clemenceau openly accused the Minister of treason
in the Senate,[4] and he resigned on 31 August.

This did not satisfy Daudet: when Malvy failed to produce a
formal justification of his behaviour (as he had promised on leaving
office), Daudet sent a letter to the President of the Republic on
30 September charging Malvy with betraying military secrets to the
enemy through the intermediary of Almereyda, Duval, etc., and
with playing a part in fomenting the unrest in the army. The letter
created an uproar when it was read aloud in the *Chambre* on
4 October.[5] An attempt was made to hush up the affair, and a
clumsy counter-attack was launched against Daudet and *L'Action
Française* which took the form of the supposed discovery of a
royalist plot to overthrow the government.[6] The alarm proved to
be a false one, and Daudet was left free once more to pursue
Malvy.[7]

---

[3] See Appendix I, *M. Almereyda*, p. 168, n. 7.

[4] "Je vous reproche d'avoir trahi l'intérêt de la France" (*Discours de Guerre*,
Paris, revised edn. 1968, p. 120). Though Clemenceau's speech is entitled "Le
Défaitisme" in this collection, it was originally published separately as "L'Antipatriotisme devant le Sénat" (see p. 65). He does not use the terms *défaitiste/
défaitisme* but refers throughout to *les antipatriotes, l'antipatriotisme*, and *la
propagande antipatriotique*. Cf. below, 2.10, p. 99.

[5] The text is reproduced by G. Bonnefous, *La Grande Guerre*, pp. 313-14.

[6] The incident became known as *le complot des panoplies*. *L'Action Française*
was suspended for a week; Painlevé summoned Daudet and Maurras to the Ministry
of War and warned them to "mettre un terme à des attaques passionnées qui seraient
de nature à déchaîner, en France, une sorte de guerre civile". Later, the premises of
L'Action Française were searched and a number of pistols, rapiers and other arms
confiscated. See G. Bonnefous, *La Grande Guerre*, pp. 317-18.

[7] On 22 Nov. 1917, Malvy requested to have the allegations made in the press
against him examined by the High Court of the Senate. The case was heard in July
1918; Daudet's accusations of treason were rejected, but the ex-Minister was found
guilty of dereliction of duty and banished for five years. See E. J. Weber, *Action
Française*, pp. 105 ff. Daudet's own account of his role in the affair is given in

The official move to silence Daudet gave his opponents in the left-wing press a unique opportunity to take their revenge: adopting an extremely self-righteous, ultra-patriotic stand, they accused him and other reactionaires of demoralizing the country by talking so much about spies and traitors. Daudet paraphrases their arguments as follows in his retrospective account of those weeks:

> Daudet a agi en défaitiste, quand il a dénoncé le défaitisme. Il n'y a pas de pire trahison que la dénonciation de la trahison, car elle répand la panique dans l'armée.[8]

H. Bérenger was quick to pour scorn on this specious reasoning: beginning on 10 October, he led a short, sharp campaign against "les Arsinoés du patriotisme" and "les vertueux Tartuffes du défaitisme". These new-found labels obviously pleased him, for he sustained the comparison, elaborating most appropriately on his theme:

> Certaines Arsinoés du patriotisme continuent de s'étonner que l'on ne couvre d'aucun voile les tableaux de la trahison.... Nos bons Tartuffes, réformés ou non, s'écrient devant l'apparition de la vérité toute nue: "Cachez ce sein que je ne saurais voir!" (*Paris-Midi*, 1 Nov. 1917)

The same argument was to be used against M. Barrès by P. Renaison a few months later:

> Mais est-ce que toute vérité est toujours bonne à dire? ... Mais est-ce que Barrès à son tour ferait du défaitisme?[9] Le défaitisme de Barrès serait le pire car il ressort plus affligeant d'une argumentation pâteuse qui tend à le dissimuler ... Signalons ce défaitisme d'un nouveau genre au rasoir vigilant de M. Maurras (*Le Pays*, 26 Apr. 1918)

The scandal which caused the "Arsinoés du patriotisme" to reiterate their cries of indignation was the discovery of the role played by a certain Bolo Pacha in the "purchase" with German money of one of France's largest daily papers, *Le Journal*.[10] German

---

Le Poignard dans le dos, pp. 173-334. Malvy puts his case in *Mon Crime,* Paris, 1921. Daudet's political activity in the autumn of 1917 boosted the sales of *L'Action Française* to unprecedented heights: from 42,500 on 1 July they rose to 48,000 on 1 Oct. (at a time when the doubling of the officially imposed price for dailies caused the sales of other papers to drop), and to 156,000 on 1 Nov. See Appendix III.

[8] *Le Poignard dans le dos,* p. 152.

[9] For the expression *faire du défaitisme,* see below, 3.6, pp. 154-5.

[10] See R. Poincaré, *L'Année trouble 1917,* p. 303. Bolo was arrested on 3 Oct. 1917 and condemned to death on 14 Feb. 1918.

financial interference was much discussed in the weeks following Bolo's arrest, and this led Lloyd George to coin the word *boloism*. Bérenger comments on it in *Paris-Midi* on 23 October 1917:

> M. Lloyd George ... vient de lancer cette formule dans son dernier discours de Londres: "*Prenez garde au boloïsme*!" [11]

—and as is typical with him, defines it to suit his own particular crusade:

> Cela veut dire prenez garde aux complaisances, plus ou moins dorées, pour les agents de l'Allemagne.... à cette tentative d'étouffement en faveur d'un pacifisme suspect, d'un neutralisme équivoque, d'un défaitisme au caviar.

It is then rapidly incorporated into existing topical expressions of his, so that one finds, for instance, "les Tartuffes du boloïsme, les Arsinoés de l'almereydisme" (24 Oct. 1917).[12] *Le boloïsme* is probably a specific variety of *défaitisme*, to judge from examples like the following:

> Aucun défaitisme de bavards, aucun neutralisme de videurs de crânes, aucun boloïsme d'embochés ne détourneront désormais nos armées de la tâche terrible et sacrée... (*Paris-Midi*, 26 Oct. 1917)

or this from G. Hervé:

> En ces temps de boloïsme et de défaitisme, on a bien le droit, après tout, d'avoir le patriotisme méfiant et soupçonneux, surtout après les catastrophes qu'ont causées les défaitistes en Russie et en Italie.
>
> (*La Victoire*, 13 Nov. 1917)

[11] F. Mackenzie treats this term as a gallicism in English: "Puis *Boloism* est employé dans un discours tenu le 22 octobre 1917 par Lloyd George: 'See what has happened in France, and look out for Boloism in all its forms'" (*Les Relations de l'Angleterre et de la France d'après le vocabulaire*, vol. ii, p. 218). In fact, *The Times* leader of 23 Oct. ascribes the coinage to Lloyd George, and Bérenger's testimony (and that of G. Valois, see below, 2.10, p. 95) confirms that the French press borrowed the word from the English.

[12] Proper names furnish a ready source of ephemeral coinages. Daudet notes: "Le président Monier, personnage indigne, trifouille les séquestres au gré du caillautisme, du malvysme et de l'almereydisme" (*Le Poignard dans le dos*, p. 336); and he refers to the supporters of Caillaux and Malvy as *les Caillaumalvystes* (ibid., p. 56). Another family of terms was created when Malvy requested to go before the High Court—as Daudet explains: "Requête insolite ... qui fit déclarer imprudemment au député vétérinaire Renaudel que 'le plus tôt possible la Haute-Cour devait laver Malvy'. D'où l'expression, devenue populaire: un 'lave-Malvy', un 'lave-Leymarie', un 'lave-Caillaux', etc., pour désigner les défenseurs éperdus et désemparés du défaitisme et de la trahison" (ibid., p. 65).

—although it is difficult to determine the precise relationship between terms which are juxtaposed for emphasis as a rhetorical device, rather than because one serves to define the other.[13]

The term *neutralisme* which Bérenger couples with *défaitisme* at this time calls for brief comment. *Neutraliste/neutralisme* first appeared in early 1915 in the debate over the stand taken by Italy;[14] M. Cachin explains:

> L'Italie hésite depuis plusieurs mois, et la lutte y est au plus vif entre interventionnistes et neutralistes. (*Le Bonnet Rouge*, 30 Mar. 1915)

G. Hervé uses the form *neutralisme* in an article headed *Lettre à Turati*:

> Comme nous vous avons maudit ici, depuis le début de la guerre, avec votre neutralisme, vous et tous les camarades italiens que là-bas on appelle le parti officiel, et dont vous êtes le chef écouté!
>
> (*La Guerre Sociale,* 20 Apr. 1915)

This form had also figured in the title of an article by P.-G. La Chesnais in the *Mercure de France* of 1 April: "Le Neutralisme en Norvège".[15] It is clear that the desire on the part of neutral countries (the terms *neutraliste/neutralisme* were rapidly applied to parties in Greece, Rumania, and Switzerland as well) to avoid involvement in the war, was regarded as the equivalent of active pacifism in countries already engaged in the fighting. G. Hervé notes the presence of "des socialistes neutralistes italiens" at the Zimmerwald peace conference (*La Guerre Sociale,* 10 Nov. 1915), and *Le Bonnet Rouge* speaks of "les prétextes dont les neutralistes couvraient leur propagande contre la guerre" (20 June 1916). Once

---

[13] Cf. below, 2.10, p. 95, n. 2.

[14] The *F.E.W.* gives 1923 (*Larousse*) for *neutraliste* glossed as "favorable à la neutralité", and 1951 for the meaning "partisan du neutralisme". *Neutralisme* (1951) has the following note: "Dieses wort ist geschaffen worden mit Bezug auf die Lage Westeuropas zwischen Russland und Amerika." This is clearly erroneous. The *Larousse Mensuel* recorded *neutraliste* in July 1916. The absence of *neutralisme* from dictionaries of the period leads J. Dubois to class it among terms in -*isme* which appear *after* the corresponding form in -*iste* (*Introduction à la lexicographie: le dictionnaire*, Paris, 1971, p. 116); he finds it first attested in the *Petit Larousse* 1960 (*Étude sur la dérivation suffixale*, p. 35). It does in fact figure in the list of neologisms supplied in 1917 by G. Gaillard, "Langue et Guerre", p. 20.

[15] Quoted in B. Quémada, *Matériaux pour l'histoire du vocabulaire français. Datations et documents lexicographiques*, 12 (deuxieme série), 1977. *Neutraliste* is dated here from 1 Sept. 1915 in the *Mercure de France*; whereas the daily press was using it considerably earlier.

Italy had joined the Allies, these same individuals became known as *pacifistes*, and later *défaitistes* (as in the passage just quoted from *La Victoire*, 13 Nov. 1917). Thus *neutralisme* joins *pacifisme, défaitisme* and *boloïsme* as a pejorative term for nefarious activities and attitudes which further the aims of the enemy.

As the net began to close more tightly around Malvy, and a growing number of associated treason cases were given publicity, *défaitiste/défaitisme* came increasingly to be used in conjunction with the term *trahison*.[16] To begin with retrospective testimony, Daudet explains that they were a euphemism for something worse:

> [nous avions demandé à Ribot] de sévir contre la propagande défaitiste (comme on disait euphémiquement alors) ...[17]

—or again:

> les progrès de la campagne dite défaitiste, en réalité de trahison ...[18]

His comments are certainly borne out by usage in the press at the time to which he refers. Once again, it seems to have been Bérenger who gave new impetus to the term *défaitisme* by redefining it to fit with the events of the moment:

> *Écrasons les Cloportes*
> Dans une guerre aussi complexe que celle-ci, la trahison est un élément essentiel de la défaite! Le mot nouveau de *défaitisme* correspond à une réalité nouvelle.
> Ce que les Allemands n'ont pu détruire par la violence, ils se flattent de le dissoudre par la trahison. Le *défaitisme* n'est pas autre chose que cet effort de dissolution morale tenté par l'Allemagne sur les nations qu'elle a attaquées. L'ancienne trahison, classique ou romantique, n'est que peu de chose auprès de cette forme moderne de la défection à la patrie quand il s'agit de la sauver. Faisons connaître sans pitié ... tout leur va-et-vient de cloportes venimeux à travers les frontières.
> (*Paris-Midi*, 7 Nov. 1917)

Throughout November, Bérenger's articles contain frequent references to "cette forme maligne de la trahison"; one finds that the two nouns are often coupled for emphasis as in: "toutes nos grandes affaires de trahison et de défaitisme" (20 Nov. 1917), or "les intermédiaires de trahison et de défaitisme" (17 Nov. 1917).

---

[16] For the beginning of this development, see above, 2.6, p. 68.
[17] *L'Hécatombe*, p. 169.
[18] *La Pluie de sang. Nouveaux souvenirs (1914-1918)*, Paris, 1932, p. 123.

Daudet also makes constant use of this double label in his various accounts of the Malvy affair:

Nous voilà devisant de Rabbat, de Garfunkel et autres lascars de défaitisme et de trahison.[19]

—and again:

Almereyda reliait les uns aux autres les différents comptoirs de défaitisme et de trahison.[20]

It is in connection with treason that Russian *défaitisme* reappears at the forefront of French news at this time, bringing the wheel round in a full circle. Lenin and his party had come to power in the October Revolution, and one of their first moves was to make an armistice and begin peace negotiations with Germany. Bérenger mentions their intentions on 30 November:

Telle est, dans sa répugnante hideur, la trahison du défaitisme russe.

—and thereafter until the treaty of Brest-Litovsk was finally signed on 3 March 1918, he never loses an opportunity of stigmatizing the band of traitors who had deprived France of one of her allies:

Puisse le grand peuple du Nord échapper à la trahison et au déshonneur que lui imposent les Judas qui se sont eux-mêmes surnommés "les défaitistes"![21] (*Paris-Midi*, 19 Dec. 1917)

In this same article, Bérenger returns to his original definition of *défaitisme*, but completes the basic element of anarchy with the notion of pro-German treason—the whole being expressed in a vivid metaphor:

Le défaitisme est le contraire de la démocratie. Le défaitisme n'est qu'une marmite anarchiste dont le couvercle a la forme d'un casque à pointe[22] et dont le contenu ne peut exploser qu'au profit de Guillaume.

---

[19] *Le Poignard dans le dos*, p. 17.
[20] *La Guerre totale*, p. 119.
[21] Bérenger was of course mistaken in thinking that the term *porazhenets* was coined by Lenin and his supporters. See above, 2.3, pp. 47ff.
[22] This expression occupied an important place in polemics against the Germans. It is found as an appellation for the German soldier: "il a fallu que les casques à pointe reculent" (*Le Matin,* 3 Nov. 1914), and it is also taken as an emblem of German militarism: "[le Dr Ostwald] s'est révélé, depuis quelques mois, comme le Baptiste du Messianisme au casque à pointe" (R. Rolland, *Au-dessus de la mêlée,* p. 119, 4 Dec. 1914).

G. Hervé too stresses the Russian associations of *le défaitisme* at the beginning of 1918 by linking the term with *bolchevisme*; after the sentencing of Bolo Pacha he comments:

> Les organes du pacifisme bêlant, du défaitisme et du bolchevisme ne sont pas très satisfaits ... (*La Victoire*, 16 Feb. 1918)

France thus saw herself threatened by treason both from Russia and from within her own frontiers. After 16 November 1917, however, she was better equipped to deal with it, for Clemenceau had replaced Painlevé as head of the Government, and was looked to by people of widely differing allegiancies to take a firm hold on the situation. Only three months after Clemenceau came to power, A. Ferry felt confident enough to proclaim that "les défaitistes sont dans la gueule du Tigre".[23] Bérenger expresses his optimism in a series of articles where he sets *le défaitisme* against *le jacobinisme* of the new Président du Conseil:

> *Soyons jacobins*!
> Allons-nous nous effondrer en défaitistes ou nous hérisser en jacobins? Dans une guerre comme celle-ci, les démocraties n'ont pas d'autre choix, à l'heure des sacrifices, que le défaitisme ou le jacobinisme. ... Que le gouvernement de M. Clemenceau ... impose comme programme à tous les Français de 1918 le cri nécessaire de 1793: *la victoire ou la mort*!
> (*Paris-Midi*, 11 Dec. 1917)

The parallel between the France of 1917 and that of 1793 is developed alongside the contrast between the French and the Russian Revolutions which Bérenger had introduced in his very first article on *le défaitisme*. On 15 December he writes:

> La question du temps de guerre [c'est]: "Etes-vous jacobin ou défaitiste?" JACOBIN, cela veut dire patriote jusqu'aux dents.... DÉFAITISTE, cela veut dire partisan de la défaite de la patrie pour lui substituer une anarchie internationale. Il faut choisir entre la Révolution de la *Marseillaise* et la révolution du *Nitchevo*.[24]

This particular drive of Bérenger's to reinvigorate national morale and to stamp out all forms of treason, brings together the two strands of *défaitisme*—Russian and French. They were never, of course, entirely separate, although some journalists were unaware of the link and others preferred not to stress it.

---

[23] *Les Carnets secrets* (1914-1918), Paris, 1957, p. 220 (10 Feb. 1918).
[24] See above, 2.6, p. 66.

2.10   Le Cheval de Troie

The account so far given of the history of the terms *défaitiste/ défaitisme* has stressed the fluctuations in usage determined by the different preoccupations which were given the greatest coverage in the press from week to week. During this experimental period, journalists were on the whole more interested in exploiting the immediate power of a new slogan than reflecting at length upon the evil which it denoted.

Soon, however, a considerable amount of systematic theorizing began to emerge on the concept of *défaitisme*. In his book *Le Cheval de Troie*, G. Valois treats *la propagande défaitiste* as part of the tactics of what he calls *la guerre d'arrière-front*—the means whereby one side, "utilisant une des grandes faiblesses des armées nationales, démoralise les défenseurs d'un front et les incite à l'abandonner".[1] He explains that German "financial investments" (i.e. moves to gain control of French newspapers etc.) also constitute this "Trojan Horse":

> Il est bien moins coûteux de monter une manœuvre d'arrière-front, avec une cinquantaine de millions, et qui a quelques chances d'ouvrir le front, que d'exécuter une préparation militaire de cinq millions d'obus, qui coûte dix fois plus, et qui ne vaut à l'assaillant qu'une bande de terrain de dix lieues carrées. Ce calcul explique la générosité de l'Allemagne dans ce que M. Lloyd George a nommé le boloïsme.[2]

To achieve complete success the enemy relies on a network of corrupt individuals (Daudet's *embochés*) who exploit revolutionary and pacifist idealism in order to sap the fibre of an army:

> Ce que l'on connaît sous le nom de propagande pacifiste et de propagande défaitiste n'a point pour objet de conduire un peuple en armes à une paix

[1] *Le Cheval de Troie*, Paris, 1918, p. 214. This chapter is dated Nov. 1917. Valois's coinage is attested by M. de Roux: "L'action politique pour la paix séparée, la propagande pour la démoralisation militaire se tiennent et font l'essentiel de ce que Georges Valois a appelé la guerre d'arrière-front" (*Le Défaitisme*, pp. 8-9).
[2] *Le Cheval de Troie*, p. 223. Judging from this quotation, *boloïsme* appears to imply "the use of Bolo and his like by the Germans", whereas for Bérenger, it referred to tolerance of, or connivance with Bolo by Malvy and his associates. Yet another interpretation is supplied by the *Larousse Mensuel* in June 1918: "Bolo ... a si bien symbolisé la propagande du pacifisme que le grand homme d'État Lloyd George a appliqué le nom de *boloïsme* aux campagnes de suggestions déprimantes." This is a good example of the "semantic autonomy" of a neologism. See above, 2.7, p. 69, n. 2.

rapide. C'est une opération militaire destinée à *vider le retranchement*....
Ces observations sont capitales; elles permettent de comprendre que
certaines affaires, classées, dans quelques pays de l'Entente, comme
affaires de "commerce" ou "d'intelligences avec l'ennemi", sont des
opérations militaires conduites par l'ennemi avec une troupe et des
cadres, et qui tendent à l'ouverture du front retranché.[3]

Valois's opinion is seconded by M. de Roux in a work entitled
Le Défaitisme et les manœuvres pro-allemandes.[4] This is exclusively
a history of the *notion* of *défaitisme* as opposed to the *word*;[5] the
author makes no distinction between a stage where certain aims,
attitudes and modes of behaviour existed, but had no specific label
in the language, and a later phase where they had been given the
name of *défaitisme*. Both Valois and de Roux seem to use the expression *propagande défaitiste* in the sense of propaganda intended
to produce discouragement and low morale. Together with *la propagande pacifiste*, it forms the chief weapon of *la guerre d'arrière-
front*, although the two are theoretically distinct—*la propagande
pacifiste* being a case of exploitation by the enemy of what is often
genuine idealism:

> L'illuminé *sincère* qui fait de la paix le souverain bien est le complice le
> plus précieux du conquérant qui menace sa patrie. Le pacifiste intégral,
> celui qui se refuse au devoir militaire, qu'il soit anarchiste, révolution-
> naire ou un chrétien dévoyé comme Tolstoï et les "conscience objectors"
> [*sic*] anglais, vaut un allié pour l'agresseur.[6]

In practice, of course, the distinction is not always clear-cut, since
soldiers are discouraged by pacifist propaganda, and *la propagande
défaitiste*, if successful, would tend to make them more receptive to
pacifist preaching even if they were not idealistically inclined at the
outset. Besides, as one of R. Rolland's critics pointed out in a bro-
chure called *Monsieur Romain Rolland, initiateur de Défaitisme*:

> Il ne faut pas oublier que le pacifisme, en temps de guerre, devient
> nécessairement une trahison envers la Patrie ... Les écrits et les actes de
> M. Romain Rolland auraient pu affaiblir le moral de ceux qui combat-
> taient pour l'existence de la France: c'est à ce point de vue qu'il encourt
> une grave responsabilité ...[7]

---

[3] *Le Cheval de Troie,* pp. 219-20.
[4] Completed in Feb. 1918, shortly after *Le Cheval de Troie* appeared.
[5] For discussion of the "retrospective" use of words, see below, 2.12, pp.110-11.
[6] M. de Roux, *Le Défaitisme,* pp. 17-18.
[7] Quoted by R. Rolland, *Journal,* p. 1502 (20 June 1918).

Overlap of this sort explains examples like the following chapter heading in de Roux's book: *Le défaitisme des réfugiés russes—Les premières manifestations du pacifisme défaitiste en France*[8]—where the author has in mind the use of pacifist doctrine to destroy an army's will to fight.

This interpretation of the role of pacifist propaganda appears to remain fairly constant, even among writers who use the term *défaitisme* rather differently. The former is always viewed as a trap set by the enemy to catch the naïve. As Bérenger explains:

> Les Boches s'appuient sur quelques misérables Français ou Russes qui, sous couleur pacifiste ou humanitaire, leur servent d'intermédiaires de trahison et de défaitisme. (*Paris-Midi*, 17 Nov. 1917)

Daudet has much the same to say:

> La manœuvre allemande consiste à entretenir une équipe d'agents qui fournissent les thèmes de polémique, les exploitent et les font développer par les naïfs.[9]

In the vocabulary of Bérenger and Daudet, *le défaitisme* often denotes the overall strategy of enemy agents; it is therefore similar to what Valois and de Roux call *la guerre d'arrière-front*. All four of them use *la propagande pacifiste* to denote one of the particular means which fall under this general heading. To make matters more confusing, however, another of these tactics—deliberate discouragement of others—which is unequivocally known as *défaitisme* or *propagande défaitiste* by Valois and de Roux, is sometimes also given this label by Bérenger and Daudet.[10]

The idea that a country at war must use every possible means to overcome the adversary had of course been voiced for some considerable time by Daudet in his campaign for *une guerre totale*. As soon as it became widely recognized in France that interference in civilian activities was an essential part of military strategy, one finds a corresponding extension of military terminology to other domains of public life. Daudet saw the function of *La Gazette des Ardennes* as being to "affaiblir et déprécier ce que l'on a appelé l'armée française de l'arrière".[11]

[8] *Le Défaitisme*, p. 24.
[9] *Le Poignard dans le dos,* p. 86.
[10] See below, 2.11, pp. 101-2.
[11] *Le Poignard dans le dos,* p. 179.

The word *front* had evolved considerably since the beginning of the war, with the traditional *guerre de mouvement* being replaced by a *guerre de stabilisation* or *guerre de tranchées*. The events of 1917 led people to conceive of the target of subversive attacks—i.e. a fighting nation's morale—as a kind of front in its own right. On 19 October Bérenger heads his leader in *Paris-Midi* "Le Front de l'intérieur", and the idea is developed on the following day:

> Il y a un front de l'intérieur qui doit être gardé chez nous contre les complices d'Almereyda, de Duval, de Bolo, etc.

A similar image occurs in Marchand's book:

> C'est alors que s'est constitué, derrière le front militaire, le front diplomatique et le front économique, un front moral ... Cette bataille a, comme l'autre, ses assauts, ses élans, ses avances, ses reculs, ses feintes, ses pièges, sa tactique, ses défaites, ses victoires, ses lâches, ses traîtres et ses héros. Ses engins sont le journal, la revue, le tract, le livre, le discours, le simple mot qu'on glisse à mi-voix dans l'oreille, la rumeur qui se répand comme un gaz asphyxiant et qui propage le découragement, l'indiscipline, la terreur ou le désespoir.[12]

—and also in the *Larousse Mensuel* for September 1918, where the writer of an article on the *Bonnet Rouge* affair says:

> Au *Bonnet Rouge* [Duval] allait s'ingénier, par l'emploi de l'argent de Marx comme par sa plume, à attaquer "notre front moral".

G. Hervé, like Marchand, pictures enemy propaganda as a poison gas:

> Des journaux défaitistes sont comme des usines de gaz asphyxiants installées à l'arrière ... (*La Victoire*, 3 Oct. 1917)

R. Rolland quotes one of his detractors as writing:

> M. Romain Rolland rappelle l'aviateur ennemi qui jette par une nuit brumeuse, sur les routes de l'arrière, des dragées contaminées du virus de la peste, et qui regagne ses lignes ...[13]

L. Daudet notes:

> Ce ne serait pas forcer l'image que de se representer ces positions d'argent, d'affaires et d'opinions de l'Allemagne chez nous ainsi que des tranchées économiques et bancaires. (*L'Action Française*, 3 May 1915)

---

[12] *L'Offensive morale*, p. 1.
[13] *Journal*, p. 1502 (20 June 1918).

and he describes *Le Bonnet Rouge* as "un tank [tout indiqué pour] jeter le trouble dans les esprits, puis dans la rue" (*L'Action Française*, 26 Apr. 1917).

The analysis of *le défaitisme* proposed by Valois etc. as the means used by the Germans to wear away the *front moral* or *front de l'intérieur* of their adversaries (thereby enabling them ultimately to break through the *front militaire*) provides the unifying link which helps to explain how the one word can be defined, by the people who use it, with reference to such seemingly diverse ideas as anarchy, treason and discouragement. It also throws light on the collocation of *défaitiste/défaitisme* with another group of terms: *antinational, antipatriote/antipatriotique/antipatriotisme*, and *antimilitariste/ antimilitarisme*. Thus, writing of the work of *les défaitistes*, L. Marchand says:

> Dans cette guerre "totale" notre front intérieur n'est pas défendu. Il est urgent d'établir une ligne de résistance morale qui mette l'opinion française à l'abri des campagnes antinationales.[14]

H. Bérenger reminds his readers of his "rapport sur les menées antipatriotiques et la sûreté nationale", and refers to it later in the same article as "ma longue enquête contre le défaitisme" (*Paris-Midi*, 13 Dec. 1917). A similar association is made by L. Daudet when he says that Sébastien Faure was "convaincu par la police spéciale du G.Q.G. de propagande défaitiste et antipatriotique",[15] or that thousands of "tracts défaitistes" had been distributed by a group of "antimilitaristes et antipatriotes".[16] In his speech to the Senate on 22 July 1917, Clemenceau uses *antipatriotique* in the sense in which other writers use *défaitiste*—i.e. as distinct from *pacifiste*; he mentions

> ... tous ceux qui feraient de la propagande, je ne veux pas dire pacifiste, ce n'est pas le mot, mais de la propagande antipatriotique en France.[17]

M. Barrès does not hesitate to qualify *Le Bonnet Rouge* as *antifrançais*:

---

[14] *L'Offensive morale*, p. 333.

[15] *Le Poignard dans le dos*, p. 118.

[16] Ibid., p. 127. The activities of the self-styled *antimilitaristes* and *antipatriotes* in early years of the century are fully discussed by J. -J. Becker, *Le Carnet B*. See esp. Text A 8 (p. 188): "Résolution du Congrès de la C.G.T. d'Amiens sur l'antimilitarisme (13 oct. 1906)" for the expression *propagande antimilitariste et antipatriotique*.

[17] *Discours de Guerre*, p. 67.

Ce journal, je veux, puisqu'il semble subsister certains doutes, établir avec précision quelle fut sa besogne défaitiste, antifrançaise, et étroitement accordée avec l'effort mondial allemand.[18]

Given that people accused of *défaitisme* regard their critics as *nationalistes, chauvins, jusqu'auboutistes*, etc.—all general terms of abuse in the language of the Left—the antonymy thus set up between these and *défaitiste* contributes to broadening the meaning of the latter, and making it a vague designation for the left-wing enemy. *Le Canard Enchaîné* plays on the status of such terms for humorous effect:[19]

Le Petit Café
Les verres ne "tiennent" pas beaucoup, et les liquides ne vont pas jusqu'au bout! C'est donc un café défaitiste? (23 Jan. 1918)

2.11 Seeds of future development

What has now to be examined is how *défaitiste*, which first designated people who deliberately or inadvertently worked towards the defeat of their country by (among other things) demoralizing soldiers and civilians (without necessarily being in any way discouraged themselves), came also to be used of the victims who had become demoralized and believed that defeat was inevitable. The relationship between these two meanings is neatly paralleled by the difference between the active *bourreur de crânes* and the passive *crâne bourré*;[1] and indeed, in 1918 one finds that the latter does collocate with *défaitiste*. H. Bérenger writes:

S'il reste encore dans Paris un seul crâne bourré défaitiste pour s'imaginer que la guerre finit en palabres ... (*Paris-Midi*, 31 Aug. 1918)

Although, as previous discussion has shown, when journalists began to use *défaitiste/défaitisme* of Frenchmen, they were frequently alluding to features of the situation other than demoralization, the terms did develop associations at this time which point to the direction in which their meaning was to become specialized later.[2] A word which figured in the press at the time of the mutinies

---

[18] *En regardant au fond des crevasses*, p. 93.

[19] Cf. the quotation from this paper below, 2.12, p. 108.

[1] Although *videur de crânes* is closer in meaning to *défaitiste* (see above, 1.7, pp. 39-41), I have not found the form *crâne vidé*.

[2] In his article "L'Opinion française et le défaitisme pendant la Grande Guerre" A. Kupferman seems to make the anachronistic assumption that the word *défaitisme*

alongside expressions already examined was *le cafard*. *L'Action Française* notes:

> Gustave Hervé revient sur la funeste propagande qui déclancha une vague d'assaut de cafard pacifiste dès le début de la dernière offensive.
>
> (12 July 1917)

Hervé had indeed given a prophetic warning at the end of 1916:

> *Dans le piège allemand*
>
> Nos zimmerwaldistes vont se retourner vers le pays, vers ces pauvres poilus qui, dans la boue des tranchées, sont sans cesse guettés par le cafard; vers nos ouvriers d'usine à tendance humanitaire et internationa-liste ... ils vont faire appel à la pitié et à la lâcheté, aux plus nobles et aux plus vils sentiments de la foule, et une immense vague pacifiste va déferler sur la France. (*La Victoire*, 18 Dec. 1916)

L'Action Française announces the same theme again on 8 September in a headline "La propagande du cafard"; neither this article nor the one from 12 July contains the terms *défaitiste/défaitisme*, but the implicit connections are very strong: *le cafard* has been deliberately induced by the unnamed individuals intent on stirring up trouble who are regularly called *défaitistes* elsewhere. This is made plain by L. Daudet when he comments on Barbusse's novel *Le Feu*:

> Maurice Pujo, notre vaillant et cher "Biffin", l'a défini et châtié d'un mot: "Du sirop de cafard". C'est un bréviaire du défaitisme, dont la victoire actuelle démontre le néant.[3]

Here, *le cafard* is the state of mind induced in others by *le défaitisme* which, since it is pictured as having its *bréviaire*, is in some respects an organized movement—as the following example confirms:

> Barrès ... a marqué la bande de quelques traits de feu. L'Allemand et le défaitisme à sa solde ne s'y sont pas trompés ...[4]

---

was closely associated with *pessimisme* from the outset, and that its use in 1917 to refer to treasonable activity has somehow to be explained. The linguistic evidence shows on the contrary that this latter use came first.

[3] *Le Poignard dans le dos*, p. 84. *Le Feu* was the subject of bitter controversy in the press, as regards both its documentary value and the political opinions of its author. For divergent assessments, see J. Norton Cru, *Témoins. Essai d'analyse et de critique des souvenirs de combattants édités en français de 1915 à 1928*, Paris, 1929, pp. 555-65; and F. Field, *Three French Writers and the Great War: Barbusse. Drieu La Rochelle. Bernanos. Studies in the Rise of Communism and Fascism*, Cambridge, 1975, pp. 40-5.

[4] *Le Poignard dans le dos*, p. 82.

Towards the beginning of 1918, one finds *défaitisme* coupled with the term *démoralisation* itself, a highly significant development in view of the fact that the latter can denote both verbal action and the resulting state produced by that action. Bérenger writes:

> ... si certains empoisonneurs de l'arrière—traîtres ou lâches, ou simplement imbéciles, mais dans tous les cas complices de l'ennemi,—étaient laissés libres d'accomplir leur sale besogne de démoralisation et de défaitisme en pleine nation qui se bat ... (*Paris-Midi*, 22 Jan. 1918)

Likewise, G. Hervé speaks of the "campagne pacifiste ou défaitiste démoralisante" organized by *Le Bonnet Rouge* (*La Victoire*, 31 July 1918), and L. Marchand observes:

> Les articles de propagande pacifiste, défaitiste et démoralisatrice passent, de plus en plus nombreux, de la seconde à la première page du *Bonnet Rouge*.[5]

In examples like these, *défaitiste/défaitisme* still have what one might call their "active" meaning (backed by the adjectives démoralis*ant* and démoralis*ateur*). It is impossible to tell whether Bérenger, for instance, regards *démoralisation* and *défaitisme* as synonymous, or if each is chosen to highlight a different aspect of a given phenomenon. The problem has already been encountered in connection with the relationship between *défaitisme* and *trahison*, and it seems that this "linking" of terms is a constant of polemical style; with a recent neologism, the device contributes to building up its meaning.[6]

An unequivocal case of the use of *défaitisme* to imply the discouragement and lack of faith in the possibility of victory which result from subversive propaganda is found in the evidence given by Daudet at the Malvy trial:

> Le procédé consiste à reprendre ces éléments, à les regrouper par le moyen du chantage, à les remettre en mouvement, de telle sorte que, par la banque, par la presse, par la parole clandestine, il se produise dans les pays visés par l'Allemagne une espèce d'affaissement du moral et qu'il s'y produise ce que l'on a appelé si justement des vagues de défaitisme.[7]

Now the kind of *affaissement du moral* which he describes had

---

[5] *L'Offensive morale*, p. 331.
[6] Stylistic "linking" is treated fully below, 3.7.
[7] *Le Poignard dans le dos*, p. 186. Daudet's statement is dated 19 July 1918.

existed and been labelled long before the word *défaitisme* came
into French. Harking back to 1870, Henry Bérenger writes:

> Le plus grand mal de la défaite pour un peuple, c'est qu'elle lui façonne
> pour longtemps des âmes de vaincus, des âmes par avance inclinées vers
> la résignation à ce qu'elles considèrent comme la fatalité.
> (*Paris-Midi*, 1 Mar. 1915)

A. Ferry uses the same expression *âme de vaincu* in another historical parallel:

> 1793 était tout enthousiasme. L'Empire était épopée. Nous, nous
> sommes tout devoir. Nous ne nous sentons ni une âme de vaincus ni une
> âme de conquérants.[8]

G. Hervé links it first with *pacifiste bêlant*:

> A la victoire, ils [les pacifistes bêlants] n'y ont jamais cru; et parce qu'ils
> ont une âme de vaincus, ils ont semé le doute et la démoralisation dans
> le pays ... (*La Victoire*, 11 July 1917)

and then with *défaitiste* when he adopts the word:

> Il faut être atteint de neurasthénie aiguë, de crétinisme intégral, ou avoir
> une âme de vaincu et de défaitiste, pour avoir le moindre doute sur
> l'issue de la lutte ... (*La Victoire*, 10 Dec. 1917)

or again:

> De ce garçon qui était d'une bravoure folle et qui n'avait point une âme
> de vaincu, vous avez fait, parce que ses besoins d'argent l'ont mis sous
> votre dépendance, une loque de défaitiste. (*La Victoire*, 25 Nov. 1917)

In this last example, Hervé is blaming Caillaux for corrupting
Almereyda (Hervé's one-time associate); and he goes on to accuse
him of the downfall of Malvy. The growing hostility to Caillaux in
the press at the end of 1917, building up to his arrest in January
1918, was the occasion for much discussion of a new brand of
défaitisme.[9] Hervé contrasts "le léninisme révolutionnaire" with

---

[8] *Carnets secrets*, p. 81 (4 June 1915).
[9] This also seems to have been the point at which the English words *defeatist/
defeatism* made their appearance in *The Times*, initially in translations of French
debates and newspaper articles. At first, journalists borrow the French form
défaitiste, e.g. "the chief *défaitistes* of Italy" in a translation from Clemenceau
(8 Nov. 1917), or *France and the "Défaitistes"*—this time as a headline (12 Nov.
1917). The English calque occurs when an adjective is needed to translate a
declaration by Caillaux: "I have not taken part in any 'defeatist' palavers in Italy"

"le défaitisme sous sa forme caillautiste" (*La Victoire*, 11 Dec. 1917), and declares in his letter "J'accuse M. Caillaux":

> Vous êtes l'âme, l'espoir de tous les défaitistes français, de tous ces malheureux qui, désespérant de vaincre, l'Allemagne impériale, sont prêts à accepter du Kaiser une paix sans vainqueur ni vaincu, qui serait le déshonneur et la ruine de notre pays. (*La Victoire*, 24 Nov. 1917)

Later, he explains how this attitude constitutes treason:

> Parce que [Caillaux] avait besoin de la défaite pour remonter sur la scène, il crut à la défaite, ou, ce qui revient au même, à l'impossibilité de la victoire.
> De là à s'entendre avec l'ennemi pour organiser secrètement, en France, à l'aide de la presse, une campagne défaitiste, il n'y avait pas loin: quelle honte pour la France si la justice a bien en mains, comme l'arrestation semble l'indiquer, la preuve d'une si monstrueuse trahison!
> (*La Victoire*, 15 Jan. 1918)

M. Barrès voices a similar opinion in his diary for January 1918; under the heading "Catilina-Caillaux" he notes:

> Il a inventé une nouvelle espèce de trahison. Ce n'est pas celle de Judas ... Non, c'est un manque de foi dans son pays. Quand on ne croit pas à la victoire de son pays, il faut s'en aller...
> Tous ces serpents à sonnettes n'attirent plus personne à la chapelle puante du défaitisme.[10]

Caillaux's supporters contended that his political enemies had trumped up the charge of *défaitisme*—a totally groundless one—for sordid polemical motives. P. Boulat argues:

> *Patrie et Humanité*
> Cette guerre a créé de déplorables malentendus, soigneusement entretenus et exagérés par les nationalistes. On inventa le mot défaitisme pour le jeter comme un outrage, un soupçon, à la face des humanitaires qui,

---

(12 Nov. 1917). *Defeatist* is used spontaneously in the leader a few days later: "Behind [the Socialists and the Syndicalists] and among them, lurk the 'defeatists' and those international financiers who manipulate them for private ends of their own" (17 Nov. 1917). When *defeatism* first appears, it is linked with *boloism*: "The feeling that [Clemenceau] alone was fitted to deal with the requisite firmness with Boloism and 'Defeatism'" ...(22 Nov. 1917). The English version of Alexinsky's *La Russie et la guerre* was translated from the manuscript of the French first edition (and appeared simultaneously with it); it therefore did not contain the word *defeatist*. Thus this neologism was not introduced to the English public in the same way as to the French (see above, 2.3, pp. 49ff.).
[10] *Mes Cahiers*, vol. xi, Paris, 1938, pp. 315-16.

d'ailleurs, ne cessent de déclarer qu'ils n'accepteraient jamais une paix à tout prix, humiliante pour la France. (*Le Pays*, 2 Dec. 1917)

However, explanations such as this did little to remove the sting from the accusation of *défaitisme*; Caillaux himself was always to resent it most bitterly:

Contre le terme abject de défaitisme je ne cesserai de protester tant qu'on le prendra dans son sens littéral, tant que l'on n'entendra pas que l'épithète n'a été imaginée que pour essayer de déshonorer les politiques de mesure et de bon sens qui s'opposent naturellement à celles de M. Clemenceau et de *l'Action Française*. Je ne cesserai de répéter que je défie qu'on prouve que j'aie jamais espéré la défaite de mon pays,—je ne suis pas, grâce aux dieux! capable d'un sentiment monstrueux. Je défie qu'on prouve qu'un écrit signé de moi, une parole publique, une seule, ait jamais découragé les efforts de nos citoyens ou encouragé ceux de nos ennemis.[11]

It seems to have been the military situation at the outset of 1918 which was decisive in cementing the connection between *défaitisme* and *pessimisme*. By an ironical twist of fate, the very man who had done so much to combat the earliest manifestations of *défaitisme* in France—Pétain—was himself to be labelled a *défaitiste* barely a year after the mutinies; his attitude to the war and the Germans remained unaltered, but the neologism had meanwhile evolved sufficiently to account for this paradox. By this time, the army and the country at large were growing impatient with the prudent approach which Pétain had proved to be so successful as a means of restoring confidence after the troubles of May and June 1917.[12] On the occasion of the German offensive of 21 March 1918, Pétain was accused of acting in sheer panic and giving way to dangerous pessimism. Poincaré relates a conversation between himself and Clemenceau on 26 March:

[11] *Mes prisons,* 2nd edn., Paris, 1920, p. 279.
[12] Pierrefeu notes that "le général n'était pas sans inquiétude. Cette vague d'*offensivite* était arrivée jusqu'à lui. Il sentait avec netteté qu'une sorte d'impopularité l'atteignait et minait son crédit" (*G.Q.G. Secteur 1,* vol. ii, p. 118). He quotes another general as saying: "Pétain perd la France. Son esprit de temporisation éternelle est en train de nous jeter dans l'abîme" (Ibid., p. 116). R. Griffiths stresses that "one must closely examine the accusations of 'pessimism' and 'defeatism' flung at Pétain during this war. Only too often they mean that Pétain is not in agreement with the opinions of the writer, and that he is avoiding a useless offensive" (*Marshal Pétain,* p. 76).

Clemenceau dit: "Pétain est agaçant à force de pessimisme. Imaginez-vous qu'il m'a dit … 'Les Allemands battront les Anglais en rase campagne; après quoi ils nous battront aussi.' Un général devrait-il parler et même penser ainsi?"

His entry for the following day runs:

Loncheur est très mécontent de Pétain qu'il trouve tout à fait défaitiste et qui lui a dit il y a quelques jours: "Il faudrait entamer des pourparlers de paix."[13]

Pétain is a *défaitiste* not because there is any question of his acting in concert with the Germans, but simply because he believes that defeat is unavoidable.[14] The term *défaitiste* is given a similar interpretation by General Fayolle on 30 April:

Déjeuner à Beauvais avec Pétain (Hôtel Continental). … Il dit des choses déplorables, montrant qu'il ne croit pas à la possibilité de l'attaque, disant qu'il est inutile de se rapprocher à bonne distance. Cet homme ne croit pas à l'offensive. Encore un peu il serait défaitiste! Il se fait du tort et il est douteux qu'il finisse la guerre comme commandant des troupes françaises …[15]

The implications are clear: Pétain has completely lost his fighting spirit and is almost prepared to *accept the idea of defeat*—"encore un peu il serait défaitiste".

2.12 Contemporary awareness of a neologism

It is instructive to establish whether people are aware of using or hearing a neologism, or whether it passes unnoticed into their vocabulary. In many cases, the fact that a word is felt to be new is shown by the various precautions which speakers employ to introduce it into their sentences.[1] These may take the form of typographical devices such as italics or quotation marks if one is dealing with written material, as for instance when H. Bérenger writes

---

[13] *Au Service de la France,* vol x, *Victoire et Armistice 1918,* Paris, 1933, pp. 92-3.
[14] R. Griffiths distinguishes between "two forms of 'pessimism' in Pétain. One, which was a rational belief in the importance of the defensive and the difficulty of the offensive, and which was qualified as 'pessimism' by his colleagues, was purely a tactical sense supported by strong arguments as to the dangers of the alternatives. The other, with which we are dealing here, is true pessimism in the face of a threat from the enemy; a belief that all is going as badly as it possibly can" (*Marshal Pétain,* p. 74). It was this latter which came to be termed *défaitisme.*
[15] *Cahiers secrets de la grande guerre,* Paris, 1964, p. 272.
[1] See M. Riffaterre, "La Durée de la valeur stylistique du néologisme", pp. 284 ff.

"l'heure est passée du 'défaitisme'";[2] or the presence of a near synonym or explanation to accompany the neologism, as in "toutes nos grandes affaires de trahison et de défaitisme";[3] or even comments on the word from the individuals who first start using it.

It will be remembered that when L. Daudet adopted the terms *défaitiste/défaitisme*, he used them without any of these precautions[4] right from the outset. Nothing suggests that he had only recently borrowed them from H. Bérenger. However, it seems more than likely that he knew who was responsible for launching the new slogan in the press; not only might he have read *Le Matin* along with other papers on 6 June 1917 when Bérenger's first dramatic article appeared, but he would also have taken a personal interest in Bérenger himself.[5] The two men reestablished contact after a lapse of time in September 1917, when Bérenger lent Daudet the report he had drafted on the troubles in the army, and asked him for information about certain suspect foreigners naturalized in France.

It is some time after this meeting that one finds Daudet first alluding to the novelty of the word *défaitisme*. In a leader which appeared in *L'Action Française* on 21 November 1917, he asks:

Est-ce le grand nettoyage?
Le réquisitoire du 22 juillet 1917 au Sénat qui vient de faire Clemenceau premier ministre était, à sa façon, un programme. Il s'agit maintenant de le remplir. Une chose est certaine: de ce grand et indispensable nettoyage dépendent la libération et le salut du pays.... La guerre actuelle est une guerre *totale*, où le défaitisme—comme dit Henry Bérenger, créateur du mot—est l'arme la plus dangereuse des Allemands.

Was Daudet aware that the term originated as a calque from the Russian, or did he believe that Bérenger had coined it independently? He refers again to the matter in March 1918 in *La Guerre totale*; this time, however, his testimony is hesitant. In one place he states:

Ces fonds étaient destinés ... à organiser des mouvements de révolte et, si faire se pouvait, des séditions, des mutineries et des émeutes, par une

---

[2] See above, 2.6, p. 66.
[3] See above, 2.9, p. 92.
[4] See above, 2.7, p. 69.
[5] "Je connais de longue date Henry Bérenger, qui venait autrefois assidûment chez Alphonse Daudet. Mon père appréciait fort son agrément personnel, son intelligence et sa culture. Une interruption de nos relations, due à des divergences politiques, n'avait nullement affaibli une sympathie réciproque, fortifiée de souvenirs communs" (*Le Poignard dans le dos,* p. 17).

série de manœuvres concertées, que le sénateur Henry Bérenger a très heureusement baptisées "manœuvres défaitistes".[6]

—whereas later in the same book he writes:

La guerre totale ... comporte de fortes, périodiques et systématiques pressions sur le moral de l'adversaire .... D'où l'expression fort juste— elle est, je crois, d'Henry Bérenger—de manœuvre défaitiste.[7]

The discrepancy between the two statements is typical of Daudet: he was a prolific, repetitive and sometimes careless writer, and there are often errors of detail from one book or article to the next. It is clear that he was not entirely sure where the expression originated, although he believed Bérenger to have been responsible for it. Moreover, Daudet had originally said "créateur du mot", whereas in *La Guerre totale* he merely credits Bérenger with applying the expression *manœuvre défaitiste* to the subversive activity of German agents.

Other writers were also aware that the terms *défaitiste/défaitisme* were being exploited as part of a deliberate campaign. *Le Canard Enchaîné* was ever quick to spot topical neologisms:

DÉFAITISTE!

La langue française s'est encore enrichie, depuis le début de la guerre, de quelques vocables tels que *pinard, gniole, jusqu'auboutiste*, etc., qui n'en sont pas le moins bel ornement. A ce collier, il faut maintenant ajouter une nouvelle perle, le mot *défaitiste*, dont le besoin, d'ailleurs, se faisait vivement sentir, n'est-ce pas?

Quel en est l'inventeur? Je n'en sais fichtre rien! Que veut-il dire? Quant à cela, je suis heureusement à même de vous renseigner.

On est *défaitiste*:

Quand on ne pense pas comme Gustave, Maurice, Charles et Léon ... et autres Sires de Framboisy. (11 July 1917)

The remaining paragraphs were unfortunately obliterated by "Anastasie". Writing in a more serious vein, J. Gerbault observes in the *Larousse Mensuel* for August 1917 (article "Guerre 1914-17"):

Quelques publicistes courageux ... secouaient rudement ceux que l'un d'eux avait fustigés du nom de "défaitistes"—les semeurs de panique, artisans conscients ou inconscients d'une paix qui ne serait pas française.

[6] p. 43.
[7] p. 244.

Bérenger is not mentioned by name, but Gerbault may well have been following the campaign closely enough to know who initiated it.

Perhaps the most satisfying testimony comes from Bérenger himself. In February 1918 he gives over a number of articles to sizing up the events of the past year; his retrospective appraisal includes comments on the word *défaitisme*. He begins by offering apologies:

> Ce sera l'honneur de notre patrie d'avoir crevé en temps utile le *défaitisme*, "mot ignoble", certes,[8] mais chose plus ignoble encore, que la Russie a connue et subie ... (*Paris-Midi*, 5 Feb. 1918)

Later, in connection with a fresh distribution of tracts at Saint-Étienne, Bérenger claims credit for putting the term *défaitisme* into circulation:

> *Un nouveau coup de l'Allemagne*
> Ceux qui nous reprochaient d'avoir exagéré cette entreprise quand nous l'avons dénoncée sous le nom de *défaitisme* il y a quelques mois, ceux-là comprendront-ils aujourd'hui la terrible gravité des faits dénoncés par M. Renaudel? (*Paris-Midi*, 19 Feb. 1918)

Now it could conceivably be argued that *nous* is ambiguous, that Bérenger may mean himself and other journalists as well. However, this seems unlikely in view of the unequivocal way he uses *nous* to refer to himself in an article on the following day concerned with the same subject:

> Ce n'est plus nous, ce n'est plus Clemenceau, ce n'est plus Léon Daudet, qui donnons ces avertissements. C'est M. Renaudel lui-même ...
> (*Paris-Midi*, 20 Feb. 1918)

Bérenger supplies further confirmation of his role in the affair a few months later:

> Nous n'en sommes plus, heureusement, aux heures d'équivoque néfaste où des gouvernements sans courage politique faisaient une part, derrière les champs de bataille, à cette chose ignoble que nous dûmes stigmatiser un jour du vocable de *défaitisme*. (*Paris-Midi*, 25 Apr. 1918)

There seems no cause to doubt that this is indeed how the terms *défaitiste/défaitisme* were popularized in French.

---

[8] Expressed hesitation on the part of the writer is one of the criteria of non-assimilation mentioned by Riffaterre (see above, p. 106, n. 1). It is interesting in this case that Bérenger did not begin to express scruples or to comment on the neologism until it had become widely accepted.

It is worth noting that awareness that a word is new does not necessarily place any restrictions on the use to which it is put. Once speakers have adopted a neologism, they do not hesitate to apply it "retrospectively" to matters which they designated in a different way before it was coined or became current. There is no means of determining to what extent Frenchmen in 1915 or 1916 thought of certain attitudes and patterns of behaviour as belonging together in some kind of identifiable category. Though it is clear, for instance, that Ch. Sancerme was denouncing the same individuals for the same activities as H. Bérenger and L. Daudet were, it is an open question whether he viewed these in a different light because he lacked the labels *défaitiste/défaitisme* in his vocabulary.[9] Similar uncertainty would attend discussion of the way in which de Roux envisaged *at the time* the behaviour he was to call *défaitisme* when the word became available. The point at issue here, however, is rather different: once de Roux had made the new acquisition, he not only applied it to current preoccupations, but he also identified past happenings as examples of the same phenomenon—hence his "retrospective" use of the term *défaitiste*:

Le 11 mars 1915 une première condamnation pour distribution de tracts défaitistes.[10]

—or again:

Politiquement, voici la situation à l'aurore de 1916. Le gouvernement sait qu'une campagne défaitiste se poursuit, associant les agents et les bénéficiaires de la corruption allemande aux tenants des chimères pacifistes.[11]

The first of these quotations is particularly likely to mislead, since

[9] One could take *défaitiste/défaitisme* as belonging to the category of "mots qui désignent *autrement* [my italics] des faits anciens" (A. Darmesteter, *De la Création actuelle de mots nouveaux dans la langue française et des lois qui la régissent,* Paris, 1877, p. 32), or as a word by means of which "s'est concrétisée, cristallisée ... [une] idée qui était 'dans l'air'" (G. Matoré, "Le néologisme: naissance et diffusion", *Le Français Moderne,* xx (1952), 89). L. Guilbert argues that one must not make the mistake of identifying "la date d'apparition d'un concept nouveau avec celle de la dénomination par une unité lexicale créée postérieurement au concept ou à la chose" (*La Formation du vocabulaire de l'aviation,* Paris, 1965, p. 331). The notion of semantic gap or void that such a view might give rise to can be avoided if one adopts T. E. Hope's principle of "comparative efficiency". See *Lexical Borrowing,* p. 709, and above, 2.3, p. 51, n. 19.

[10] *Le Défaitisme,* p. 35.

[11] Ibid., p. 83.

once might assume it to contain a verbatim echo of the sentence passed, whereas the text in question would undoubtedly have referred to *tracts pacifistes* or *tracts révolutionnaires.* A further example of this kind of usage occurs in an article by L. Daudet— significantly, the *first one* in which the new term figures:

> Le gouvernement ne s'est pas ému des renseignements que j'ai publiés ici, au moment de l'offensive de Verdun, sur l'origine des rumeurs défaitistes. (*L'Action Française*, 21 June 1917)

There is nothing surprising about this; one is, after all, dealing with a continuing situation in which *le défaitisme* of 1917 is merely the eruption of something which had been smouldering for a long time, and it seems quite natural that these early manifestations should be viewed and labelled as harbingers by anyone looking back into the past. All that needs to be stressed is that the possibility of retrospective extension is present right from the start, and does not appear to depend on people's forgetting how recent a particular term is.

Final confirmation that a neologism has been assimilated comes when it finds its way into dictionaires, though the extent to which this postdates its general acceptance will depend on the stylistic register to which it belongs and the policy of the lexicographers of the period. *Défaitiste/défaitisme* were included in the *Larousse Mensuel* in March 1918. The definition is a synchronic one, and there is no mention of Russian politics:

> DÉFAITISME (fè-tissm'—rad. défaite) n.m.
> Opinion et politique de ceux qui jugent la défaite inévitable, ou qui l'estiment moins onéreuse que la continuation de la guerre: *La guerre actuelle est une guerre totale, où le DÉFAITISME—comme dit Henry Bérenger, créateur du mot—est l'arme la plus dangereuse des Allemands.* (Léon Daudet)[12]

The example given is, of course, the quotation from *L'Action Française* discussed earlier.[13] Unfortunately, this first dictionary article is doubly misleading. In the first place, since nothing is said about the origin of the term, readers are bound to assume that the quotation supplies the necessary information. Was the writer so unfamiliar with articles appearing in the daily press just after the

---

[12] *Défaitiste* is defined with reference to *défaitisme.*
[13] See above, p. 107.

February Revolution that he did not know of the Russian doctrine of *défaitisme*? If he was aware of it but considered it irrelevant for his purposes, he was guilty of serious inaccuracy in implying that Bérenger was the "créateur du mot". In the second place, the example as it stands does not elucidate the definition, and it is doubtful whether Daudet would have subscribed to this interpretation of what he meant by *le défaitisme* of *Le Bonnet Rouge*. The definition given here corresponds rather to the kind of *défaitisme* that had come in certain circles to be associated with Caillaux and then Pétain; in which case one can only regret that the lexicographer did not find a more suitable example on which to base his article.

These different interpretations of *défaitisme* are not, of course, unrelated.[14] But in order to see this, one has to make a conscious effort to recreate the atmosphere of 1917-18, to remember that calling someone a *défaitiste* in time of war is a very different matter from using the same term in an extended sense in peacetime (when military defeat is not an issue of the moment) to imply that a person gives in rather too easily in a struggle of one sort or another. Many people would argue that when a country is at war, any kind of weakening of will among its citizens, any slight readiness to countenance defeat, is *ipso facto* a treacherous attitude which plays straight into the hands of the enemy. Individuals who have succumbed to enemy propaganda and become demoralized will themselves discourage others; not only that, they constitute a potential threat to security, for they are obvious candidates for treacherous agents to approach, and if the opportunity presents itself they may well join the network in the hope of bringing hostilities to an end as quickly as possible. Thus the chain of *défaitisme* runs unbroken from enemy agent to victim; from a certain point of view they both do the same work and are equally reprehensible.

If one is obliged to present the early history of *défaitiste/défaitisme* in summary form, it may look as though the problem in hand is one of semantic change.[15] This is no doubt true of the transition from phase one: *le défaitisme de Lénine* to phase two: *le défaitisme*

[14] See above, 2.8, pp. 86-7.
[15] Cf. T. E. Hope, "Loan-words as cultural and lexical symbols" (1963), 41: "Gradually certain contexts predominate and are felt to be typical; use defines the signification more and more precisely. A restrictive choice is made, or rather a series of choices which, viewed diachronically, appear as a shift in meaning."

des embochés; however, once the ties with Russian revolutionaries have been severed, it becomes difficult on close examination of the material to talk convincingly about *change* of meaning. What is involved in this experimental period is surely *acquisition* of meaning—the shaping of usage for a term which, only a few months previously, had not impinged at all on the linguistic consciousness of the majority of French speakers.

Part Three

LA RÉACTION

3.1   *Les réactionnaires*

> ... abrités sous la bannière de l'union sacrée, les réacteurs
> de droite et de gauche (car il y en a), chaque jour plus
> audacieux, terrorisent ce qui reste de gouvernement et
> dictent des ordres à leurs créatures.
>
> LE PAYS, 6 Sept. 1917

The attack mounted by the Left in 1914-18 on reactionaries of
various sorts drew upon a well-stocked arsenal of pejorative labels
which had been built up progressively since the French Revolution,
and had received considerable reinforcement from the verbal
excesses of the Dreyfus Case.[1] The phraseology of the left-wing
press in the First World War seems remarkably stereotyped when
contrasted with that of its adversaries, and this can be explained
in part by the fact that most of the component forces of *la réaction*
were enemies of long standing, whereas *les défaitistes* represented
a new threat calling for fresh linguistic weapons.

The terms *réaction/réactionnaire/réacteur* entered political vocabulary in the revolutionary period.[2] In First World War polemics

---

[1] For an analysis of the French Right in the nineteenth and early twentieth cen-
turies, see R. Rémond, *La Droite en France de la première restauration à la Ve
République*, vol. i: 1815-1940, 3rd edn., Paris, 1968.

[2] The political meaning of *réaction* dates from 1795 (*Bloch-Wartburg*); according
to Brunot, at this period "le sens est toujours abstrait; le mot ne désigne pas les
gens, mais l'esprit qui les anime, le mouvement auquel ils poussent" (*Histoire de la
langue française*, vol. ix. 2, p. 844). Later, it comes also to denote collectively the
holders of reactionary opinions. *Réactionnaire* (modelled on *révolutionnaire*) goes
back to 1796 (The *Dauzat-Dubois-Mitterand* gives 1790; there seems to be some
difficulty in interpreting Brunot's dates); the *Bloch-Wartburg* notes that it "a
éliminé *réacteur,* de la même époque. However, the latter was still in use in 1848:
M. Tournier observes that *réacteur* (and *réac*) belong to the vocabulary of the
workers, while *réactionnaire* is used by historians ("Éléments pour l'étude quantitative
d'une journée de 48", p. 88). J. Dubois has examples of its use in 1869-72 (*Le
Vocabulaire politique et social*, p. 398), and the *Dauzat-Dubois-Mitterand* suggests

the choice between them depends largely on considerations of emphasis or simple variety. The collective noun *réaction* is especially well suited to feature in headlines like "La Réaction à la Chambre", with the form *réactionnaires* or *réacteurs* occurring in the text of the article. In some cases the collective or abstract term could not be replaced by either of the others, as for instance in the following example:

Les Tranchées de l'Arrière

"Les tranchées de la Réaction" ... M. Gustave Téry a relevé cette expression dans un article du *Bonnet Rouge* et le voilà désolé.

(*Le Bonnet Rouge*, 21 Sept. 1916)

The familiar abbreviation *réac*[3] occurs sporadically in R. Rolland's diary, as does the form *ultra-réac*; he mentions

le système de compromis, d'alliances secrètes entre le gouvernement et les partis ultra-réacs.[4]

Réactionnaire and its cognates are abusive labels, whereas *conservateur/conservation/conservatisme* need not be.[5] J. Longuet contrasts

le conservatisme équilibré et prudent des tories anglais et le réactionnarisme[6] enragé et aveugle de nos propres gens de droite—les opinions de l'*Écho de Paris* our de l'*Action Française.* (*Le Pays*, 14 Aug. 1917)

The same distinction is made by G. Hervé:

---

that it did not become obsolete until the second half of the nineteenth century. In fact, it was still being used in 1914-18 as a stylistic alternative for the more common form *réactionnaire*.

[3] Popularized at the beginning of 1849; see M. Tournier, "Éléments pour l'étude quantitative d'une journée de 48", p. 88.

[4] *Journal,* p. 1627 (Oct. 1918).

[5] *Conservation* and *conservateur* began to be used as political terms during the eighteenth century. F. Brunot notes that they became quite common during the revolutionary period, but without any hint of pejorative meaning; he quotes expressions like "la politique conservatrice de la liberté", where what is being preserved is specifically the changes brought about by the Revolution and threatened by reactionary forces (*Histoire de la langue française,* vol. ix. 2, pp. 796-8 and 840). During the nineteenth century, when the monarchy was re-established, the terms came to imply support for this, and counter-revolutionary attitudes in general. Only then did the word *conservatisme* appear: the *F.E.W.* dates this from 1868. From the July Monarchy onwards the Right called itself *le parti conservateur.* See J. Dubois, *Le Vocabulaire politique et social,* pp. 73-4.

[6] This derivative (obviously modelled on *conservatisme*) does not appear to figure in dictionaries. I have found no other example of it.

Le *Temps* est, on le sait, l'organe qui reflète avec le plus d'autorité la pensée de cette bourgeoisie conservatrice—je ne dis pas réactionnaire—dont la doctrine est que moins l'État s'occupe d'une affaire, mieux elle marche. (*La Guerre Sociale*, 20 July 1915)

The full implications of the parenthesis become clearer if one compares it with something he had written two months earlier:

certains milieux que nous appelions réactionnaires avant l'union sacrée
(*La Guerre Sociale*, 25 May 1915)

Hervé repeats this comment with monotonous regularity, varying it occasionally by putting *réactionnaire* in quotation marks—a rather unsubtle device whereby he pretends to eschew a loaded word which evokes internal quarrels of the pre-war years (now supposedly set aside), and yet contrives to use it all the same. Hervé's view of the status of the term is given independent confirmation by L. Marchand:

En dépit de "l'Union Sacrée [le *Bonnet Rouge*] mène de violentes campagnes contre ceux qu'il appelle "des réactionnaires" et contre les prêtres.[7]

Le Bonnet Rouge, it should be noted, had no scruples about employing the word *réactionnaire*: the quotation marks are Marchand's.

The distinction between the two sets of terms is of course frequently neutralized, and *conservateur* etc. convey much of the same odium that attaches to *réactionnaire* etc. When H. Barbusse writes:

Deux partis: celui des réformes et celui de la conservation, celui du progrès et celui de la réaction[8]

conservation and *réaction* are synonymous in the context. Another indication of this equivalence is afforded by the fact that both families have antonyms in common; for instance, one finds, often within the writings of a single person, oppositions of the following kind: *conservateurs* v. *républicains* and *réactionnaires* v. *républicains*; or *les forces conservatrices* v. *la Révolution prolétarienne* and *réactionnaires* v. *révolutionnaires*. On the other hand, a term like *radical* is more likely to be contrasted with *conservateur*, and

[7] *L'Offensive morale,* p. 58.
[8] *Paroles d'un combattant,* p. 75 (article in *Le Populaire,* 3 July 1918).

pacifiste with *réactionnaire*—in the latter case, because the intensive anti-pacifist campaign of 1917 provoked a virulent response from the papers under attack. *Le Bonnet Rouge* carries recurrent headlines like "Le 'Pacifisme' et la Réaction" (28 June 1917), and its articles are full of this sort of language:

> S'il faut considérer comme pacifistes les gens qui n'épousent point l'admiration religieuse et fanatique des réacteurs pour la guerre ...
>
> (2 July 1917)

Réactionnaire etc. are undoubtedly more important terms than *conservateur* etc. in the polemical writings of the Left during the First World War; one must now take a closer look at the characteristic ways in which they were used. Speaking of *la réaction*, Barbusse writes:

> Entre l'extrême gauche et l'extrême droite, entre les socialistes, qui sont des républicains dans leur expression la plus stricte et la plus humaine, et la coalition monarchique, cléricale, nationaliste, qui représente un dogme opposé ...[9]

It is explained here as consisting of a kind of "coalition" of different elements.[10] Elsewhere, Barbusse analyses the situation more fully:

> Le parti réactionnaire se présente actuellement sous une forme renouvelée: le nationalisme ... Le nationalisme intégral de l'*Action Française*, un des foyers les plus actifs de ces théories, est le seul qui soit conséquent avec lui-même: il est en même temps royaliste et catholique—naturellement.
>
> (*Le Pays*, 2 June 1917)

It is not uncommon to find writers making this dependency plain with a straightforward gloss of the term in question:

> Quiconque, dans les pays neutres, est réactionnaire, c'est-à-dire clérical et contre-révolutionnaire, quiconque admire l'*Action Française* déteste la France. (*Le Bonnet Rouge*, 3 Aug. 1915)

---

[9] Ibid., p. 75.

[10] *Réaction* might perhaps be interpreted as one of those collectives "which are superordinate to sets of lexemes in a hierarchical relationship that is ambivalent with respect to the distinction of hyponymy and the part-whole relation" (J. Lyons, *Semantics*, vol. i, Cambridge, 1977, p. 316). But its co-hyponyms *nationaliste/ royaliste/clérical* etc. are clearly not incompatible (cf. *priest/bishop* v. *table/chair*), and the relationship between them is not of a rigorous and systematic kind.

In an article headed "Les Français diffamés par la Réaction", G. Clairet deplores

> ... tout le mal qu'ont fait à notre pays les réactionnaires de tous poils, cléricaux ou nationalistes. (*Le Bonnet Rouge*, 3 Aug. 1915)

On a later occasion, he presents an elaborate picture of "les forces de la réaction" in which their composition is expressed in a number of alternative formulations: "républicains et réacteurs" are contrasted, and the latter then become "les hommes de l'Église et du Roy",[11] after which it is "la presse monarchiste et cléricale" which is opposed to "la presse républicaine".[12] The corporate body is sometimes viewed as exercising control over the actions of its dependent members; Clairet mocks

> ... les frocards que la Réaction a embusqués dans les hôpitaux ou les bureaux. (*Le Bonnet Rouge*, 22 Jan. 1916)

As one would expect of a generic name, *réaction* can also be given a specific qualification, and used to designate one of the constituent parts of the whole. In a letter published in *La Tranchée Républicaine*, H. Barbusse writes:

> Vous vaincrez l'effort maladif des anciens régimes, des anciennes religions, et cette néo-réaction de la dangereuse et malfaisante utopie nationaliste. (9 May 1917)

A. Charpentier singles out two features which distinguish a subgroup:

> Heureusement que le Parti Socialiste est là qui, une fois de plus, s'est dressé contre la réaction nationalo-royaliste en lui criant: "Halte-là! tu ne passeras pas." (*Le Pays*, 12 Sept. 1917)

It would appear, then, that *la Réaction* in its broadest sense is made up of a number of individually specifiable *réactions*.[13]

Finally, there is an idiomatic use of the term which stands apart from the common pattern just outlined. With examples of the type "quelques feuilles de calotte et de réaction" (*Le Bonnet Rouge*, 24 Oct. 1915), it remains open to interpret *réaction* as being more inclusive than *calotte*;[14] at any rate, there is no means of telling

---

[11] See below, 3.2, p. 119, n. 1.

[12] See Appendix II, text 5.

[13] J. Dubois gives an example of similar usage in 1871: "partisans de toutes les réactions" (*Le Vocabulaire politique et social*, p. 398, quotation 4363).

[14] See below, 3.3, pp. 124-5.

exactly what the terms are intended to refer to when they are primarily linked for rhetorical emphasis. However, a different analysis suggests itself if one compares this (and the many other similar instances which appear in *Le Bonnet Rouge* at this time) with the following:

> Contre la calotte et contre la réaction, contre les gens du Pape et contre les gens du Roy, défendons la République: c'est le salut de la France qui l'exige. (*Le Bonnet Rouge*, 10 Nov. 1915)

Here, *la réaction* is equated with *les gens du Roy*, in other words it replaces what is sometimes called *la réaction royaliste*, and loses its status as a superordinate term in this context.[15] The same interpretation is undoubtedly called for when G. Hervé mentions

> un organe d'opposition républicaine, destiné ... à combattre la "calotte", la "réaction", le "chauvinisme". (*La Victoire*, 6 July 1917)

This specialization is understandable, in that royalism was regarded as the quintessential and most dire manifestation of reactionary opinion.

3.2   *Les gens du Roy*[1]

In 1914-18 royalists and their doctrine were referred to by various terms which were not synonymous at earlier periods, for reasons that become apparent from a glance at their history.

Monarchiste/monarchisme[2] and *royaliste/royalisme*[3] were broadly equivalent at the time of the French Revolution.[4] Once the Empire had been established, they parted company because *monarchiste* could then also quite properly be applied to a supporter of the Emperor, whereas *royaliste* could not. This distinction was obviously extremely important at a time of constitutional upheaval

---

[15] The significant point is not that *la réaction* can be used instead of *les gens du Roy*, but that it can be co-ordinated with *la calotte* which it normally includes.

[1] Ch. Bally notes that the spelling *roy* "ressuscite la majesté le l'ancien régime ('les camelots du *roy*')" (*Linguistique générale et linguistique française*, 4th edn., Bern, 1965, p. 133, n. 1). In the language of the Left, this conscious archaism indicates scorn on the part of the writer.

[2] Dated 1738 by the *Bloch-Wartburg*.

[3] First attested in 1589, *royaliste* became current during the Revolution; *royalisme* appeared in 1770 (*Bloch-Wartburg*).

[4] After commenting on *royaliste*, F. Brunot observes: "on disait aussi 'monarchiste'" (*Histoire de la langue française*, vol. ix. 2, p. 838).

such as 1869-72.[5] Later, when the deaths of the Prince Imperial in 1879 and the comte de Chambord in 1883 had left the Orleanist comte de Paris as the only candidate for the throne, *monarchiste* and *royaliste* came once more to refer to the same individuals. This drastic narrowing of the field made the range of terms available for designating the supporters of the sole surviving Pretender correspondingly wider, and in 1914-18 one finds a whole battery of words whose meanings were previously distinct being deployed against *L'Action Française* without any discernible nuances between them. *Le Bonnet Rouge* refers to Ch. Maurras and L. Daudet indifferently as *royalistes* or *monarchistes*, and also as *néo-royalistes* or *néo-monarchistes*. The doctrine they preach is either *royalisme* or *monarchisme*; with typical panache, G. Clairet declares:

> Seuls, imaginait-on, les néo-chouans, intoxiqués de royalisme doctrinal, ont l'esprit assez faussé par le fanatisme pédantesque pour penser déjà à tirer de la guerre un profit politique.

—and a few lines later he calls the same people

> les factieux du monarchisme orléaniste. (*Le Bonnet Rouge*, 27 Apr. 1916)

However, *monarchiste* and *royaliste* are not always interchangeable, particularly in registers other than the highly emotive and pejorative. The wider meaning of *monarchiste* is readily invoked; in a letter to Ch. Maurras, M. Barrès employs it as the proper term to set against *républicain*:

> Je voudrais montrer (pour la glorifier) ce qu'est la vie spirituelle à l'armée ... Il s'agit de faire connaître non pas les monarchistes (je n'ai pas pris les républicains; je ne me mets pas sur le plan politique), mais les patriotes, les nationalistes, les hommes qui parlent de la terre française et de la grandeur française ...[6]

The didactic prose of Maurras himself provides an instance of full weight being given to the word's etymology:[7]

[5] J. Dubois stresses that "les 'partis monarchiques' sont ceux qui préconisent le rétablissement d'une monarchie qu'elle soit celle des Bourbons, des Orléans ou des Bonapartes". whilst "les 'royalistes' ne sont que les partisans de la 'monarchie bourbonienne' ou 'orléaniste'" (*Le Vocabulaire politique et social,* pp. 31 and 65).

[6] *La République ou le roi. Correspondance inédite (1883-1923)*, Paris, 1970, pp. 565-6 (15 Oct. 1916).

[7] Cf. the use of *anarchie* by Proudhon in his *Confessions*: "La véritable forme du gouvernement est l'an-archie" (quoted by M. Tournier. "Éléments pour l'étude quantitative d'une journée de 48", p. 93).

Tous les Français (ou peu s'en faut!) sont unifiés par la guerre. Ils vivent sour le gouvernement d'une seule chose: la guerre. C'est *mon-archie*, non d'une être, mais d'une événement.

(*L'Action Française*, 19 Apr. 1916)

The term *chouan* was revived in the First World War as a variant for *royaliste*.[8] *Le Bonnet Rouge* writes of its enemy *L'Action Française*:

Ces nouveaux chouans,[9] traîtres et fils de traîtres, racontent que la France est menacée à l'intérieur par un péril grandissant, le péril antimilitariste.

(4 Aug. 1915)

—and G. Hervé affirms patriotically that

La France républicaine peut, en toute sécurité, faire face au militarisme prussien sans craindre qu'aucune chouannerie, cette fois, n'essaie de venir la poignarder dans le dos. (*La Guerre Sociale*, 8 July 1915)

Other stylistic alternatives for *royaliste* include a number of expressions based on the form *Roy*: in an article entitled "Rodin et les chouans" which appeared on 1 October 1916, G. Clairet refers to "le parti du Roy ... la clique du Roy ... les gens du Roy ..."[10] It should be remembered that the *Action Française* movement had a body of volunteers known as *les camelots du roi* whose avowed function was to hawk the newspaper in the streets of Paris, but who also acted as agitators and street fighters.[11] Their name, too, occurs as an appellation for royalists; G. Hervé writes:

En vérité, je me sens à l'heure actuelle beaucoup plus près des républicains les plus modérés, je dirai plus, je me sens plus près des conservateurs les plus cléricaux, je me sens plus près des camelots du roi—et Dieu sait si je suis royaliste!—que de ces messieurs de l'Église de saint Karl Marx et du pacifisme bêlant. (*La Victoire*, 26 Dec. 1916)

On the facetious level, *Le Bonnet Rouge* turned *les orléanistes* into

---

[8] Initially the name given to the participants in the Western uprising against the Revolution in 1791, *chouan* rapidly became a label for "un réactionnaire quelconque" (F. Brunot, *Histoire de la langue française*, vol. ix. 2, p. 868), and was a commonly used form of insult—no doubt popularized by Balzac's novel *Les Chouans* (1829). J. Dubois notes that the term was given a new lease of life at the time of the Commune: "Les Versaillais, confondus sous le nom de monarchistes, redeviennent des 'chouans' ..." (*Le Vocabulaire politique et social*, p. 107).

[9] Cf. the form *néo-chouan* used by G. Clairet on 27 Apr. 1916.

[10] Further examples are given above, 3.1, pp. 118-19.

[11] See E. J. Weber, *Action Française*, pp. 53-6.

les Orléânons (e.g. 19 Aug. 1915)—a pun which was to serve as a model for other ephemeral creations.[12]

The style of government advocated by *les royalistes* or attributed to them by their detractors was regularly known as *césarisme*[13]—a term originally used of *les bonapartistes* and later applied to *les orléanistes* along with other supporters of *un régime du sabre.* In a leader entitled "Liberté ou dictature?" H. Bérenger deplores the rod of iron with which his country was being ruled, particularly in the matter of press freedom:

> Il ne resterait plus dans le pays silencieux qu'un gouvernement et qu'une armée. Ce serait le *césarisme sans César,* c'est-à-dire sans ce qui peut faire comprendre le césarisme, sinon l'excuser et encore moins le justifier.
> La doctrine n'est pas nouvelle! *L'Action Française,* organe des royalistes, la développe tous les matins par la plume abondante de M. Ch. Maurras. Et nous en avons vu, par ailleurs, l'essai d'application pendant les six premiers mois de cette guerre où le Parlement fut forclos et la presse enchaînée. (*Paris-Midi*, 26 Jan. 1916)

Césarisme/césarien found special favour with G. Clairet at the end of 1915 and beginning of 1916. Under the heading "L'union Sacrée. N'oublions pas la République" he writes:

> Or, si nous laissons les hommes de la calotte et du césarisme défigurer la France ... (*Le Bonnet Rouge*, 10 Nov. 1915)

Later, expounding the misdeeds of "les gens du Pape et du Roy", he calls them "gazetiers césariens" and their papers "feuilles césariennes ou orléanistes" (*Le Bonnet Rouge*, 24 Feb. 1916).[14]

The terms *impérialiste/impérialisme* which were used unambiguously in 1869-72 of a particular kind of *monarchiste*—supporters of the Second Empire—had come by 1914-18 to denote extreme militarists (expansionists) and their doctrine.[15] There may, however,

[12] The title of a regular column "Censuriania" became "Censuriâneries" on 24 Oct. 1915. For *vaticâneries*, see below, 3.3, p. 125.

[13] *Césarisme* is dated 1849 (Proudhon) by the *T.L.F.* J. Dubois quotes a definition supplied by M. Block in 1863: "un gouvernement absolu appuyé sur l'armée, et plus ou moins dénué des sympathies des populations"; *césarien* and, less commonly, *césariste,* are also used (*Le Vocabulaire politique et social,* pp. 130 and 243).

[14] See also Appendix II, text 5.

[15] First attested in 1525 with the meaning "partisan de l'empire d'Allemagne" (Bloch-Wartburg), *impérialiste* was extended in the nineteenth century to. cover supporters of the Napoleonic dynasty. *Impérialisme,* modelled on the English *imperialism,* first appeared in 1836; in 1880 it took on the meaning "prépondérance de la puissance britannique dans le monde" (E. Bonnaffé, *Dictionnaire étymologique*

be a few odd survivals of the meaning "bonapartiste". With examples like the following:

> Que les royalistes, les impérialistes, les cléricaux formulent leurs griefs contre le Parlement, nous leur répondrons (*La Bataille*, 20 Feb. 1916)

—and these lines from H. Barbusse:

> ... la campagne qu'en violation de l'union sacrée, les impérialistes, les royalistes, et les ennemis du progrès n'avaient cessé de mener contre les vrais républicains[16]

—the wider context is a discussion of internal politics and constitutional structure, and *impérialiste* is explicitly linked with terms belonging to this sphere and not to the domain of foreign policy. Did these writers have in mind any particular group of individuals still nostalgic for the Empire, or is one perhaps dealing with a mere figure of rhetoric in which an association of terms has become a *cliché* and outlives the situation it formerly reflected?[17]

3.3 *Les gens du Pape*

Some of the most typical representatives of reactionary opinion singled out for criticism in 1914-18 were the supporters of the established Church. The main point to be stressed about the words used for this purpose is not that the relationships between them are of particular interest, but simply that they are all essentially political terms, denoting attitudes which are connected primarily with affairs of State, and only secondarily with religious matters in so far as these impinge on the former.

Clérical/cléricalisme are the central terms in this series.[1] G. Clairet contrasts "les républicains d'extrême-gauche" with "les ennemis de la République et de la Démocratie, cléricaux et conservateurs"

---

et historique des anglicismes et des anglo-américanismes, Paris, 1920). *Impérialiste* acquired the sense "expansionist" in 1893, again under English influence. Cf. J. Touchard, *Histoire des idées politiques,* 3rd edn., Paris, 1967, vol. ii, pp. 701-2. See below, 3.5, p. 136.

[16] *Paroles d'un combattant*, p. 54 (article published in *La Vérité*, 31 Jan. 1918).

[17] The collocation of *impérialiste* with *royaliste* in 1871 is illustrated by J. Dubois, *Le Vocabulaire politique et social,* p. 320 quotation 2624.

[1] The *Dauzat-Dubois-Mitterand* gives 1815 for the political use of *clérical* (first attested in the twelfth century), and 1863 for the appearance of the term *cléricalisme*. For the period 1869-72, J. Dubois notes that "les hommes de gauche, comme J. Vallès, voient dans les 'cléricaux' des adversaires de la République" (*Le Vocabulaire politique et social,* p. 33).

(*Le Bonnet Rouge*, 7 Jan. 1916), and G. Bazile has hostile words for

> ce cléricalisme qui, profitant du couvert de l'*Union Sacrée*, essaie, par une manœuvre désespérée, de regagner le terrain perdu. On calomnie nos officiers, on critique nos institutions, on nous accuse de tous les crimes ... (*Le Bonnet Rouge*, 17 Feb. 1915)

G. Clemenceau sums up the significance of "clerical" opinion as follows:

> Chacun sait que nous n'avons, en France, que deux partis organisés: le parti clérical et le parti socialiste révolutionnaire.
>
> (*L'Homme Enchaîné*, 17 Feb. 1915)

One also finds the adjective *clérical* linked directly with words like *anti-républicain*: *Le Bonnet Rouge* mentions

> la propagande cléricale et anti-républicaine qui est faite sur le front.
>
> (17 July 1916)

Anticlericalism was not, of course, exclusively an attitude of the Left;[2] but *clérical/cléricalisme* feature more consistently as pejorative terms in their vocabulary than in that of other groups.

Les cléricaux were known collectively as *la calotte*.[3] When G. Hervé asks:

> Est-ce qu'on ne continue pas à répéter, dans certains milieux qui se croient avancés, que les poursuites contre Caillaux sont un coup de la réaction et de la "calotte"? (*La Victoire*, 22 Dec. 1917)

—he is alluding to the language of left-wing papers like *Le Pays* which had stepped in to fill the gap created by the suspension of *Le Bonnet Rouge* in July 1917. The term *calotte* had appeared quite frequently on the pages of the latter in such expressions as "quelques

---

[2] See R. Rémond, *L'Anticléricalisme en France de 1815 à nos jours,* Paris, 1976, p. 41: "On peut être anticlérical et républicain—c'est même l'association la plus fréquente—mais aussi anticlérical et bonapartiste, anticlérical et royaliste ...".

[3] First attested in 1394, *calotte* became a pejorative designation for priests at the end of the eighteenth century; *calotin* (sometimes spelt *calottin*) dates from 1717 (*Dauzat-Dubois-Mitterand*). F. Brunot notes that during the Revolution shouts of "À bas la calotte" were heard in the streets, and explains that "*calotin* était déjà le synonyme courant d'ecclésiastique, voire de chrétien" (*Histoire de la langue française,* vol. ix. 2, pp. 893 and 898). For the use of these terms in 1869-72 see J. Dubois, *Le Vocabulaire politique et social,* p. 95. In 1906 A. Lorulot founded *La Calotte,* a satirical paper which became the chief organ of anticlerical opinion; see R. Rémond, *L'Anticléricalisme,* p. 214.

feuilles de calotte et de réaction" (24 Oct. 1915), or "les Boches du
Vatican—toute la calotte romaine" (14 Oct. 1915), or toujours la
Calotte germanophile" (22 Dec. 1915).[4] The form *calotin* is also
found (as on 15 Nov. 1915), but seems to be far less common.

Les cléricaux and *la calotte* have a number of minor synonyms
which proliferated on the pages of *Le Bonnet Rouge* and papers of
that ilk in the second half of 1915 and then fell into relative disuse—
the explanation being that *Le Bonnet Rouge* was conducting a particularly virulent anticlerical campaign during those months, and
clearly needed all the verbal ammunition it could muster.[5] The
phrase *gens du Pape*[6] dates from this period. One also finds *papiste*
and *papalin*:[7]

> Les cléricaux et les papistes entendaient n'être point les "jobards" de
> l'union sacrée. (*Le Bonnet Rouge*, 10 Nov. 1915)

An article in this paper on 17 August 1915 headed "Embusqués en
soutane" includes "des papalins" among other designations for
the clergy. *Frocard*[8] is a favourite with G. Clairet: he jibes at "les
frocards alarmistes" on 18 October 1915 and at "les frocards royalistes" two days later.[9] The expression "journaux bondieusards"[10]
occurs in an article entitled "Les menées pacifistes du clergé catho-
lique" (*Le Bonnet Rouge*, 15 Aug. 1915). Material dismissed as
religious nonsense becomes *Vaticâneries* on 23 November 1915,
according to a formula that had already proved productive in the
colums of *Le Bonnet Rouge*.[11]

---

[4] See also the examples given above, 3.1, p. 119, and 3.2, p. 122.

[5] In conjunction with *La Dépêche de Toulouse*, it launched what became known
as "la rumeur infâme: le décompte des prêtres embusqués et l'insinuation que le
clergé attendait, à l'abri du danger, la fin d'une guerre qu'il avait contribué à
déclencher" (R. Rémond, *L'Anticléricalisme*, p. 235).

[6] Usually linked with *gens du Roy*; see above, 3.1, p. 119, and 3.2, p. 122.

[7] Neither appears to have functioned as political terms during the Revolution.
The *F.E.W.* supplies as glosses for *papalin*: "qui se rapporte au Pape (péjor.);
soldats du Pape; partisans du Pape (péjor.)", and "ca 1670; seit 1868" as dates.
Papiste is dated 1526 (*Bloch-Wartburg*). J. Dubois discusses *papisme* (*Le Vocabulaire
politique et social*, pp. 161 and 166), but gives no examples of *papiste* or *papalin*.

[8] Dated "vers 1700" by the *Bloch-Wartburg,* but not found by F. Brunot or
J. Dubois in the revolutionary period or 1869-72 respectively.

[9] See also the example given above, 3.1, p. 118.

[10] First attested in 1865 (Bloch-Wartburg), *bondieusard* is not given by J. Dubois.
It was used by Catholics to refer to bigoted coreligionists.

[11] See above, 3.2, pp. 121-2.

3.4 *Les professionnels du patriotisme*

A number of gradations of extreme patriotism are recognized by writers in 1914-18. Most of the terms in this series were well established in French by then; they form a relatively uniform and stable pattern of relationships common to the language of different left-wing groups.

An overall picture of the use of *patrie* and its derivatives has already been given.[1] The present discussion is concerned with the variety of *patriotisme* characteristically referred to by *La Gazette des Ardennes* as "ce pseudo-patriotisme étroit, haineux".[2] As terms of abuse in the First World War, *patriote/patriotisme* will generally either occur with other pejorative words in "linking constructions"[3] or be qualified explicitly as in the following examples:

> Les farouches et belliqueux patriotes de cafés, de coulisses et de rédactions... (*Le Bonnet Rouge*, 28 July 1916)

> Les patriotes professionnels ... qui restèrent bravement à l'arrière ...
> (*Le Bonnet Rouge*, 29 June 1917)

> Ce patriotisme factice ... (*Les Nations*, 20 June 1917)[4]

> Il tire argent de son patriotisme affecté ...
> (*Le Bonnet Rouge*, 15 Dec. 1915)

> Ces appels pseudo-patriotiques ... (*Le Bonnet Rouge*, 28 June 1917)

On the whole, since most people claim to be *patriotes*, the word is rarely used as an insult without some kind of further definition. An exception to this is of course R. Rolland; he writes with heavy irony:

> De grands patriotes réclament que l'eau de Cologne soit nommée eau de Pologne[5]

and again:

> Anatole France et Hervé ayant eu, en flétrissant la destruction de Reims, quelques mots généreux sur la victoire future qui saurait ne pas user de représailles, les patriotes écument et aboient de rage.[6]

---

[1] See above 1.1.
[2] See above 1.1, pp. 11-12. According to F. Brunot, at the beginning of the Revolution the term "n'impliquait aucune haine de l'étranger", but *patriote* became pejorative under the Directory (*Histoire de la langue française*, vol. ix. 2, p. 663).
[3] See below, 3.7.
[4] Quoted by L. Marchand, *L'Offensive morale,* p. 224.
[5] *Journal,* p. 86 (16 Oct. 1914).
[6] Ibid., p. 62 (Sept. 1914).

The form *ultra-patriote*, which dates from the Revolution,[7] reappears in 1914-18, but exclusively as a label for the Right. The revolutionary H. Guilbeaux says of G. Hervé whom he regarded as a renegade:

> Il est aujourd'hui ultra-patriote, militariste, anti-internationaliste, policier, *jusqu'au bout*.[8]

The ephemeral superlatives *surpatriote* and *superpatriotisme*[9] are also used of right-wing extremists: R. Rolland criticizes "le manque de logique et le superpatriotisme de Loyson",[10] and *Le Bonnet Rouge* casts a slur on "les surpatriotes de l'arrière" (14 July 1916). *Patrouillotisme*, first applied to Lafayette in 1789,[11] occurs sporadically in 1914-18 as a pejorative variant of *patriotisme*, as in this passage from *La Feuille* of 6 June 1918:

> Eh bien, Messieurs du Roy, du nationalisme intégral, de la Frrrrance aux Frrrrançais, Messieurs du Panama, du Boulangisme, de l'antidreyfusisme et du patrouillotisme revanchard, vous avez bien travaillé.[12]

Of greater significance is the form *patriotard*, explicitly pejorative by virtue of its suffix.[13] G. Hervé predicts that some of his socialist friends who have made a stand in favour of continuing the war "seront traités sans doute de réactionnaires et de patriotards" (*La Victoire*, 20 May 1918). The word can also function adjectivally; M. Cohen asks:

---

[7] See F. Brunot, *Histoire de la langue française*, vol. ix. 2, p. 664. J. Dubois gives no examples of it for 1869-72. The hyphen is optional.

[8] Introduction to *Le Général et le lieutenant. Correspondance entre Gustave Hervé et Charles L. Hartmann*, Geneva, 1917, p. 12.

[9] Not attested in dictionaries.

[10] *Journal,* p. 1616 (16 Oct. 1918).

[11] Its formation is explained by F. Brunot as "un calembour sur le service de gardes et de patrouilles qu'il imposait à la garde nationale. Mais peut-être est-ce aussi une déformation péjorative destinée à montrer chez lui l'absence de vrai patriotisme?" (*Histoire de la langue française,* vol. ix. 2, p. 666). M. Rheims (*Dictionnaire des mots sauvages,* Paris, 1969) gives *patrouillotisme* as a neologism invented by Rimbaud in 1870, and comments: "De 1870 à 1918, ce mot a constamment été réutilisé, réinventé pour stigmatiser le patriotisme belliqueux de certains groupes".

[12] Quoted by R. Rolland, *Journal*, p. 1484.

[13] First attested in 1904 (*F.E.W.*), *patriotard* was coined by the Left in response to the Right's use of *sans-patrie*. See T. J. Field, "The Concept of La Patrie", pp. 245-50. Cf. the declaration made by G. Hervé in September 1912: "Et la France d'aujourd'hui, n'est-ce pas nous encore, les prétendus 'sans-patrie' et les prétendus 'antipatriotes' qui l'aimons d'un amour ardent et éclairé? ... Oui, c'est nous, et non pas les patriotards, qui sommes les vrais patriotes, au sens où nos pères de '93 entendaient ce mot" (quoted by Almereyda, *Le Bonnet Rouge,* 17 Mar. 1916).

Qu'importe dans un temps de patriotisme aussi épuré, des insanités de presse et quelques accès de pudibonderie patriotarde? [14]

The attitude for which the French Right is best known in the early years of the twentieth century is its nationalism: "le nationalisme est désormais [à partir de 1900] un élément si caractéristique de la droite qu'il lui tient lieu de programme, d'étiquette, de drapeau".[15] The term *nationalisme*, which had been used for much of the nineteenth century in connection with the question of nation states for oppressed minorities (*le principe des nationalités*, as it was referred to), came in the 1870s to denote a "préférence aveugle et exclusive pour tout ce qui est propre à la nation à laquelle on appartient".[16] Nationalism as it was understood in the First World War could imply the very opposite of what it implied formerly; with no apparent contradiction, G. Clairet describes his opponents as

les nationalistes exclusifs et belliqueux ... contempteurs des idées qui font aimer la France, l'idée de Justice et l'idée de Droit, *le principe des nationalités* [my italics] et le respect de la personnalité humaine.

(*Le Bonnet Rouge*, 6 Oct. 1916)

In so far as people like M. Barrès and Ch. Maurras referred to themselves as *nationalistes*,[17] the use of the term by the Left is not automatically pejorative; however, since the attitude in question prompts reactions of such loathing, the word readily becomes a term of abuse applied quite widely to individuals regardless of how they view themselves. G. Hervé rejects the epithet *nationaliste* in favour of *national*:

---

[14] Quoted by R. Rolland, *Journal*, p. 545 (Sept. 1915).

[15] R. Rémond, *La Droite en France*, p. 160.

[16] *Larousse*, 1874. This meaning is classed as a neologism. J. Dubois finds no attestations of it in 1869-72, but notes that "quelques années après 1871, 'nationaliste' remplacera 'national'" (*Le Vocabulaire politique et social*, p. 165). F. Brunot does give an example from 1798 in which *nationalisme* is used to imply dislike of foreigners, and is described as a variety of *patriotisme* (*Histoire de la langue française*, vol. ix. 2, p. 639 n.6), but this appears to be an isolated instance. *Nationaliste* is first attested in 1837 (Bloch-Wartburg).

[17] Writing in 1900, Maurras claimed that Barrès first used the terms *nationaliste/ nationalisme* in their new meaning in an article in *Le Figaro* on 4 July 1892 entitled "La querelle des nationalistes et des cosmopolites", in which he outlined the debate between the admirers of the French classical tradition in literature and the partisans of European romanticism (*Dictionnaire politique et critique*, Paris, 1932, s.v. *nationalisme intégral*).

"Socialisme nationaliste!" nous font dédaigneusement les socialistes de Zimmerwald.

Non! socialisme national seulement, et ce socialisme national n'a, en France, qu'à remonter à ses sources, à Blanqui, à Saint-Simon, à la Révolution française ... (*La Victoire*, 3 Apr. 1916)

The ephemeral form *nationalard*[18] was coined on the model of *patriotard*. Almereyda writes of "les niaiseries du vocabulaire nationalard" (*Le Bonnet Rouge*, 20 May 1916).

The most extreme manifestations of *patriotisme* and *nationalisme* were stigmatized by the Left as *chauvinisme*, the offenders in question being *chauvins*.[19] These terms are virtually always pejorative; apparent exceptions like the following:

Il faut accepter que le patriotisme, tant que durera la guerre, soit du chauvinisme. Il ne faut pas être pacifiste.[20]

can be explained as a case of someone countering an attack by deliberately and defiantly accepting the charge laid against him.[21] R. Rolland uses the verb *chauviniser*:

Jusqu'au vieux [*sic*] antipatriote Rémy [*sic*] de Gourmont qui chauvinise! Il écrit dans *La France* son *mea culpa* pour avoir méconnu le grand rôle de la Ligue des Patriotes.[22]

Closely associated with *chauvin/chauvinisme* are the terms *exclusif/exclusivisme*[23] which feature in the language of *Le Bonnet Rouge*. G. Clairet warns of the dangers awaiting those socialists prepared to

---

[18] Not attested in dictionaries.

[19] *Chauvin* originated in about 1830 from the proper name Chauvin, "type du soldat des armées du premier Empire, célébré pour son enthousiasme naïf" (*Bloch-Wartburg*). *Chauvinisme* is first attested in 1834. Both terms were widely used in 1869-72 as "superlatifs péjoratifs de 'patriote' et de 'patriotisme'" (J. Dubois, *Le Vocabulaire politique et social*, p. 91). The form *chauviniste*, first found in the *Larousse* (1867), was derived from *chauvinisme* when the latter became a political doctrine, but it did not oust *chauvin* as a noun. There are only isolated occurrences of *les chauvinistes* in 1914-18.

[20] Ch. Sancerme, *Les Serviteurs de l'ennemi*, p. 10.

[21] Cf. below, 3.6, p. 146.

[22] *Journal*, p. 173 (Dec. 1914).

[23] The political connotations of *exclusif* are a legacy from the Revolution; see F. Brunot, *Histoire de la langue française*, vol. ix. 2, pp. 832-3. *Exclusivisme*, first attested in 1835 (*Petit Robert*), was used in 1869-72 to refer to "ce que l'on nommerait maintenant le sectarisme" (J. Dubois, *Le Vocabulaire politique et social*, p. 165).

... suivre, dans la voie de l'exclusivisme chauvin, ceux d'entre eux qu'a gagnés le nationalisme, affecté mais point sincère, des cléricaux

(7 Aug. 1916)

and a different permutation appears in an article on art signed "L'Iconoclaste":

Que, sous le couvert artistique, on ne tente pas de développer un de ces courants de chauvinisme exclusif et dangereux ... (29 June 1916)

Distinctions between *patriote, nationaliste* and *chauvin* are frequently exploited by journalists for polemical purposes. The relationship of *chauvin* to *patriote* noted by J. Dubois[24] continues to hold in the First World War: *La Bataille* mentions

des hommes résolus à se mettre en garde contre les fautes du passé, c'est-à-dire ardemment patriotes, ou plutôt chauvins ... (15 Feb 1916)

However, the new meaning acquired by *nationaliste* had brought a third term into the hierarchy; this also serves as a kind of superlative of *patriote* in 1914-18—witness the following examples:

Là encore les nationalistes, les professionnels du patriotisme, auront nui à la patrie. (*Le Bonnet Rouge*, 5 Mar. 1916)

Le confrère en question n'est pas, comme l'*Action Française*, un journal nationaliste. C'est simplement un journal patriote.
(*Le Bonnet Rouge*, 17 Feb. 1916)

A Nancy, un ancien notaire de cette ville, patriote à tous crins, et même nationaliste ... (*La Guerre Sociale*, 14 Aug. 1914)[25]

The same connection can be observed between *patriotisme* and *nationalisme*:

Les femmes ne font aucun cas de ce patriotisme factice qui, en créant l'animosité commerciale, engendre le nationalisme outrancier.
(*Les Nations*, 20 June 1917)[26]

Chauvin appears to be stronger than *nationaliste*, to judge by these lines from Ch. Maurras:

Ma jeunesse a connu des socialistes presque chauvins.... L'hypothèse d'un socialisme nationaliste n'était pas plus improbable qu'une autre vers l'année 1894. (*L'Action Française*, 2 Aug. 1914)

[24] See above, p. 129, n. 19.
[25] See Appendix II, text 1.
[26] Quoted by L. Marchand, *L'Offensive morale*, p. 224.

Patriotard is also situated on the scale *patriote* → *nationaliste* → *chauvin*, although it is hard to assess how it compares in strength with *nationaliste* or *chauvin*. Ch. Maurras notes in the language of his adversaries

> des distinctions subtilement introduites entre les patriotes et les patriotards (*L'Action Française*, 1 Nov. 1916)

and Ch. Sancerme associates *patriotard* with *chauviniste* when he comments on the use of the word *patriote* by Almereyda:

> On voit que Vigo ne dit même plus: les patriotards ou les chauvinistes. C'est bien aux patriotes qu'il en a.[27]

Revanchard is likewise a term used in conjunction with *nationaliste* and *chauvin* in 1914-18. One might have expected it to belong to the series centering on *militariste*, in view of its obvious affinities with *annexionniste*. In fact, it collocates more closely with *nationaliste*—understandably, given the importance of the emotive term *la Revanche*[28] in the language of a man like M. Barrès, who could proclaim triumphantly when the French entered Mulhouse in August 1914:

> Nous tenons la Revanche. Le mot pendant quarante-trois ans répété, fatigué, quasi-discrédité, que nous étions fous de maintenir, que nous eussions été mille fois plus fous d'abandonner, il est devenu un fait. Revanche, ce matin, c'est un mot tout neuf, tout rayonnant de vérité, de joie et de gloire. (*L'Écho de Paris*, 10 Aug. 1914)

G. Hervé uses *revanchard* in conjunction with *nationaliste*:

> On était presque reconnaissant aux revanchards et aux nationalistes d'avoir toujours eu l'œil ouvert sur l'armée prussienne.
> (*La Victoire*, 2 Aug. 1916)

> La plupart des nationalistes et des revanchards—c'est ainsi, vous vous en souvenez, que nous appelions, avant l'union sacrée, les chauvins un peu trop belliqueux de chez nous ... (*La Guerre Sociale*, 15 July 1915)

Explicit comments of this nature about usage provide welcome confirmation that terms which stand out as particularly significant

---

[27] *Les Serviteurs de l'ennemi*, p. 234. I have not found *chauviniste* used by Almereyda, only *chauvin*. Clearly, Sancerme did not distinguish between the two.
[28] According to J. Dubois, the political meaning of *revanche* is discernible in July 1871, although neither *Littré* nor the *Larousse* mention it (*Le Vocabulaire politique et social*, pp. 135 and 406). *Revanchard* dates from the end of the nineteenth century (*Dauzat-Dubois-Mitterand*).

when studied retrospectively did indeed appear so to people at the time. Hervé makes frequent reference to the fact that *nationaliste* is characteristic of pre-war polemics, and this is borne out by L. Marchand's commentary on his selection of excerpts from *Le Bonnet Rouge* and *La Gazette des Ardennes*:

> N'est-ce pas avec intention que Clairet emploie le terme de "nationaliste" qui rappelle les dissensions d'avant-guerre que l'agression allemande avait complètement effacées et dont le réveil ne peut que profiter à l'ennemi?[29]

and again in a note accompanying another occurrence of the term:

> Décidément, Clairet tient autant que l'État-Major allemand à ce terme de désunion française.[30]

The use of the word *chauvin* elicits similar remarks from Marchand: quoting from an article by J. Longuet:

> Il est grand temps ... de désavouer les échauffés et les chauvins qui compromettraient la plus noble des causes (*Le Bonnet Rouge*, 10 Apr. 1915)

he adds:

> C'est la première fois que nous rencontrons, dans le journal d'Almereyda, ces expression de "chauvins", d' "échauffés", etc., chères à la *Gazette des Ardennes*, et qui désormais, en descendant de plus en plus bas dans l'injure, vont faire partie du langage courant du *Bonnet Rouge*.[31]

When a few weeks later Longuet writes:

> Seippel fait ... entendre à nos chauvins et à nos fous furieux la voix de la raison (*Le Bonnet Rouge*, 1 May 1915)

Marchand notes:

> On voit tout de suite le crescendo dans l'emploi des termes qui désignent les patriotes. Les "échauffés" du 10 avril sont devenus des "fous furieux". Nous sommes déjà en plein vocabulaire de la feuille d'État-Major éditée à Charleville [i.e. *La Gazette des Ardennes*].[32]

As has been shown, there are a number of potential distinctions which writers can draw between terms if this suits their particular needs, but it should not be assumed that they always choose to do

---

[29] *L'Offensive morale*, p.232.
[30] Ibid., p. 234 n. 1.
[31] Ibid., pp. 307-8.
[32] Ibid., p. 308 n. 1.

so. In many instances these subtle differences are neutralized, and two or more closely related words function as quasi-synonyms. An example from G. Hervé—

> Je ne serai pas surpris qu'on leur ait représenté Paris livré à la fureur nationaliste, les chefs socialistes assassinés. Avouez que l'assassinat de Jaurès pouvait, de loin, apparaître non comme le crime d'un aliéné, mais comme le triomphe du chauvinisme français
>
> (*La Guerre Sociale*, 13 Aug. 1914)

—gives *le chauvinisme français* quite simply as alternative phrasing for *la fureur nationaliste*. Likewise, when a journalist writes in *Le Bonnet Rouge*:

> Que reproche Gohier à Jaurès?
> Il lui reproche de ne pas être chauvin. Il met en doute son patriotisme. C'est au nom du nationalisme qu'il l'a fait assassiner.... Or, en 1903, Urbain Gohier attaquait déjà Jean Jaurès, mais ce qu'il lui reprochait, c'était tout le contraire. Il faisait un crime à Jaurès d'être trop chauvin, trop nationaliste, pas assez antimilitariste (28 Dec. 1915)

he is hammering home his point by repeating it in slightly varying form, but with the emphasis clearly on the features which the words have in common. The rhetorical effect of accumulating near synonyms is to suppress the finer nuances which at other times distinguish them.

Another stylistic feature which tends to highlight the similarities rather than the differences between the words in this series is their collocation with the term *professionnel*. It is a favourite idiom of *Le Bonnet Rouge* (especially G. Clairet) and *La Gazette des Ardennes*, and reflects their view that the most vociferous of patriots were men who were raking in comfortable profits from their writings, safely *embusqués* away from the danger line. Mention has already been made of *les patriotes professionels* and *les professionels du patriotisme*;[33] on the same model as the former expression, one also finds:

> L'irresponsable propagande des calomniateurs professionnels, des propagateurs de légendes haineuses ...
>
> (*La Gazette des Ardennes*, 31 Oct. 1916)

> Ces services le préparèrent à jouer le rôle lucratif de chauvin professionnel, de dénonciateur hebdomadaire de pacifistes et de mauvais patriotes.
>
> (*Le Bonnet Rouge*, 6 Dec. 1915)

[33] See above, pp. 126 and 130.

Nationalisme and *chauvinisme* occur as alternatives to *patriotisme* in the expression *les professionnels du ...*

> Telle fut l'attitude que prirent, vis à vis des bons patriotes qui dénon-çaient l'invasion les professionnels du nationalisme, les nationalistes intègres de l'*Action Française* ... (*Le Bonnet Rouge*, 7 Sept. 1915)

> Les obscènes caricatures imaginées par les professionnels du chauvinisme à la ligne ... (*Le Bonnet Rouge*, 12 July 1916)

There is no discernible difference of strength according to which of the three is chosen.[34]

It is worth noting that this use of *professionnel* is still found today in similar contexts; the satirical weekly *Charlie Hebdo* declares:

> Question patriotisme tous ces gens-là en connaissent un rayon. Ce sont des professionnels, si j'ose dire. La nation, ils n'ont que ce mot-là à la bouche. (12 June 1972)

and it refers some lines later to "les super-patriotes qui nous gouvernent". The relationships between *patriote, chauvin,* and *nationaliste* which began to develop when the latter took on a new meaning at the end of the nineteenth century, and which First World War polemics must have played a large part in consolidating, seem to have become a stable feature of the language.

3.5   *Les éléments militaristes*

The terms used in 1914-18 to denote the supporters of the army, or those who believed in the use of force to further their country's aims, are varied in origin; some of them were well established in the language by then, while others were new creations, not all of them destined to last. They all occur in explicit opposition to words like *paix, pacifiste* and *pacifisme.*

The most general terms in this series are *militariste/militarisme.*[1]

---

[34] It is tempting to regard this idiom as what J. Dubois calls an "unité sémantique complexe" in which "le deuxième élément joue le rôle d'une variable que l'on peut commuter, sans que rien ne soit changé au contenu sémantique de l'unité totale" ("Problèmes de méthode en lexicologie. Les notions d'unité sémantique complexe et de neutralisation dans le lexique", *Cahiers de lexicologie*, ii (1960), 63. Cf. *Le Vocabulaire politique et social*, pp. 185-7). However, the analogy with the slogans discussed by Dubois cannot be convincingly sustained.

[1] The *Bloch-Wartburg* gives 1845 for *militarisme* and 1892 for *militariste.* F. Brunot notes the use of the former some time before 1817 (*Histoire de la langue française*, vol. ix. 2, p. 961 n. 1), and J. Dubois cites an isolated example of the latter from 1870 (*Le Vocabulaire politique et social*, p. 343).

One of the chief aims invoked by the French Socialists (who claimed to be *pacifistes* and *antimilitaristes*) to justify their participation in the war effort was the defeat of German militarism. Thus a typical occurrence of the word *militarisme* at this period is illustrated by the following:

> Cette guerre c'est la guerre à la guerre, c'est la guerre au militarisme sous sa forme la plus odieuse et la plus grotesque: le militarisme prussien.
>
> (G. Hervé, *La Guerre Sociale*, 2 Jan. 1915)

But while this hated attitude was regarded as quintessentially German, the French Left accused the Right of sharing it. Since they were anxious that there should be no confusion between their own motives for support of the war and those of their political opponents, they lost no opportunity of laying the charge of militarism at the latter's door to make the contrast as sharp as possible. *Le Bonnet Rouge* praises

> ... des hommes qui font leur devoir de soldat sans tomber dans le militarisme belliqueux; c'est à dire, sans aimer la guerre pour elle-même, sans la croire nécessaire au bien de l'humanité, sans la considérer, ainsi que certains l'ont dit, comme une institution d'essence divine. (6 June 1915)

The term is not exclusively pejorative; some writers are happy to class their own ideals under this heading. R. Rolland mentions an open letter addressed to him by A. Séché with the following comment:

> On y lit des aphorismes dans ce genre: ''Le militarisme est une manifestation naturelle de la vitalité d'un peuple.''[2]

A number of stylistic variants are used for the term *militariste*. R. Rolland favours the neologism *belliciste*.[3] In a note to an entry in his diary dated 15 October 1914 he writes of

> ... nombre d'Allemands notoires, qui, dès les premiers jours de la guerre, se révélèrent les plus implacablement germanistes et bellicistes[4]

Bellicisme occurs on 23 September 1918:

> On n'a pas plus le droit de m'annexer au bolchevisme qu'au bellicisme ...[5]

---

[2] *Journal*, p. 1056 (28 Jan. 1917).

[3] According to the *Dauzat* (1st edn., 1938), the terms *belliciste/bellicisme* were "formés d'après le latin *bellicus*, belliqueux, par opposition à *pacifisme, -iste*", and applied to Bismarck in 1871; they were coined again in 1915.

[4] *Journal*, p. 1840; the date of the note itself is uncertain.

[5] Ibid., p. 1618.

The traditional epithet *belliqueux* is also found. When H. Barbusse writes:

> En réalité, il y avait des deux côtes des éléments belliqueux et des éléments pacifistes; mais en Allemagne les éléments militaristes étaient dirigeants et tout-puissants....[6]

he is clearly equating *belliqueux* and *militariste*.

The form *va-t-en-guerre* appears in the press in the early months of the First World War.[7] *Le Bonnet Rouge* refers to the Kronprinz as "le terrible va-t-en-guerre" (6 Dec. 1914), and G. Hervé writes of "des gens qui, en temps de paix, étaient de farouches va-t'en-guerre" (*La Guerre Sociale*, 19 June 1915). He later contrasts "certains va-t'en-guerre du temps de paix" with "la C.G.T., repaire de l'antimilitarisme" (*La Victoire*, 26 Dec. 1917).

Closely related to *militariste/militarisme* are the terms *impérialiste/impérialisme*. As has been noted, the latter had come by 1914 to be applied to any country with an aggressive foreign policy.[8] Thus one finds R. Rolland writing:

> Le pire ennemi n'est pas au dehors des frontières, il est dans chaque nation ... C'est ce monstre à cent têtes qui se nomme l'impérialisme, cette volonté d'orgueil et de domination, qui veut tout absorber, ou soumettre, ou briser, qui ne tolère point de grandeur libre, hors d'elle.[9]

As in the case of *militarisme*, Germany was regarded as the prime offender, though right-wing elements in France came in for considerable criticism for their "imperialist" war aims. The label *impérialiste* does not seem to be one which people were prepared to welcome; Ch. Maurras expresses his indignation in an article headed "L'impérialisme français":

> Ceux qui auront à faire l'histoire de la guerre seront d'autant plus ébahis de lire dans nos feuilles, parfois officielles ou officieuses, qu'un pays comme la France, indéniablement attaqué et, depuis près de quatre ans, envahi sur une étendue de dix départements, se voit forcé de se défendre de buts de guerre im-pé-ri-a-lis-tes! (*L'Action Française*, 15 May 1918)

---

[6] *Carnet de guerre (1915)*, Paris, 1965, p. 298.
[7] Its origin appears to be unknown, but it probably comes from the popular song *Malbrouk s'en va-t'en guerre*. The *Robert* (1956) gives it with the gloss "belliciste", but with no example or date; the *Dauzat-Dubois-Mitterand* notes "XXe siècle, journaux". The spelling varies.
[8] See above, 3.2, pp. 122-3.
[9] *Au-dessus de la mêlée*, p. 85 (15 Sept. 1914).

An *annexionniste*[10] was a particular kind of *impérialiste* whose ambitions were to appropriate portions of his foreign neighbours' territory. The significance of this term in the First World War is plain: *la Revanche*—the question of Alsace-Lorraine—had been pending since 1870-71, and the recovery of the lost provinces was an aim which united many shades of opinion within France. For the majority, this did not constitute an act of *annexion*, since they considered that Germany had snatched the provinces from France in the first place. The term *désannexion* was coined to express this view.[11] However, in the minds of the left-wing extremists who endorsed the conclusions of the Zimmerwald Conference and preached "la paix immédiate sans annexions ni indemnités", there was no doubt that some of their fellow countrymen deserved the name of *annexionnistes* as richly as the most grasping of German warmongers.

The ultimate expression of militarism in Europe at this time was of course felt by many to be pangermanism. H. Bérenger defines *le pangermanisme* as "ce surimpérialisme et ce surmilitarisme" (*Paris-Midi*, 21 June 1918). *Pangermaniste/pangermanisme*[12] are not terms used to label the Right in France in 1914-18, but they are discussed here because words like *nationaliste, militariste* and *impérialiste* collocate with *pangermaniste* when they are applied to the Germans:

> Récemment [le *Berliner Tageblatt*] englobait sous la méprisante appellation de *clique nationaliste* l'ensemble des partis impérialistes et pangermanistes. (*Le Bonnet Rouge*, 3 Oct. 1916)

Moreover, explicit parallels are frequently drawn between French nationalists or royalists, and pangermanists across the frontier. In the words of J. Longuet:

> Intellectuellement, nos monarchistes à la Paul Bourget, à la Maurras,

[10] The *T.L.F.* gives "fin XIVe" for *annexion* and 1853 for *annexionniste*, questioning the eighteenth century datings usually proposed for the latter. I have found no example of the form *annexionnisme* which is given by the *Petit Robert* under *annexionniste*.

[11] It is glossed as follows by the *Larousse Mensuel* (April 1918): "Restitution d'un territoire annexé à l'État auquel il était rattaché avant l'annexion (mot créé par le ministre belge Vandervelde): 'Le retour de l'Alsace-Lorraine à la France est une *désannexion* et non une annexion' (Vandervelde)".

[12] Whereas *pangermanisme* is attested in 1845 (*Bloch-Wartburg*), the form in *-iste* is apparently not found until 1908 (*Petit Robert*). But see above, 2.3, p. 48, n. 6.

sont les frères et les congénères des pangermanistes et des Junkers, les
disciples qui s'ignorent des Treitschke et des Bernhardi
(*Le Bonnet Rouge*, 1 May 1915)

H. Barbusse writes:

Répète-toi ce jugement de bon sens, que le nationalisme français ne vaut
pas mieux que le pangermanisme et tous les pans du monde. Abats le
militarisme allemand, non pour y substituer le tien, ni pour abattre
l'Allemagne, mais pour abattre le militarisme.[13]

Pangermanist rule is sometimes referred to as *le sabre prussien*:
G. Hervé speaks of "la guerre de la démocratie universelle contre le
sabre prussien" (*La Victoire*, 4 July 1917). As has been noted, *le
césarisme* or *régime du sabre* was a form of government also associated with French royalists and nationalists.[14]

Almereyda uses the prefix *pan-* to express his fears:

Les "Pans"
On en connaissait deux (le Dieu bouc mis à part): le panslavisme et le
pangermanisme.
—Mais voici qu'un troisième "pan" surgit à l'horizon … c'est le pan-
britannisme….
Mais par grâce! ne prenons pas exemple sur eux pour ajouter aux trois
"pans" un quatrième: le "pangalisme" [*sic*].

He continues to exploit *pan-* for humorous effect throughout this
editorial; criticizing the imperialist aims of Lloyd George, he
declares:

Le peuple de France, qui se bat quand on l'y force mais qui veut la paix,
dira qu'il ne mange pas de ce "pan"-là! Ah …
(*Le Bonnet Rouge*, 15 June 1916)

Clearly, the appeal of the form *pan-* in this kind of context lies in
its strongly right-wing, imperialist connotations: *Le Bonnet Rouge*
coined the label *pandiffamateur* for Ch. Maurras and L. Daudet to
indicate that their slander embraced everything; in his statement in
one of the many court cases involving the two papers, Almereyda
declared:

Ce ne sont pas des diffamateurs, ces gens-là, ce sont des pandiffamateurs!
Tout le monde y a passé … (*Le Bonnet Rouge*, 16 Mar. 1916)

---

[13] *Paroles d'un combattant*, p. 19 (June 1917).
[14] See above, 3.2, p. 122.

The prefix of course also serves to stress the political colour of *L'Action Française*, and is used to good effect in some of the more extravagant fantasies of *Le Bonnet Rouge* such as this preview of one of its own publications:

> Ce qu'on trouve dans *Les Naufrageurs de la Patrie* (brochure de 64 pages)
> Le Rêve des Bons Messieurs de l'*Action Française*.
> Les Pandiffamateurs et l'Union Sacrée.
> Le Dégorgement de l'Égout. Chapitre emprunté—titre en moins—à l'A. Fr. (25 July 1916)

Finally, it is worth noting that the orthodox terms in *pan-* have their antonym: R. Rolland preached the need for what he called "le Panhumanisme", in order to combat the proliferation of these pernicious nationalistic movements:

> Nous devons prendre aujourd'hui l'humanisme dans sa pleine acception, qui embrasse toutes les forces spirituelles du monde entier:—*Panhumanisme*.[15]

3.6 *Les jusqu'auboutistes*

Jusqu'auboutiste[1] is known to be a First World War coinage, although its origins, like those of *défaitiste*, have never been investigated. According to A. Dauzat, "*jusqu'auboutiste* fut en 1915-17 une création de circonstance".[2] It does not appear in the *F.E.W.*, the *Bloch-Wartburg* or the *Robert*. The *Petit Robert* dates it "avant 1922", and gives the following gloss:

> Personne qui va jusqu'au bout de ses idées politiques. V. *Extrémiste*.
> "Il était ce que Brichot appelait un jusqu'au-boutiste" (PROUST).

The use of the term by Proust is no doubt what qualifies it for inclusion in the *Petit Robert*. But the definition is anachronistic and misglosses the citation it was presumably devised to explain. Reference to the preceding lines leaves no doubt about the meaning of *jusqu'auboutiste* for Proust:

> M. Bontemps ne voulait pas entendre parler de paix avant que l'Allemagne eût été réduite au même morcellement qu'au moyen âge, la

---

[15] *Les Précurseurs,* p. 333 (15 Mar. 1918).
[1] Graphies vary, even within the practice of a single writer. I have respected the author's (or printer's) spelling in quoting.
[2] *Le Génie de la langue française,* Paris, 1947, p. 80.

déchéance de la maison de Hohenzollern prononcée, et Guillaume ayant reçu douze balles dans la peau. En un mot, il était ce que ... etc.[3]

"Partisan de la guerre jusqu'au bout"[4] is in fact the only gloss applicable to the term as used in the First World War. The most precise dating to hand seems to be that offered by A. J. Greimas and R. Monnot; they give an example of *jusqu'auboutiste* used by R. Rolland in his diary on 7 May 1917.[5] However, this date proves little, since the text of the diary referred to consists of excerpts from April and May 1917 only, which were published in *La Table Ronde* in December 1952 before the complete edition was available. As will be seen, Rolland in fact uses the term *jusqu'auboutiste* considerably earlier.

Unlike *défaitiste, jusqu'auboutiste* has not come into common usage; its survival in present day French is chiefly as a historical term in works dealing with the 1914-18 war, but it is sometimes found in other contexts. In a radio programme about Bangladesh in December 1971, the commentator said of President Bhutto of Pakistan: "c'était lui l'intransigeant, le jusqu'auboutiste" (Europe I, 20 Dec. 1971), referring to the uncompromising hostility he had shown to India. The term can also be applied analogically to people involved in confrontations other than war. The hard-liners in an industrial dispute were referred to in a radio news bulletin as "les jusqu'auboutistes de la grève" (Europe I, 30 Apr. 1971). It is significant that the announcer immediately explained the term as "les partisans de la grève à outrance"—an indication of its presumed unfamiliarity. Similar usage is found in *Le Monde*, this time without comment:

> M. Feather ... prévoyait que la base ... abandonnerait les jusqu'auboutistes. (24 Aug. 1972)

The rather restricted use of this term in modern French is aptly summed up in the *Nouveau Larousse Universel* (1948):

---

[3] *Le Temps retrouve,* Pléiade edn., vol. iii, p. 728.
[4] A. Dauzat, *Précis d'histoire de la langue et du vocabulaire français,* Paris, 1949, p. 179.
[5] "Datations nouvelles. Notes lexicologiques", *Le Français Moderne,* xxiii (1955), 140. The entry *jusqu'auboutiste* in B. Quémada, *Matériaux pour l'histoire du vocabulaire français* (deuxième série, 2, p. 131) adds no new information, but merely refers to Greimas and Monnot.

jusqu'au-boutiste Fam. Partisan du jusqu'au-boutisme.

jusqu'au-boutisme Fam. Nom par lequel on désigne parfois, dans une guerre, dans un conflit d'intérêts quelconque, l'attitude prise par ceux qui se refusent à tout compromis et veulent mener la lutte *jusqu'au bout* (d'où le nom).

The morphological process involved in the formation of a derivative from a phrase rather than a single word is not itself new; in the category of "dérivés de noms composés" Kr. Nyrop gives *jemenfichisme* and *jemenmoquiste*.[6] What is particularly interesting is that there appears to be a precedent for forming a derivative from the expression *jusqu'au bout*. Nyrop cites *jusqu'auboutien* with the following comment:

> Dans l'ordre du jour qu'adressait Mac-Mahon à l'armée, le 9 juillet 1877, se trouvait la phrase: J'irai jusqu'au bout. Les journaux qui soutenaient la politique du maréchal s'appelaient ironiquement *jusqu'au boutiens*.[7]

The word is listed with other

> créations éphémères, nées de circonstances politiques ou littéraires, et qui n'ont de chance de reparaître que si des circonstances semblables se représentent.[8]

The particular circumstances here were presumably the election campaign following the *coup d'État* known as *le 16 Mai*.

Nyrop's general observation about trends in political vocabulary is lent an almost prophetic note in retrospect by events in 1914-15. The expression *jusqu'au bout* again became a slogan and produced a derivative, this time in *-iste*. The origins of the slogan can be traced to a *mot historique* of General Gallieni. With the Germans advancing rapidly on Paris, and the exodus of the government to Bordeaux, Gallieni made the following proclamation:

---

[6] *Grammaire historique de la langue française*, vol. iii, Copenhagen, 1908, p. 40. Nyrop does not separate derivatives of a verb-phrase from derivatives of a compound noun, e.g. *fait-diversiste*. *Jemenfichisme* dates from 1885 according to the *Petit Robert*; the *Bloch-Wartburg* supplies 1884 for the variant *je-m'en-foutiste/ je-m'en-foutisme*.

[7] *Grammaire historique*, vol. iii. p. 40.

[8] Ibid., p. 41.

Habitants de Paris,
Les membres du gouvernement de la République ont quitté Paris pour donner une impulsion nouvelle à la défense nationale.
J'ai reçu le mandat de défendre Paris contre l'envahisseur. Ce mandat, je le remplirai jusqu'au bout.

Paris, le 3 septembre 1914

Le gouverneur militaire de Paris, commandant de l'armée de Paris,
GALLIENI
(reproduced by *le Matin*)

These words were immediately taken up with enthusiasm by the press. In an article devoted to the General, *L'Illustration* writes:

Lui, sans le vouloir, s'est exactement dépeint: "jusqu'au bout" a-t-il dit, et ce pourrait être sa devise, et c'est sa psychologie. (19 Sept. 1914)

The label was to remain. H. Bérenger reminds readers of *Paris-Midi* in November 1915 that Gallieni had been nicknamed "le général *Jusqu'au bout*", and in the obituary he wrote for him he takes this as his theme:

Quel Français oublierait sa déclaration comme Ministre de la Guerre en décembre 1915, déclaration que le Sénat fit afficher sur tous les murs de France: "Il y a 2 ans la France voulait la paix: aujourd'hui la France veut la guerre et elle la poussera jusqu'au bout."
Jusqu'au bout! C'est le seul testament que Gallieni laisse à la France.
(*Paris-Midi*, 28 May 1916)

As the conflict took on the character of a *guerre de tranchées*, and it became increasingly apparent that France was in for a long struggle, *jusqu'au bout* established itself as a rallying cry.[9] It occurs frequently as a newspaper headline, either on its own or in a more elaborated formula of the type: "Tous ensemble jusqu'au bout!" (*Paris-Midi*, 27 Jan. 1915); or "Jusqu'au bout pour l'écrasement du Boche et la victoire de l'Indépendance!" (*Paris-Midi*, 17 Dec. 1915). *L'Association fraternelle des anciens combattants de la Marne* (*6ᵉ Armée*) chose to entitle its monthly bulletin *Jusqu'au bout*! The slogan was even thought to have commercial potential, judging from an advertisement which appeared in *L'Illustration* on 19 December 1914:

[9] "Jusqu'a à la victoire, jusqu'au bout devint le mot d'ordre" (J. Bainville, *Histoire de France,* Paris, 1924, p. 555).

A NOËL ET AUX ÉTRENNES
Pour jouer en famille et dans les tranchées
Offrez le *JUSQU'AU BOUT*
Nouveau jeu de la guerre, 63 illustrations en couleurs
Amusant, historique, instructif
Modèle spécial entoilé et plié pour les soldats

Left-wing newspapers also have their share of articles headed "Jusqu'au bout!", though here the intention is quite different. Without explicitly repudiating the aim, some writers set out to discredit it surreptitiously:

> Il faut que ... les Alliés sachent bien quel est le terme de la lutte. Car "jusqu'au bout" n'est qu'un mot, une formule encore plus vide que sonore, si les uns visent ce bout avec des vues de myope, les autres, de presbyte. (*Le Pays*, 6 July 1917)

La Gazette des Ardennes is more outspoken:

> On ira jusqu'au bout! Jusqu'au bout aboutit à cette signification sinistre: jusqu'à ce que les mâles n'y soient plus qu'enfants et vieillards! Jusqu'au bout veut dire jusqu'au dernier homme, jusqu'au dernier sou!
>
> (3 Feb. 1917)

With growing opposition towards the continuation of the war, and the weakening of the *Union Sacrée* pact, *jusqu'au bout* becomes established as a pejorative expression in the vocabulary of the strongly pacifist elements of the Left, and is readily used to characterize their opponents. M. Badin expresses his alarm in the form of a nightmare where

> Des individus à l'aspect terrifiant allaient et venaient, avec une allure saccadée et inquiète de fauves emprisonnés. Ils avaient la face convulsée, ils se dépensaient en gesticulations menaçantes, et hurlaient ... "Haine! Revanche! Représailles! Jusqu'au bout!"
>
> (*Le Bonnet Rouge*, 12 July 1916)

Readers at the time would not have had any difficulty in recognizing figures such as M. Barrès, Ch. Maurras, and L. Daudet in the above description. This strong, almost automatic association was readily exploited by humorists for satirical effect. Under the heading "L'Immortelle", *Le Canard Enchaîné* makes the following prediction:

> Au train dont ça va, et d'après les probabilités établies par les compagnies d'assurances, si la guerre dure encore seulement dix ans, il ne nous restera plus un seul académicien.

Si pourtant. Il en restera un: M. Maurice Barrès. M. Maurice Barrès
a promis de tenir jusqu'au bout. (25 Aug. 1916)

Likewise, V. Snell, the anonymous author of a parody called "*Le
Jardin de Marrès*, par Bérénice", published as a serial by *L'Humanité*,[10] makes use of the same device to introduce and at the same
time caricature his hero. The first scene of the story takes place in
a tram a few days before the outbreak of war:

> Puis, s'adressant au voisin de celui-ci, [le conducteur du tramway] avait
> demandé:
> - Jusqu'où, Monsieur?
> Alors une voix un peu lasse, mais énergique, répondit:
> - Jusqu'au bout.
> Il y avait dans ces simples mots tant de volonté concentrée, et l'accent
> dont ils étaient marqués était tel que, par un phénomène singulier, ils me
> parurent avoir une importance formidable, gigantesque, et sous laquelle
> je me sentis écrasée.
> A ce "jusqu'au bout", simple réponse à une simple question, les
> railleurs feindront de s'étonner que quelqu'un n'ait pas répliqué par un
> "Déjà?" anticipé autant qu'irrévérencieux. (*L'Humanité*, 18 Oct. 1915)

Once *jusqu'au bout* is established as a war slogan, it can be sub-
stantivized. On 15 February 1916 R. Rolland writes of a nationalistic
journalist:

> Il voulait faire un coup de théâtre et brusquement, au nom de la France,
> proclamer devant la salle stupéfait le "jusqu'au bout!" de ceux qui font
> marcher les autres.[11]

There is a similar example from the pen of L. Daudet:

> Il faut un caractère héroïque pour prononcer le "jusqu'au bout" quand
> on a une partie de sa fortune à Hambourg, à Francfort ou à Berlin.
> (*L'Action Française*, 2 Dec. 1916)

It seems highly probable that this studied and conscious use of the
expression facilitated the creation of a derivative in -*iste*. The word
jusqu'auboutiste appears in a letter written to R. Rolland in August
1915 by R.L., "jeune homme d'une famille protestante distinguée".
The absence of any comment leads one to assume that the term
must have been current at the time, even if only in a limited circle:

> L'état d'esprit des hommes du front m'a stupéfié. Je m'attendais bien à y

[10] It appeared in book form in 1916.
[11] *Journal*, p. 658.

trouver plus de bon sens, plus d'humanité, que chez les jusqu'auboutistes de l'arrière, les dilettantes du carnage, avec leur mysticisme féroce. Mais je n'osais espérer ce bouillonnement contenu à peine de révolution.[12]

Rolland soon adopts it into his own vocabulary; on 23 September 1915 he writes:

J'étais devenu, sans l'avoir cherché et sans même le savoir, le chef invisible d'un parti, de tous ceux qui s'opposent aux jusqu'auboutistes forcenés.[13]

Thereafter, the word becomes increasingly frequent in Rolland's diary, as does the form *jusqu'auboutisme* which first appears in May 1916. It is hardly surprising that he makes such use of these terms, since they designate an attitude which was anathema to him, and which he took every opportunity to attack in his writings.

It is not until December 1915 that one finds a specific name being given in the press to the people who believed in fighting Germany to the bitter end. E. Langevin, writing in *La Bataille* on 3 December, claims that

nous, syndicalistes, nous ne sommes ni des "jusqu'au bout" ni des "pacifistes à tout prix",

but this use of *jusqu'au bout* to refer to people appears to be an isolated example. It may have had a brief existence as an alternative to the form in *-iste*, but it was soon to be ousted by the latter. The occasion which was responsible for giving widespread publicity to an expression that must already have been in restricted circulation was the annual Socialist Party Congress in December 1915. A split had developed between members who favoured *une politique de défense nationale* and the fraction which was sympathetic to the ideals voiced at Zimmerwald the previous September;[14] this gave rise to heated discussion at the Congress, in the course of which the minority accused their opponents of being *jusqu'auboutistes*. Since one of the chief of these was G. Hervé, readers of *La Guerre Sociale*[15] were treated to a full editorial on the subject on 29 December:

Jusqu'auboutiste
Jusqu'auboutiste! c'est l'épithète que les Pères-la-défaite et les Pères-

[12] Ibid., p. 495.
[13] Ibid., p. 528.
[14] See above, 2.4, pp. 57-8.
[15] Due to change its name to *La Victoire* on 1 Jan. 1916. See Appendix I.

la-panique[16] lancent dans les milieux avancés à ceux qui veulent la guerre "jusqu'au bout"!

Far from rejecting the label as the insult it was intended to be, Hervé welcomes it gratefully;[17] in a series of paragraphs beginning *Jusqu'à ce que ...*, he lists the *sine qua non* of victory, and then proceeds, as was his wont, to look for a historical parallel:

> Jusqu'auboutistes! Nous sommes fiers de l'injure, comme nos pères les patriotes du siège de Paris, ceux qui devaient plus tard faire la Commune pour protester contre ceux qu'ils appelaient les Capitulards—étaient fiers qu'on les appelât les "guerre à outrance". Guerre à outrance, jusqu'auboutistes: il n'y a pas d'offense. Ce qui serait pour nous une offense, c'est qu'un jour quelqu'un pût venir traiter notre Parti de parti de capitulards![18]

The term *guerre à outrance* had been used by Hervé on 30 July 1914 when comparing the stand taken by the French Socialist Party over the threat of German aggression with that of the defenders of Paris in 1870.[19] It remained in his vocabulary (not only as a historical term, but also to refer to contemporaries) after he had adopted *jusqu'auboutiste*, and he clearly regarded the two as equivalent, as the following example indicates:

> Heureusement, il y eut Gambetta. Un "jusqu'auboutiste" celui-là! En ce temps-là, ça s'appelait un "guerre à outrance".
>
> (*La Victoire*, 23 May 1916)

J. Dubois does not mention this form, but gives *outrancier*. He quotes from L. Cladel (1871), who describes Gambetta as

> l'ardent patriote que les capitulards ont honoré, voulant l'en flétrir, de ce surnom immortel: "l'Outrancier"![20]

The only examples of *outrancier* that I have found in 1914-18 are adjectival: *Le Bonnet Rouge* mentions

> ... un échantillon de prose outrancière découpée dans un journal mondain
>
> (29 June 1916)

[16] See above, 2.8, pp. 78-9.
[17] Cf. M. Tournier, "Éléments pour l'étude quantitative d'une journé de 48", p. 93: "Renverser ainsi le vecteur affectif d'un terme, assumer l'étiquette infâmante, c'est, en religion comme en politique, retourner l'infâmant pour s'en faire un drapeau, désamorcer l'injure et polémiquer en sens inverse".
[18] Hervé himself was to resuscitate the label *capitulard* for this very purpose. See above, 2.8, pp. 78 and 86.
[19] See above, 1.1, p. 9.
[20] *Le Vocabulaire politique et social*, p. 361.

and

> ... un quotidien parisien aussi habile aux pires démagogies qu'au "jusqu'auboutisme" outrancier. (11 Aug. 1916)

Both *guerre-à-outrance* and *outrancier* derive from slogans of the type *la guerre/la lutte à outrance*, which were revived in 1914-18; G. Clemenceau writes of

> ... les conditions éventuelles d'une lutte à outrance dont nul encore ne peut prévoir la durée. (*L'Homme Enchaîné*, 2 Jan. 1915)

and R. Rolland describes *The Suffragette* as

> ... un gramophone assourdissant de guerre à outrance.[21]

However, the new alternative *la guerre jusqu'au bout* proved to have far more widespread appeal.

G. Hervé's ostentatious acceptance of the label *jusqu'auboutiste* was immediately commented upon by *Paris-Midi* in its review of the morning press on 29 December 1915:

> Hervé est enchanté de l'étiquette que ses amis socialistes lui ont collée: "jusqu'auboutiste" lui plaît énormément. "Jusqu'auboutiste" il est, "jusqu'auboutiste" il sera. D'ailleurs, Hervé a toujours été "jusqu'auboutiste". Il est né "jusqu'auboutiste".

Thereafter, *Paris-Midi* frequently refers to him as "le jusqu'auboutiste Hervé", and this humour at his expense must have helped to popularize the word. It should be noted that this newspaper refrains from using *jusqu'auboutiste* when writing purely in its own name; it merely reports the emotive usage of other people.

Three months later, *Le Bonnet Rouge* published an important front-page article headed "Paix boiteuse ou jusqu'auboutisme?" in which the writer, General Percin, makes the following statement—striking in view of the subsequent evolution of the paper:

> Au moment où, en Allemagne, on recommence à parler de paix, je suis heureux de constater l'unanimité avec laquelle nous sommes décidés, en France, à pousser la guerre jusqu'au bout. Sur l'autel du *jusqu'auboutisme*, pacifistes et militaristes ont réalisé l'Union Sacrée.

In case his readers should be in any doubt, he goes on to add:

[21] *Journal,* p. 373 (20 May 1915).

Saluons cette union sacrée qui, sous la même bannière range des adversaires politiques: le lieutenant-colonel Driant qui s'est fait pacifiste, comme le *Bonnet Rouge*, et le *Bonnet Rouge* qui s'est fait jusqu'auboutiste comme le lieutenant-colonel Driant.

(Le Bonnet Rouge, 29 Mar. 1916)

Contemporaries seem to have reacted quickly to the adoption of this neologism by the press. In a column devoted to "La guerre et le langage", *Le Bonnet Rouge* notes:

Un humoriste inventa le "jusqu'auboutisme". Cette locution-là, au moins, finira avec la guerre. (16 Apr. 1916)

M. Bouchor goes so far as to publish some verse on the subject in *La Bataille*:

> *Jusqu'au bout*
> Pour nous tous, qui voulons que la France persiste
> Sans se lasser, dans son effort le plus viril,
> Ces messieurs ont créé le mot: *Jusquauboutiste*
> Dont ils usent avec un bonheur puéril.
>
> Ce mot, tant applaudi par ces auteurs, veut dire
> Que nous nous obstinons, par délire chauvin,
> A vouloir prolonger l'universel martyre
> En soutenant un âpre effort qui sera vain.
>
> A quoi bon leur répondre et plaider notre cause? etc.

(1 May 1916)

In the early summer of 1916, there is a marked change of tone in *Le Bonnet Rouge*. Up till then, while conducting a virulent polemical campaign against reactionary enemies—in particular *L'Action Française*—it had remained at least nominally in favour of *la guerre jusqu'au bout*. When it shifts its position, one of the chief indications of this is the fact that its contributors reject *jusqu'auboutiste* as an epithet which they are happy to see applied to themselves; it becomes a pejorative term in much the same way as it is in the vocabulary of R. Rolland. G. Clairet writes:

On les appelle en Italie les guerrafondiers. En France, ce sont les jusqu'auboutistes. Je ne sais quel est le nom dont on les affuble en Allemagne .... Quel que soit son nom, quels que soient ses thèmes, l'engeance, vous le voyez, sévit partout. (*Le Bonnet Rouge*, 29 July 1916)

On 23 September, Almereyda took an unequivocal stand in his editorial:

La paix allemande? ... jamais!
Mais le jusqu'auboutisme aveugle qui, sans certitude de victoire totale,
interdit à nos gouvernements d'abréger le cauchemar, jamais non plus!

—so much so that "Anastasie" only saw fit to let the first line of
the above pass, thus rendering the article completely innocuous.[22]
La Gazette des Ardennes was also engaged in denigrating *jusqu'auboutistes* at just about this time. The close similarity between
material appearing in *Le Bonnet Rouge* and articles such as the
following:

Pour juger sainement la situation, il faut savoir regarder les réalités en
face et non pas à travers les lunettes de l'illusion "jusqu'auboutiste" qui
s'obstine à vouloir l'impossible écrasement d'une force vitale aussi puis-
sante et aussi élémentaire que le peuple allemand.
                                      (*La Gazette des Ardennes*, 19 Nov. 1916)

—was one of the chief factors which led L. Marchand to suspect
collusion between the two papers.[23]
Perhaps one of the surest indications that the term *jusqu'auboutiste* had become established in the register of topical polemics
is to be found in the use made of it by *Le Canard Enchaîné*. On the
pages of this weekly it produces a family of ephemeral variants,
the comic potential of which quite clearly assumes familiarity with
the parent term. Readers learned of

les théories plus-loin-que-jusqu'auboutistes de Campois (18 Aug. 1916)

they were introduced to

un fervent lecteur de l'*Écho de Paris*, grand héros de l'arrière, chasseur
d'embusqués, plus-loin-que-le-boutiste convaincu (8 May 1918)

and they were even treated to a poem about a young lady nicknamed

> *Presqu'auboutiste*
> Elle était blonde, plutôt rousse,
> Avait des yeux bleus, presque verts, etc.
>   (21 Aug. 1918)

Towards the end of the war, the neologism *exterministe/exter-
minisme* came into circulation as a variant for *jusqu'auboutiste/
jusqu'auboutisme*. It does not appear to figure in dictionaries; the

---

[22] The uncensored text is given by L. Marchand, *L'Offensive morale*, p. 168.
[23] See above, 2.7, pp. 72-3.

earliest example I have found dates from January 1918, in R. Rolland's diary:

> L'"Exterminisme" des uns, le "Défaitisme" des autres, n'est qu'un masque. L'ennemi, pour eux, c'est d'abord le rival.[24]

His comment on the form *exterministe* implies that it is a recent coinage:

> Le stupide entêtement des jusqu'auboutistes Alliés porte ses fruits. On dit maintenant "exterministes"—et c'est la vérité.[25]

It occurs sporadically in the left-wing press: *Le Pays* points to

> ... les fureurs anti-ouvrières des amis de Maurras (toute la presse exterministe). (16 Feb. 1918)

Its meaning is close to that of *belliciste/bellicisme* and *va-t'en-guerre*. R. Rolland writes:

> On n'a pas plus le droit de m'annexer au bolchevisme qu'au bellicisme comme l'ont tenté récemment ces bons socialistes exterministes de la *France Libre*[26]

—where *bellicisme* is quite straightfowardly the attitude of the *exterministes.* Similarly, under the heading "L'exterminisme musical" he notes:

> Mes amis musicologues ... ne sont pas moins va-t'en-guerre que les autres.[27]

When *jusqu'auboutiste/jusqu'auboutisme* are used as terms of abuse, they clearly belong among *les éléments militaristes*; they collocate with words like *réactionnaire, annexionniste, impérialiste, tenant d'un militarisme à la prusienne.* V. Leriche says of the right wing of the Socialist party:

> Avec quelle précipitation les réactionnaires, les jusqu'auboutistes, les majoritaires avaient-ils écrit et clamé sur tous les toits qu'ils répudiaient l'entrevue de Stockholm parce qu'elle ne constituait qu'un piège grossier du Kaiser! (*La Tranchée Républicaine*, 31 May 1917)

Annexionniste and *jusqu'auboutiste* are particularly closely con-

---

[24] *Journal*, p. 1395 (17 Jan. 1918).
[25] Ibid., p. 1419 (28 Feb. 1918).
[26] Ibid., p. 1618 (23 Sept. 1918).
[27] Ibid., p. 1458 (8 May 1918).

nected, since the recovery of Alsace-Lorraine constituted one of the principal objectives of those who preached *la guerre jusqu'au bout*. Writing of just such a person, R. Rolland calls him "un jacobin jusqu'auboutiste", and then refers to him again as "cet intrépide annexionniste".[28] In Rolland's vocabulary, *patriote*, a strongly negative term,[29] is often linked with *jusqu'auboutiste*:

> Même ceux qui, foncièrement patriotes et jusqu'auboutistes, ont reconnu l'impossibilité d'employer une autre voie.[30]

More common in such contexts is the superlative *ultrapatriote*; A. Lunacharsky writes in a letter to Rolland:

> Mais si le gouvernement russe, aidé par ces libéraux ultrapatriotes et jusqu'auboutistes ... concluait maintenant une paix séparée ...[31]

On the whole, the terms linked with *jusqu'auboutiste* when it is intended as an insult are never used by people to describe themselves.[32] Indeed, their enemies often attribute to them views and ideals which they expressly reject (e.g. Prussian-style militarism). Among the "positive"[33] words opposed to *jusqu'auboutiste/ jusqu'auboutisme* which do not feature in contrast with them elsewhere, one finds *humanitaire* and *paix juste et humaine*.

In the vocabulary of someone like G. Hervé who claims to be a *jusqu'auboutiste*, the word is a member of a positive set comprising such terms as *patriote, "guerre à outrance", "union sacrée",*[34] and it is contrasted with *pacifiste bêlant, zimmerwaldien*, and *défaitiste* (after July 1917); similarly *jusqu'auboutisme* is opposed to *paix boiteuse* (*blanche, allemande*) and *défaitisme*. The terms in this second set are nearly always pejorative. Of the aims explicitly put forward by these self-styled *jusqu'auboutistes*, the most

---

[28] Ibid., p. 1617 (16 Oct. 1918).

[29] See above, 3.4, p. 126.

[30] *Journal,* p. 1166 (7 Apr. 1917).

[31] Ibid., pp. 888-9 (26 Aug. 1916).

[32] *Patriote* is an exception, R. Rolland's refusal to accept it as a label being highly idiosyncratic.

[33] M. Tournier calls such polarization "le poids social du mot"; he argues that "tout syntagme polémique dépend non de deux pôles (auteur et récepteur) mais de trois, car il fait appel à une sorte de code référentiel de valeurs qui joue un rôle d'étalonnage des énoncés. C'est par rapport à une valeur-étalon des termes choisis, sociologiquement déterminée, que le locuteur situe sa parole" (Éléments pour l'étude quantitative d'une journée de 48", pp. 92-3).

[34] Examples of these last two terms used to refer to people are given above, p. 146, and 1.2, p. 17.

representative are probably "la fin du militarisme prussien", "la force à outrance pour sauver le droit", or "la guerre pour tuer la guerre".

The dual status of *jusqu'auboutiste* is acknowledged by some writers who comment on the neologism. P. H. Loyson regards it primarily as an insult, but is prepared to see it applied to himself provided he can supply his own definition:

> Un "jusqu'au-boutiste outrancier", c'est ainsi que m'étiquète Louis Lévy.... Je défie qu'on puisse me citer un seul passage qui justifie cet opprobre d'être rangé parmi les tenants d'un militarisme à la prussienne.... Se c'est être "jusqu'au-boutiste" d'applaudir au geste du Président Wilson tirant L'épée pour son idéal ... si enfin c'est être "jusqu'au-boutiste" que d'avoir foi en notre cause, en cette cause une et indivisible de la Démocratie et du Droit, je le serai jusqu'à mon dernier souffle, quelle que puisse être la durée, l'issue et les conséquences de la guerre. (*La Tranchée Républicaine*, 20 May 1917)

R. Rolland coined a special term for this somewhat milder shade of opinion; he mentions

> les malheureux qui prônent (pauvres naïfs!) la guerre pour la paix (nommons-les *bellipacistes*), et les pacifiques tout court, ceux de l'Évangile ...[35]

and it is clear from an entry he made in his diary in the same month (December 1916) that he distinguished this attitude from *jusqu'auboutisme* proper:

> Je vois la tactique: ... compromettre [la brebis émancipée, i.e. himself] dans un groupe oscillant du pacifisme au bellipacisme, et de celui-ci, si l'occasion s'en présente, au jusqu'auboutisme.[36]

It should be added that usage is not as clear-cut as the preceding outline of the collocations of *jusqu'auboutiste/jusqu'auboutisme* might imply, since by no means all of the words which are associated with the neologism are "polarized" in the sense that *zimmerwaldien* or *chauvin* are. The existence of terms such as *antimilitariste* or *pacifiste*, which like *jusqu'auboutiste* can be either "positive" or "negative", and are usually contrasted with the latter, means that it is often only the general context which enables one to determine the "polemical charge" carried by a particular occurrence of one of these oppositions. To complicate the picture further, writers will

---

[35] *Les Précurseurs,* p. 194.
[36] *Journal,* p. 1008 (15 Dec. 1916). I have not found *bellipacisme* elsewhere.

deliberately exploit the indeterminacy in the relationships between such terms, setting up idiosyncratic contrasts between them to suit their own purposes.[37] For instance, General Percin sees the term *jusqu'auboutiste* as superseding the old labels *pacifiste* versus *militariste*,[38] whereas for R. Rolland, *pacifiste* remains outside what he calls "la mêlée de haines" in which *défaitiste* is opposed to *jusqu'auboutiste*, etc.:

> Guilbeaux accusé d'avoir été l'instrument du "défaitiste" Hartmann... lequel, au demeurant, n'est ni un défaitiste, ni un jusqu'auboutiste, ni un germanophile, ni un francophile, mais un pacifiste, socialiste, ancien ami et admirateur d'Hervé.[39]

In conclusion, a few comments are called for on certain features of the syntactic environment in which *jusqu'auboutisme* figures. A comparison with the term *défaitisme* serves as a useful means of highlighting what is peculiar about the behaviour of each. Both words are neologisms of the period, and might be thought of as antonyms. It is true that there is a striking difference in their frequency of occurrence: *défaitisme* was adopted into general usage in the press within a matter of months in 1917, and spread in a way that *jusqu'auboutisme*, popularized at the beginning of 1916, was never to do; but if this is taken into account, one might still have expected them to be used in much the same manner, as is indeed the case with the corresponding forms in *-iste*.[40] What one actually finds is that whereas *défaitisme* is most commonly used without further qualification—*une politique de défaitisme, combattre le défaitisme, les agents du défaitisme*, etc.—people tend to talk about the *jusqu'auboutisme* of a particular individual or group:

> —le jusqu'au-boutisme farouche de la population civile[41]
> —expliquer mon "jusqu'auboutisme" actuel par ...
> (G. Hervé, La Guerre Sociale, 28 Dec. 1915)

> —appuyer son jusqu'auboutisme sur mon article[42]
> —la justification de notre jusqu'auboutisme
> (G. Hervé, La Victoire, 17 May 1916)

---

[37] On the importance of "persuasive definitions", see above, 1.1, pp. 7-8.
[38] See above, pp. 147-8.
[39] *Journal*, p. 1450 (April 1918).
[40] See the passage from R. Rolland just quoted.
[41] J. de Pierrefeu, *G.Q.G. Secteur 1*, vol. ii, p. 29.
[42] R. Rolland, *Journal*, p. 784.

Examples of this kind with *défaitisme* are comparatively rare.[43]
When *jusqu'auboutisme* does not occur with a possessive or with
de + noun, it is usually qualified by an adjective:

> —Clemenceau représente le jusqu'auboutisme le plus aveugle, le plus
> forcené (*Le Pays*, 16 Nov. 1917)
>
> —le donjon du jusqu'auboutisme tedescophobe[44]
>
> —c'est le jusqu'auboutisme défaitiste[45]

Défaitisme, on the other hand, tends to be coupled with one or
more abstract nouns if it needs reinforcement or explanation:

> —les défenseurs éperdus du défaitisme et de la trahison[46]
>
> —la sarabande du défaitisme, du bolchevikisme et de la trahison[47]
>
> —leur sale besogne de démoralisation et de défaitisme[48]

Of the cases where *jusqu'auboutisme* is used absolutely, a fair
number can be accounted for as instances of definition:

> —le "jusqu'auboutisme" n'est pas une théorie raisonnable si ...
>
> (*Le Pays*, 17 Feb. 1918)
>
> —un groupe oscillant...[du bellipacisme]...au jusqu'auboutisme[49]

This leaves very few examples of expressions like "sur l'autel du
jusqu'auboutisme",[50] which represent the sort of unqualified use
most commonly found with *défaitisme*. Finally, there is a con-
struction in which both words function identically:

> —l'ancien correspondant allemand à Paris qui fait aujourd'hui du
> jusqu'auboutisme (*Le Bonnet Rouge*, 23 Aug. 1916)
>
> —combien de fripouilles faisant chez nous du défaitisme[51]

Faire du défaitisme seems to be a favourite idiom of Barrès;[52] he

---

[43] A few are given above, 2.9, p. 89, and 2.11, p. 104.
[44] R. Rolland, *Journal*, p. 1061.
[45] See above, 2.4, p. 61.
[46] L. Daudet, *Le Poignard dans le dos*, p. 65.
[47] Ibid., p. 337.
[48] See above, 2.11, p. 102.
[49] See above, p. 152.
[50] See above, p. 147.
[51] M. Barrès, *En regardant au fond des crevasses*, p. 44.
[52] Judging from the way in which one of his critics, P. Renaison, takes him up on
it. See above, 2.9, p. 89.

also uses the expression *favoriser le défaitisme* as in "des feuilles qui favorisent le défaitisme",[53] or the following:

> Si [M. Caillaux] se borne à se défendre d'avoir favorisé et prêché le défaitisme ... (*L'Écho de Paris*, 18 Dec. 1917)

Jusqu'auboutisme does not seem to collocate with *favoriser*; nor does there appear to be a parallel to the idiom *verser dans le défaitisme* which Hervé uses:

> Le Bonnet Rouge versait dans le défaitisme. (*La Victoire*, 29 Nov. 1917)

The reason for all the differences just outlined in the use of *jusqu'auboutisme* and *défaitisme* is probably to be found in the fact that while both words denote a personal attitude, these attitudes had quite different consequences. *Défaitisme* gave rise to specific nefarious activities (as witnessed by the mutinies and scandals of 1917), and the term rapidly took on the function of designating them. It must be assumed that anyone who followed political developments with a reasonable degree of alertness would have known what kind of thing was being alluded to when L. Daudet wrote of "une trame souterraine de défaitisme",[54] or H. Bérenger of "le plus bel exploit du défaitisme" (*Paris-Midi*, 20 Nov. 1917). Nothing comparable occurred in the case of *jusqu'auboutisme*: it remained an opinion or state of mind the most concrete manifestations of which were the endless outpourings of what *Le Bonnet Rouge* called "prose outrancière".[55]

3.7   Rhetorical linking of terms

It is tempting to pursue discussion of the various components of *la Réaction* by trying to draw up a list of the objectives associated with each group.[1] Could it be shown, for instance, that *la Revanche* was an aim attributed exclusively to people who were termed *nationalistes* or *chauvins*? or that avowed hostility to the Stockholm peace conference was the prerogative of *les jusqu'auboutistes*? Analysis of this kind is rendered impossible in practice by a recurrent

[53] *En regardant au fond des crevasses*, p. 19.
[54] *La Guerre totale*, p. 210.
[55] See above, p. 146.
[1] Cf. G. Provost's article "Approche du discours politique: *socialisme* et *socialiste* chez Jaurès", where she reduces the "énoncés politiques" of her corpus to the form "les socialistes veulent que x soit", and examines the class of terms that can be substituted for x. See above, Introduction, p. 6, n. 21.

feature of polemical style: writers will hurl as many abusive names as they can at their opponents in a way which blurs the distinctions between the different terms used, and makes it difficult to disentangle what any one of them implies individually. The neutralization of fine nuances has already been discussed in cases where two or more terms function as equivalents in a short stretch of text.[2] What must now be considered is the linking of such terms within a single sentence—composite phrases like *les monarchistes, les cléricaux et les nationalistes,* or *les patriotes, les nationalistes et les chauvins.*[3]

Examples like these can be understood in more than one way. When a sequence of related terms is used to describe a single individual, each one may be interpreted as adding a new dimension to the portrait—shifting the perspective, however slightly. But it is much more likely that such a reading is over-refined, and that the accumulation of terms of opprobrium is purely rhetorical, being designed primarily to leave its target reeling under a sledgehammer attack. A more real difficulty arises if the words appear in the plural. The collocation *les monarchistes, les cléricaux et les nationalistes* may refer to three distinct groups of people, a sort of *coalition monarchique, cléricale, nationaliste,* or may refer collectively to a single group whose members each qualify as *monarchiste, clérical et nationaliste.* In practice, of course, the choice of interpretation is of small consequence, since it is highly improbable that polemical journalists or their readers would have paused to worry about implications of this sort. A certain degree of indeterminacy is inherent in their usage.[4]

The terms most readily linked for emphasis are drawn from different sub-groups of *la Réaction* (e.g. *nos nationalistes, nos*

---

[2] See esp. 3.1, p. 116, and 3.4, pp. 132-3.

[3] The linking of *défaitiste/défaitisme* with other terms has already been touched upon (see above, 2.9, pp. 90-93, and 2.11, p. 102; this stylistic device will be illustrated at some length here as it seems particularly prevalent in the language of the Left.

[4] J. -B. Marcellesi makes passing reference to this problem in connection with the interpretation of collocations such as *ouvrier et socialiste, socialiste et révolutionnaire,* etc., in the vocabulary of the Congrès de Tours. See "La Délimitation des unités lexicales dans le vocabulaire politique et social", *Wissenschaftliche Zeitschrift, Martin-Luther Universität Halle-Wittenberg,* xix, 3/4 (1970), 46. It is important to recognize this feature of "linking" for what it is: a trick of style; and not to draw unwarranted conclusions from it as J. Dubois seems to be doing when he equates terms in the glossary of *Le Vocabulaire politique et social.*

réactionnaires, nos cléricaux), but one does find some combinations of terms belonging to a single sub-group. This only seems to be possible where the terms are sufficiently distinct to be able to contrast with one another in some contexts, or—better still— to form an explicit hierarchy. The sub-groups which provide the most striking examples of linking are *les professionnels du patriotisme* and *les éléments militaristes*. Expressions like **les cléricaux, les calotins et les frocards* do not appear to be attested, perhaps because the various names for *les gens du Pape* function purely as alternatives, and do not have any separate identity when set against one another.

Writers concerned to attack extreme forms of patriotism frequently select two or more items from the series *patriote → nationaliste → chauvin*. *Patriotisme* can be linked with *nationalisme*:

> Urbain Gohier, aujourd'hui, fait profession de dénoncer ceux qu'il appelle les ennemis de l'Intérieur. Il tire argent de son patriotisme affecté, de son nationalisme d'emprunt. (*Le Bonnet Rouge*, 15 Dec. 1915)

and *nationalisme* with *chauvinisme*:

> Deux ou trois journaux connus pour leur nationalisme intempérant, leur chauvinisme affecté, leur haine intéressée pour tout ce qui est étranger ...
> (*Le Bonnet Rouge*, 23 June 1916)

Similarly, *nationaliste* can be coupled with *revanchard*.[5] The greatest effect is achieved, however, when all three principal terms are involved, as in these lines from G. Hervé:

> Pendant 44 ans, les chauvins, les nationalistes et les patriotards, avec des exagérations qui souvent nous parurent grotesques ou dangereuses, exaltèrent le sentiment patriotique, rappelèrent l'amputation subie après Metz et Sedan. (*La Guerre Sociale*, 6 Sept. 1915)

or this magnificent tirade from *Le Bonnet Rouge*:

Exploits d'embuscomanes[6]

> Les patriotes en chambre, les chauvins qui restent le ventre à table et le dos au feu, les nationalistes "chauffe-la-couche" n'estiment jamais que leurs concitoyens sont assez dévoués au salut du pays. (18 Dec. 1915)

In the case of *les éléments militaristes*, the lexical items in question seem to be differentiated according to areas of specialization rather

---

[5] See above, 3.4, p. 131.
[6] See above, 1.3, pp. 23-4.

than degrees of intensity,[7] but this kind of proximity also enables words to reinforce one another effectively in polemical usage. *Impérialiste* is often coupled with *pangermaniste*, even though the latter would appear to imply it automatically:

> Nous faisons la guerre non au peuple allemand, mais à la caste militaire impérialiste et pangermaniste qui nous vaut les horreurs actuelles.
> (*La Guerre Sociale*, 27 Sept. 1914)

Annexionniste is also found in conjunction with *impérialiste* and *pangermaniste*. Strictly speaking, *pangermaniste* is only applicable to the Germans and to their supporters in other countries. Thus, J. Bainville says of the Russians:

> On sait que, dans la guerre présente, le parti national-libéral s'est montré aussi "annexionniste", aussi pangermaniste, aussi outrancier, que les plus qualifiés des conservateurs[8]

However, the parallel with right-wing attitudes in France remained uppermost in many people's minds. A. Charpentier writes:

> [La paix de Lénine] sera combattue par les pangermanistes, par les impérialistes, par les annexionnistes de tout crin, par ceux qui, en Allemagne, ont la mentalité de nos Barrès et de nos Daudet—car la bêtise humaine n'a pas de patrie. (*Le Pays*, 7 Jan. 1918)

When used pejoratively, the neologism *jusqu'auboutiste* collocates with terms denoting militarists.[9] R. Rolland links it with *militariste*:

> nos plus notoires antipacifistes, militaristes et jusqu'auboutistes d'aujourd'hui ...[10]

and with *impérialiste*:

> Le ministre des Affaires étrangères, Milioukoff, est un impérialiste et jusqu'auboutiste notoire ...[11]

Turning now to the rhetorical accumulation of terms denoting *different* brands of reactionaries in the First World War, one must begin by pointing out that the lines of demarcation between these various bodies are considerably less clear-cut than may have

---

[7] Except, perhaps, *pangermanisme,* although this is a restricted as well as an exaggerated form of *militarisme* and *impérialisme*.

[8] *Comment est née la révolution russe,* Paris, 1917, p. 28.

[9] See above, 3.6, pp. 150-1.

[10] Journal, pp. 1002-3 (Dec. 1916).

[11] Ibid., p. 1170 (7 Apr. 1917).

appeared so far. Some of the ways in which they seem to be connected emerge clearly from definitions and comments supplied by
writers of the time. G. Clairet sums up the characteristics of the
nationalist movement as follows:

> Ne traitez pas tous ces gens-là de malhonnêtes gens ou de diffamateurs.
> Ils vous répondraient qu'ils sont des nationalistes.
>
> Or, ces nationalistes qui voient l'Allemagne partout, ces nationalistes
> qui appellent "boches" les gens qui se font tuer pour la France[12] ... ne
> s'aperçoivent pas que c'est d'Allemagne que viennent les trois ou quatre
> idées rudimentaires qui constituent toute leur philosophie politique.
> Qu'y a-t-il dans la tête d'un nationaliste? Peu de chose; la haine des
> Juifs, le respect du clergé, le culte de l'autorité ...
>
> Ces sottises pourraient porter l'estampille "Made in Germany".[13]
> Antisémitisme, cléricalisme, néo-monarchisme, autant d'importations
> allemandes. (*Le Bonnet Rouge*, 23 June 1916)

The affinities between *les nationalistes* and *les cléricaux* are made
plain by *Le Bonnet Rouge* when it refers to

> La grande vague clérico-nationaliste qui, en quelques années, nous a
> conduits à la guerre ... (21 July 1916)

or

> Les nationalistes français et leurs compères, les cléricaux ... (8 Nov. 1916)

Nationalism taken to extremes finds expression in support for the
monarchy; as *Le Radical* observes:

> M. Ch. Maurras, adhérant à l'idée royaliste, se plut à démontrer en un
> style parfait, que le nationalisme, conduit jusqu'à son expression inté-
> grale, aboutissait à la Royauté.[14] (4 Nov. 1915)

Militarism in its varying forms is also regarded as a typical con-
comitant of nationalism. G. Hervé argues:

> Si nous faisions la paix à l'heure actuelle, j'irais trouver nos nationalistes
> et je leur dirais humblement:
> "C'est vous qui aviez raison quand vous disiez que le militarisme était
> la seule sauvegarde des peuples." (*La Victoire*, 22 Feb. 1916)

P. Boulat puts nationalism on a par with pangermanism:

---

[12] See above, 1.4, pp. 24-5.
[13] See above, 1.6, p. 31.
[14] Cf. the extract by Barbusse from *Le Pays*, above, 3.1, p. 117.

La guerre résulte d'une mentalité créée chez tous les peuples par l'éducation, depuis les temps les plus reculés. C'est une vérité qui apparaît avec évidence, quand on constate la force de propagande mise au service d'une conception particulière, fausse autant que dangereuse, du patriotisme, et qui, selon les latitudes, s'appelle pangermanisme, impérialisme ou nationalisme. Nommons-la simplement esprit de domination.

(*Le Pays*, 2 Dec. 1917)

The close connections between the different components of *la Réaction* provide good material for polemical tirades; the linking of three or more elements seems to have particular rhetorical appeal. The trio favoured by G. Hervé is a cliché in his usage:

Les conservateurs, cléricaux et nationalistes de jadis se réjouissaient de voir les socialistes les plus pacifiques et les plus pacifistes d'antan les aider à faire leur guerre de revanche. (*La Victoire*, 13 Feb. 1916)

Similarly, under the heading "Des neutres nous détestent—ce sont nos réactionnaires qui les dégoûtent", G. Clairet writes:

Nos nationalistes, nos réactionnaires, nos cléricaux, qui parlent toujours au nom du pays, ont présenté à P. Baroja une image tellement odieuse de la France qu'il s'enfuit, dégoûté, sur l'autre rive.

(*Le Bonnet Rouge*, 5 Feb. 1916)

This relentless nationalist-baiter supplies what must be an unrivalled instance of multiple linking:

Les partis cléricaux et nationalistes s'agitent et se démènent, hurlent et crient .... Barrès ou Capus ou Daudet, les royalistes xénophobes, les conservateurs enragés, les cléricaux sectaires, les nationalistes exclusifs et belliqueux, tous cyniques de la politique, contempteurs des idées qui font aimer la France, l'idée de Justice et l'idée de Droit, le principe des nationalités et le respect de la personnalité humaine.

(*Le Bonnet Rouge*, 6 Oct. 1916)

The prevalence in emotive usage of rhetorical elaborations of this kind renders many of the finer distinctions between terms inoperative, and has the effect of drawing them together in a strong network of associations, so that any one item from the series will automatically conjure up the others.[15] The picture of *la Réaction*

---

[15] As an illustration of these linguistic constraints, one might cite the care taken by E. Cahm in his book *Péguy et le nationalisme français, de l'affaire Dreyfus à la Grande Guerre* (Paris, 1972) to justify his use of the expression *nationalisme de gauche*. He is forced to admit that such a collocation "risque de choquer dans le contexte de la vie intellectuelle française" (p. 8), and that it is "contre l'usage

which emerges is that of a unified body of offenders, collectively responsible for the different actions and attitudes which are blamed on it.

linguistique français, il faut le dire" (p. 127). For French speakers, *nationaliste/ nationalisme* acquired a particular meaning through constant association with terms like *militariste, réactionnaire,* etc. in the early years of this century, and the connection has remained. As Cahm concedes (p. 8): "les Français, en lisant 'nationalisme', pensent 'Charles Maurras'."

CONCLUSION

In likening journalists to fighter pilots, *Le Canard Enchaîné* is poking fun at a widely held view of them as soldiers on the home front—"les grands chefs d'armées du 'front moral' français que sont Clemenceau, Hervé, Barrès et Léon Daudet".[2] The press in 1914-18 was the sole purveyor of news and comment to the public, and journalists were in many cases extremely influential figures. Each one had his personal style and reputation which were commented upon by others. *Le Canard Enchaîné* calls Maurras "le rasoir national"[3] (30 Oct. 1918), mocking the tedium of his prose; and Gide, writing of Copeau's patriotic zeal, says: "Les articles qu'il lit, fussent-ils de Barrès, lui paraissent insuffisants, médiocres..."[4] A man like Barrès, who could proclaim in all seriousness:

> Chacun de nous sait que les Français sont là pour qu'il y ait moins de misère entre les hommes. En ce sens, la France est pacifiste; en ce sens, la France est guerrière. L'idée que cette guerre doit être la dernière des guerres, c'est une vieille idée populaire[5]

not unnaturally laid himself open to merciless ridicule. In the fourth chapter of V. Snell's brilliant parody *"Le Jardin de Marrès, par Bérénice"* (the work in which the Master was overheard requesting a ticket *jusqu'au bout* on the tram),[6] Bérénice turns to the great man with the words:

> Devinez, cher Maître, comment on vous appelle dans une feuille que

---

[1] Military correspondent of *L'Écho de Paris*.
[2] L. Marchand, *L'Offensive morale*, p. 237.
[3] A deliberate echo of the saying of the Duc d'Orléans which *L'Action Française* had taken as its motto: "Tout ce qui est *national* est nôtre".
[4] *Journal*, p. 474 (22 Aug. 1914).
[5] *Les Diverses Familles spirituelles de la France*, Paris, 1917, p. 263.
[6] See above, 3.6, p. 144.

je lisais tout à l'heure en métro? ... On vous appelle "Guère à la guerre".[7]
(*L'Humanité*, 20 Oct. 1915)

Polemics in the press were an essential counterpart to activity in
the military sphere; they channelled energies, harnessed anxieties
to specific goals, and provided a safety-valve for the pressures that
built up in a situation of seemingly endless waiting. Concern to
keep up civilian morale was crucial in a protracted war which had
settled down so rapidly to a position of stalemate. It is hardly surprising that it produced the verbal excesses that were so aptly stigmatized as *bourrage de crânes*: a phrase that covered any pronouncement which ran counter to the ideology of the person who
so labelled it. All the words and slogans that have been discussed
in this book were regarded as *bourrage de crânes* by someone. Thus
from the standpoint of the extreme Left, it was *bourrage de crânes*
on the part of their enemies to call them *défaitistes*, or to describe
the Germans as *sales Boches*, while the Right considered the Left
to be displaying the same vice when it designated them *jusqu'auboutistes* and the Germans *Allemands, mais pas Boches*.

One of the most striking things to emerge from this study of
First World War vocabulary is the decisive role played by individual
journalists in launching words and phrases and shaping their subsequent development.[8] It is not fortuitous that this inventiveness
should be so amply illustrated in polemical registers: words, after
all, are the only weapons in this kind of battle, and the success or
failure of the attempt to convince, discredit or shout down an
opponent depends entirely on the skill with which they are handled.
The degree to which journalists' polemics are word-oriented cannot
be over-emphasized: the political evolution of *Le Bonnet Rouge* is

[7] The C.G.T. had entitled a manifesto of 18 Oct. 1912 "Guerre à la guerre"
(see J. -J. Becker, *Le Carnet B,* pp. 189-91). When war broke out this slogan became
popular with left-wing writers seeking to justify their participation in the war effort,
e.g. "Cette guerre, c'est la guerre à la guerre" (G. Hervé, *La Guerre Sociale,*
2 Jan. 1915). The formula *la dernière des guerres* used by Barrès (see above, p. 162)
was also a catch-phrase; popular speech transformed it into *la der des ders* (see
J. Marouzeau, *Aspects du français*, Paris, 1950, p. 96). The title of H. G. Wells's
War that will end War (London, 1914) was translated into French as *La Guerre
qui finira les guerres* (*Le Bonnet Rouge*, 1 Nov. 1914) or *La Guerre qui tuera la
guerre* (G. Valois, *Le Cheval de Troie*, p. 18).
[8] Cf. B. Migliorini, *The Contribution of the Individual to Language,* Oxford,
1952, p. 3: "Not only the general public, but also the majority of linguists, still
underestimate the impact on language of the creative work of individuals."

detected first and foremost through changes in its own vocabulary and in its explicit attitude to that of its adversaries. Much of the value of L. Marchand's study of this paper lies in his linguistic sensitivity.

If it is apparent that to study political vocabulary adequately, one needs to give close attention to the issues preoccupying the public at a given time, it is no less true that an understanding of the way words are used forms an essential part of interpreting the written or spoken records of any period if anachronistic judgements are to be avoided.[9] Barrès once wrote:

> Dame! il faut se servir de son intelligence et comprendre une nation par les hommes et par les idées qui lui servent de drapeau ...
>
> (*L'Écho de Paris*, 29 Sept. 1914)

To do this, one has to begin with words.

---

[9] The word *révolution* is a good case in point. See J. M. Goulemot, "Emplois du mot *Révolution* dans les traductions françaises du XVIIIᵉ siècle des *Discours* de Nicolas Machiavel", *Cahiers de Lexicologie*, xiii (1968), 75-82, and G. Mailhos, "Le mot *Révolution* dans l'*Essai sur les mœurs* et la correspondance de Voltaire", *Cahiers de Lexicologie*, xiii (1968), 84-93.

Appendix I

BIOGRAPHICAL NOTES

Grigory Alexinsky (1879-?)[1]

Grigory Alexinsky was born in 1879 in the province of Dagestan. His father was a doctor employed by the district council, and he had a French grandmother from whom he learned French at an early age. He attended school in Yaroslavl and then enrolled in the Faculty of History and Philology at Moscow University. It was a time of intense revolutionary activity among students. Alexinsky played an active part in the troubles of 1899, 1901 and 1902; he was a prominent figure at political meetings, renowned for his eloquent and witty speeches criticizing the government and the university authorities. When he was arrested and expelled from Moscow, he returned to Yaroslavl to work for local Social-Democratic Party organizations. He passed his state examinations in Moscow in 1905 and joined the Bolsheviks. After the 1905 revolution he was again forced to leave Moscow, and he pursued his political activity in Ekaterinoslav and St. Petersburg, where he contributed regularly to the Bolshevik press.

In 1907 he was elected to the Second State Duma; as leader of the Bolshevik faction he became one of its most outstanding orators. He was one of the sixteen Social-Democratic deputies whom the government sought to arrest for subversive activity: when the Duma refused its consent and was dissolved, Alexinsky managed to escape arrest and decided to emigrate, after publicly attacking his former associate Lenin at the second Social-Democratic Workers' Party Conference in July 1907.

He taught for a time in Italy before settling in Paris, where he studied philology under A. Dauzat at the École Pratique des Hautes Études. He became the leader of a group of Russian socialists hostile to Lenin, editing their publications and acting as their spokesman at conferences. When war broke out he made a definitive break

---

[1] I have been unable to discover the date of his death.

with the Bolsheviks and joined G. Plekhanov in adopting an extreme "defensist" stand. He returned to Russia in April 1917 with the help of the French and British authorities. In July of that year, at the time of the first Bolshevik uprising, he published sensational revelations in the press about the aid received by Lenin from Russia's enemies.[2] When he mounted another attack on the Bolsheviks in April 1918, he was arrested and imprisoned. Nine months later he was let out on bail and the charges against him were dropped. He refused the offer of a post in the Bolshevik government and escaped to Paris in 1919.[3] In 1921 he was condemned to death in his absence by the Revolutionary Tribunal in Moscow and became a permanent exile.

On his return to Paris he began to contribute regular articles on Russian affairs to the *Mercure de France*. He was already known to the French public as the author of *La Russie Moderne* (1912), *La Russie et la Guerre* (1915), and *La Russie et l'Europe* (1917). Other works were to follow: *Du Tsarisme au communisme* (1923), *Un Quart de siècle de régime communiste* (1941), and *La Russie révolutionnaire* (1947).

Miguel Almereyda (1883-1917)

Eugène Bonaventure Vigo was born of Andorran parents on 5 January 1883 at Béziers (Hérault). He came to Paris at the age of seventeen to work as a photographer's apprentice, but soon turned to political journalism, joining the staff of *Le Libertaire* in 1902. A militant anarchist and antimilitarist, he was convicted on a number of occasions for publicly insulting the army, as well as for incitement to murder and for sundry drug and blackmail offences. During a spell in prison in 1905-6 he struck up a friendship with G. Hervé, and soon became a close associate of his when the latter founded *La Guerre Sociale* in December 1906: Vigo was known to its readers as "le lieutenant du général [Hervé]". In 1907 he was condemned to five years' imprisonment for his antimilitarist articles in *La Guerre Sociale*; his political views are summed up in a notorious pronouncement he made in May of that year:

[2] These allegations are of course treated as vile slander in the entry devoted to Alexinsky in the *Entsiklopedicheskiĭ Slovar' Russkogo Bibliograficheskogo Instituta Granat*, 7th edn., vol. ii and supplement, Moscow, 1910 and 1936.

[3] He recounts these adventures in his *Souvenirs d'un condamné à mort*, Paris, 1923.

Actuellement, notre propagande doit se traduire par des actes sérieux. En cas de guerre, il faut prendre l'engagement de ne pas marcher. Les prolétaires ne doivent pas se borner à dire: "Nous ne marchons pas." Ils doivent faire en sorte de jeter la perturbation...

Tout citoyen doit être antipatriote: il lui doit être indifférent d'être Allemand ou Français.[4]

In 1910 he formed the *Association des jeunes gardes révolutionnaires* to combat the *camelots du roi*. Two years later he decided to join the Socialist Party—a step which was bitterly resented by his anarchist friends. In November 1913 he founded *Le Bonnet Rouge*, a weekly publication which became a daily in March 1914.

The pseudonym *Almereyda* was invented by him as a deliberate piece of bravado: M. Barrès alluded to "l'anagramme que le directeur du *Bonnet Rouge* avait voulu enclore en son nom" (*L'Écho de Paris*, 24 July 1917), and L. Daudet frequently reminded his readers that the name meant no less than *la merde y a*. As a result of his beliefs and his behaviour, his name figured prominently on the pages of the *Carnet B*—a list kept by the Ministry of the Interior of suspect individuals who were to be arrested at once in the event of war to prevent any attempt to sabotage mobilization.[5] In August 1914, however, Malvy decided not to put the *Carnet B* into effect, hoping thereby to avoid antagonizing the extreme Left, and to bring them into the *Union sacrée* pact. Almereyda boasted that he had been instrumental in Malvy's decision; in an article in *Le Bonnet Rouge* of 31 October 1915, he claimed to have persuaded the Minister not to arrest *les militants de la classe ouvrière*, promising to vouch in person for their loyalty. In spite of his age he was not called up, because, as he explained:

M. Malvy m'a dit: "Pour le moment, des hommes comme vous sont plus utiles à Paris qu'à la frontière; je vous prie de rester."[6]

The close dealings which Malvy had with Almereyda and his disreputable associates were to form the basis of the charges brought against the Minister by his opponents later in the war. In reply to Clemenceau's direct attack in the Senate, he said that he had withdrawn his support from Almereyda (payments to the tune

---

[4] Quoted by G. Clemenceau in a speech to the Senate, 22 July 1917 (*Discours de guerre,* p. 73).

[5] See J. -J. Becker, *Le Carnet B. Les pouvoirs publics et l'antimilitarisme avant la guerre de 1914,* Paris, 1973.

[6] Quoted by Clemenceau, *Discours de guerre,* p. 81.

of 8,000 francs per month, as it subsequently emerged[7]) as soon
as *Le Bonnet Rouge* had abandoned its patriotic line, but his critics
produced evidence of his continued leniency towards pacifist agitators.

Almereyda's motives for engaging in the treasonable activities
which led to his final arrest were no doubt ideological in part;
G. Hervé reports a statement which Almereyda made to their
mutual friend Dulac:

> Toi, tu es aveugle; lorsque tu verras clair, il sera trop tard, le pays sera
> perdu et toute la jeunesse fauchée par le champ de bataille; le mieux
> serait une paix immédiate avec les résultats nuls.
>
> (*La Victoire*, 25 Nov. 1917)

But he was also a reckless adventurer in need of a constant supply
of money from whatever source to provide for his expensive tastes.
In a sinister way, the unsolved mystery of his violent death in the
prison at Fresnes on 14 August 1917, in circumstances strongly
suggesting foul play, belongs wholly to the underworld of dangerous intrigue in which he had lived.

Henry Bérenger (1867-1952)

Henry Bérenger was born on 22 April 1867 at Rugles (Eure) of
Norman and Breton parents. He completed his education in Paris
at the Lycée Henri IV and at the Sorbonne, where he won the *con-
cours général de philosophie* and obtained a *licence ès lettres*. His
major works all date from the 1890s: *L'Âme moderne* (1892),
L'Effort (1893), *L'Aristocratie intellectuelle* (1895), *La Proie*
(1897), *La Conscience nationale* (1898) and *La France intellectuelle*
(1899)—the first three of which won awards from the *Académie
Française*. In 1898 he became a Dreyfusard and a virulent anticlerical. He founded his own newspaper *L'Action* in 1903; from
there he moved on to become editor of *Le Siècle* in 1908 and then
of *Paris-Midi* in 1911. He wrote regular leaders for the latter
throughout the First World War, with occasional interruptions
when he was absent from Paris on official missions.

In 1912 he became a Senator representing Guadeloupe. His

---

[7] "La vérité fut révélée, à ce sujet, quelque temps après. M. Malvy reconnut,
devant le groupe radical-socialiste de la Chambre, auquel il appartenait, avoir
subventionné mensuellement de 8000 francs, sur les fonds secrets, Almereyda sous
prétexte 'd'encourager son patriotisme'" (G. Bonnefous, *La Grande Guerre*, p. 304
n. 1).

political affiliations were to the *Radicaux-socialistes*, and in the immediate pre-war years he took part in the press campaign against Caillaux and his proposed income-tax reforms. In August 1914 he was responsible for a law preventing the press from divulging military secrets in wartime. As member of a commission set up to investigate the running of France's economy, he sponsored a bill in 1917 to introduce *la mobilisation civile*. He had campaigned relentlessly since the outbreak of war for the proper deployment of the nation's energies, particularly in ensuring a regular supply of armaments and fuel; in recognition of his talent and foresight Clemenceau appointed him *Haut-Commissaire aux essences et aux combustibles* in August 1918. His vice-presidency of the *Commission sénatoriale de l'Armée* led him to become personally involved in the attempt to establish the causes of the mutinies in the army in May 1917.

His subsequent career was equally distinguished: he was sent to Washington in 1925 as a parliamentary delegate to look into the question of Inter-Allied war debts, and became French Ambassador to the United States in 1926. In 1931 he succeeded Victor Bérard as President of the *Commission des Affaires étrangères*, and the following year he was sent to represent France at the League of Nations. He spoke out actively in *La Sémaphore* against Hitler and Mussolini, and in 1938 played a prominent part in organizing aid to Jewish refugees. In June 1940 he abstained from the vote which brought Pétain to power, and retired from political life.

There can be no doubt that Bérenger owed much of his success as a politician to his masterly command of language. His journalistic writings reveal a remarkable understanding of the suggestive power of words. The *Dictionnaire des parlementaires français*[8] describes him as "l'avocat inlassable des mesures énergiques et des décisions bien tranchées", and pays tribute to his "éloquence pleine de fantaisie et d'originalité, toujours brillante". But his was never gratuitous rhetoric; his inventiveness in devising new slogans and exploiting them to the full was always put to the service of whatever cause he might be immersed in at the time. He has two major linguistic innovations to his credit: he played a crucial role in popularizing the noun *intellectuel* in the 1890s,[9] and in 1917 his

[8] Vol. ii, Paris, 1962.
[9] See G. Idt, "'L'Intellectuel' avant l'Affaire Dreyfus", *Cahiers de Lexicologie*, xv (1969), 35-46, and W. M. Johnston, "The Origin of the Term 'Intellectuals'

initiative was responsible for launching the neologism *défaitisme*. These contributions to the vocabulary of French (and thereby to other European languages as well) deserve to go down in history.

Léon Daudet (1868-1942)

Alphonse Daudet's son Léon was born in Paris on 16 November 1867. He was educated at the Lycée Louis-le-Grand and embarked on a medical career, but soon abandoned it in favour of the literary world.[10] His novels include *Les Morticoles* (1894), *Fantômes et vivants* (1914), and *L'Hérédo* (1917), and he was elected to the Académie Goncourt in 1897. He grew up in Republican circles, and remained loyal to them at the time of the Boulangist movement; later, he made a name for himself in journalism by his antisemitic writing for *La Libre Parole*. In March 1908, won over to the *nationalisme intégral* of Charles Maurras, he joined with him in founding the daily *L'Action Française*[11] where he openly advocated the restoration of the Duc d'Orléans to the French throne. In 1891 he married Victor Hugo's grand-daughter Jeanne, but they divorced in 1895 and Daudet married his first cousin Marthe Allard in 1903.

Daudet was unquestionably one of the most gifted polemicists of the First World War period. An extremely prolific writer (he was the author of numerous books on political subjects, as well as of daily articles in *L'Action Française*), he cultivated the art of hammering home his points by endless repetition of a few well-chosen themes. His writings are racy and witty, often inaccurate, and though what he says is sometimes quite outrageous—deliberately so—he seems to sweep his readers along with him through the sheer force of his language. One of his most characteristic devices is the development of a kind of jargon or code, making use of picturesque and suggestive terms to refer to his enemies. These are not intended to be hermetic, for Daudet will redefine them periodically for the benefit of new readers or absent-minded old ones. The aim is to create a highly charged atmosphere of com-

in French Novels and Essays of the 1890's", *Journal of European Studies*, iv (1974), 43-56. The latter provides a warm appraisal of Bérenger's literary achievement, and regrets the undeserved oblivion into which he has fallen. I hope that my findings will contribute to enhancing Bérenger's reputation.

[10] According to E. J. Weber, because of "an injustice suffered, or assumed, in a competitive examination" (*Action Française,* p. 44).

[11] The Action Française movement had published a fortnightly *Revue de l'Action Française* from July 1899 to 1908.

plicity between himself and his public. He was a great coiner of words, most of them ephemeral, and showed a predilection for puns of all varieties. For instance, describing the protests raised in certain quarters about the supposedly slanderous allegations of which Caillaux had become the object, he writes:

> Ce Téry demanda ... une loi nouvelle contre 'la calomnie', ou plus exactement contre la caillaumnie.[12]

Again, expostulating about the capricious ways of officialdom, he explains that on one occasion Painlevé ordered him to hand in his newspaper article to the censorship at six o'clock on the evening before it was due to appear, only to revoke the decision on the very next day:

> Le jour suivant, la consigne était levée et même, si je puis dire, pain-levée ...[13]

Daudet's highly idiosyncratic views were coupled with a grossly inflated sense of his own importance. His "Vœux pour 1917" published in *L'Action Française* on 1 January contain a blueprint for victory in the form of wishes that all the various spies and traitors infesting France should be expelled or brought to justice forthwith. He concludes as follows:

> Je souhaite qu'on me confie l'exécution de la partie de ce programme qui relève particulièrement de ma compétence. Je me charge de la réaliser sans faiblir et sans délai.

Small wonder that he became an object of ridicule in the left-wing press: *Le Pays* calls him "le Garde des Sots" and, punning on the title of his father's book, "le Gros Chose" (7 Apr. 1918). His fanatical politics inspired such extreme hatred that he believed his son Philippe had fallen victim to it when the boy died in mysterious circumstances in 1923. Daudet's attempts to prove that he had been murdered (and had not committed suicide in an unbalanced state of mind, as his death was officially explained) led only to his own conviction and imprisonment on a charge of libel.[14] He escaped from prison to Belgium in 1927, where he continued to write; he was pardoned and returned to France in 1929. Later, in 1935, he was to follow G. Hervé's lead in championing the cause of Pétain.

[12] *Le Poignard dans le dos*, p. 46.
[13] Ibid., p. 58.
[14] For a detailed account of the case, see E. J. Weber, *Action Française*, ch. 9.

172   BIOGRAPHICAL NOTES

Gustave Hervé (1871-1944)

Gustave Hervé was born in Brest of Breton descent on 2 January 1871. A man of versatile talent, he started his professional life as an *agrégé d'histoire*, appointed first to the Lycée at Rodez in 1897 and then to Sens in 1899. His early admiration for Déroulède soon gave way to an outspoken rejection of nationalism; he joined the Socialist Party and became an active antimilitarist. He was taken to court in 1901 for an antimilitarist article which had appeared in *Le Pioupiou de l'Yonne*, a supplement to *Le Travailleur Socialiste de l'Yonne* intended for recruits. Although acquitted of the charges against him, thanks to the skill of his counsel Aristide Briand, he was nonetheless struck from the register of the University. His famous article "L'Anniversaire de Wagram", signed *un Sans-Patrie*, was published in *Le Travailleur Socialiste de l'Yonne* on 20 July 1901, a few days before his first court appearance. Commenting with disapproval on the way in which the regiment stationed at Auxerre had celebrated the anniversary of the battle of Wagram, Hervé wrote:

> Tant qu'il y aura des casernes, pour l'édification et la moralisation des soldats de notre démocratie, pour déshonorer à leurs yeux le militarisme et les guerres de conquête, je voudrais qu'on rassemblât dans la principale cour du quartier toutes les ordures et tout le fumier de la caserne et que, solennellement, en présence de toutes les troupes en tenue n° 1, au son de la musique militaire, le colonel, en grand plumet, vînt y planter le drapeau du régiment.[15]

Thereafter, the press was to associate Hervé with the slogan *le drapeau dans le fumier*,[16] and to remind him mercilessly of his famous pronouncement when he subsequently modified his views.

Forced to begin a new career, Hervé turned to Law; he qualified as a barrister in July 1905, but was struck from the register in November for the revolutionary activities which earned him a conviction to four years' imprisonment along with Almereyda and Yvetot, who were each sentenced to three. All of them were granted an amnesty on 14 July 1906. Hervé was one of the few prominent

---

[15] This "article du drapeau dans le fumier" is widely but wrongly believed to be the one for which he was taken to court. It is reproduced in *Mes Crimes,* pp. 23-9.
[16] Clemenceau refers to him simply as "l'homme du drapeau dans le fumier" (*L'Homme Enchaîné,* 3 Apr. 1916).

socialists (as opposed to anarchists) to have his name included in the *Carnet B*.[17]

In December 1906 Hervé founded his own newspaper *La Guerre Sociale*, where he continued to voice the antimilitarist and anti-patriotic ideals of the extreme wing of the French Socialist Party. By 1912, however, as he was fond of explaining to his readers in frequent attempts to justify his change of heart,[18] he had come to realize that the German Socialists would be powerless to revolt against their government, and he therefore renounced his motto *plutôt l'insurrection que la guerre*, fearing that Prussia's imperialist aims would only be furthered if the French Socialists refused to fight. From then until 1914 he preached the cause of Franco-German *détente*, and when war eventually broke out, he once more became the staunchest of patriots, moving rapidly to the right of his party and bitterly opposing the Zimmerwald peace conference of September 1915, and the *minoritaires* who supported it. Despite his claims to have remained faithful to his fundamental ideology while adapting his practical decisions to meet the demands of an evolving situation, Hervé was widely regarded by his detractors as a political chameleon unworthy of respect: Maurras referred patronizingly to him as "notre bonne girouette nationale" and "le gobe-mouche national" (*L'Action Française*, 23 Dec. 1915). At the end of December 1915 Hervé decided that *La Guerre Sociale* was unfitting as a name for his paper at a time when all Frenchmen were pledged to forget their differences in the *Union Sacrée* pact, and he rechristened it *La Victoire* with effect from 1 January 1916. But he was not allowed to forget his pre-war attitudes; Maurras, after predicting that everyone would call Hervé *le Père la Victoire*, soon had second thoughts:

> Contrairment à l'opinion exprimée ici hier, Gustave Hervé, en dépit du nouveau titre de son journal, pourrait bien s'appeler le Père la Défaite, car il n'a rien négligé pour la préparer.
>
> (*L'Action Française*, 24 Dec. 1915)

Paris-Midi observed, with reference to the internal dissensions of the French Socialist Party, that the meaning of the term *hervéisme* would have to change to fit Hervé's new stand:

[17] See J.-J. Becker, *Le Carnet B*, p. 179.
[18] See e.g. *La Guerre Sociale*, 27 Dec. 1915.

Le néo-hervéisme

Le mot "hervéisme" servait naguère à définir une certaine nuance assez grossière d'antipatriotisme. Nous l'emploierons, désormais, à d'autres fins. Il désignera le socialisme nationaliste,—ou national, comme dit Hervé en sa *Victoire*:

"Socialisme nationaliste! nous font dédaigneusement les socialistes de Zimmerwald. Non! socialisme national seulement, et ce socialisme national n'a, en France, qu'a remonter à ses sources, à Blanqui, à Saint-Simon, à la Révolution française ..." (3 Apr. 1916)

His move towards nationalism became so marked that in September 1918 he was expelled from the Socialist Party by the former *minoritaires* who had now taken over as the majority: "Je suis excommunié par l'Église socialiste", he wrote in *La Victoire* of 26 September 1918. With the loss of his revolutionary faith he returned to the fold of Catholicism in 1926. The following year he founded his own *Parti socialiste national* of strongly fascist leanings. He continued to advocate a strong, authoritarian Republic in his articles in *La Victoire*, and in 1935 he launched his famous campaign: "*C'est Pétain qu'il nous faut!*"[19] *La Victoire* was the first to become a collaborationist paper in 1940.

Hervé was a prominent figure in journalists' polemics in the First World War, renowned not only for his views but equally for his blunt and forthright expression of them. Léon Daudet acknowledged a certain flair in this "révolutionnaire sans cervelle, mais non sans talent";[20] Almereyda named him "notre Pangloss national" (*Le Bonnet Rouge*, 11 Apr. 1916) on account of his unshakable optimism, and *La Lanterne*, in a regular column given over to his exploits, paid this splendid tribute to his heavy-handed eloquence:

Gustave Hervé ou l'Homme heureux

Avec ce mépris absolu de ses lecteurs qui compose sa plus sûre originalité dans la presse française, M. Gustave Hervé, favori de tous les Hasards, va de présomption en présomption, de contradiction en contradiction, avec la grâce lourdement sonore d'un bourdon ivre d'air et divaguant entre les orties. (21 Dec. 1915)

His admirers saw in him "un caractère entier, assoiffé d'absolu, peu clairvoyant, naïf peut-être, mais sincère dans ses convictions successives et contradictoires".[21]

---

[19] See R. Griffiths, *Marshal Pétain*, pp. 175 ff.
[20] *L'Hécatombe*, p. 44.
[21] *Dictionnaire biographique du mouvement ouvrier français*, vol. xiii, Paris, 1975.

Appendix II

REPRESENTATIVE TEXTS

Text 1: G. Hervé, *La Guerre Sociale*, 14 Aug. 1914

La Peur des Espions

Il faudrait quand même que la partie du public qui a conservé toute sa lucidité intellectuelle et toute sa santé morale réagisse contre cette espèce de maladie qui s'est emparée du pays, et qui lui fait voir des ennemis partout.

Ça a commencé par cet ignoble et stupide pillage des boutiques Maggi. Parce qu'il y avait des Suisses allemands à la tête de cette grande administration, est-ce qu'il ne s'est pas trouvé de pauvres gobe-mouches pour croire que la Société Maggi était une vaste société d'espionnage et d'empoisonnement!! Les chiffres qu'on lisait sur les affiches Maggi étaient des signes cabalistiques, des indications pour les troupes allemandes! Vérification faite, c'étaient les dates et les numéros d'enregistrement des affiches!

La province est aussi malade que la capitale.

L'autre jour, à Nancy, un ancien notaire de cette ville, patriote à tous crins, et même nationaliste, qui revenait de Lorraine, racontait, sur une place, à un de ses amis, ce qu'il avait vu de l'autre côté de la frontière. Un benêt vient à passer. Il entend un bout de conversation. Pas de doute. C'est un espion. Vite, il ameute les badauds. Tous les gobe-mouches du voisinage accourent. Et c'est la ruée sur le malheureux notaire, qui reste sur le carreau, grièvement blessé.

A Versailles, c'est un consul honoraire de Belgique, M. de Meeus, demeurant avenue de Saint-Cloud, qui est arrêté à la légère comme espion, par la police, et qu'on dut relâcher après qu'on eut reconnu qu'il était Belge, marié à une Française, et, de plus, un chaud ami de la France.

A Paris, il ne se passe guère de jour sans qu'une méprise se commette à l'égard de quelque honnête citoyen.

....

Ce journal n'y suffirait pas, s'il fallait les raconter toutes.

Voyons! ça devient du maboulisme! Avez-vous jamais rien vu de plus sot que cette peur folle des espions?

Les espions?

Même s'il y en a, que diable voulez-vous qu'ils espionnent?

Comment diable voulez-vous qu'ils renseignent leur gouvernement?

Avec quoi?

Le gouvernement tient le télégraphe et les téléphones.

Il garde les lettres, par mesure de salut public.

Une auto ne peut pas franchir une porte de ville, ne peut pas circuler en rase campagne, sans que ceux qui l'occupent soient obligés d'exhiber leurs papiers.

Qu'ils fassent sauter des ponts?

Est-ce que tout n'est pas gardé, archi-gardé, depuis quinze jours?

Vraiment, ça vaut bien la peine d'avoir donné au monde l'exemple du courage et de la bonne humeur au moment de la mobilisation; ça vaut bien la peine d'avoir entre l'ennemi et nous un million de braves et de héros, qui vont étonner le monde par leur belle furie française, pour faire dans ses culottes parce qu'il y aurait un espion par-ci par-là, perdu dans le flot d'étrangers amis de la France, qui lui témoignent tous leur affection en ce moment de façon si touchante.

Si, par miracle, des espions allemands pouvaient communiquer avec leur gouvernement, la seule chose qu'ils pourraient lui révéler, c'est que ça ne se passe pas du tout comme en 70!

Que ça n'est pas comme en 70, eh! braves gens, les généraux allemands n'ont pas besoin d'espions pour le leur apprendre.

Nos soldats de l'armée de Sambre-et-Meuse et de l'armée du Rhin le leur ont déjà fait savoir!

Text 2: H. Lavedan, *L'Illustration,* 7 July 1917

Sabotage Moral

Dans un de ces accès de verve qui sont coutumiers à la malice de notre race, une expression drôle et d'argot bien venue est lancée. Elle amuse et fait rire. On l'adopte, on la propage. La voilà populaire. Mais bientôt, à force d'en user, on en abuse, on la détourne de son premier sens, on cesse de lui donner son application véritable et limitée. Du trait juste et léger qu'elle était d'abord elle devient une arme perfide et dangereuse, et quand on s'aperçoit du mal que fait cet enfant terrible du langage auquel on fut si complaisant, il est trop tard. La phrase, emportée, a le mors aux dents; vous ne la tenez plus.

C'est ce qui est arrivé pour "bourrage de crâne".

Destinée au début à marquer et à railler les bavards majestueux, les professionnels des grands mots et des clichés oratoires, ou les énergumènes du courage d'autrui, cette locution pittoresque et satisfaisante a peu à peu dévié et s'est mise à battre la campagne, jusqu'au moment où, ramassée à dessein par les esprits louches qui la guettaient, elle a commencé d'être, sous leurs menées, un moyen provocateur et sûr de dissolution, une formule de déchéance et d'épuisement.

L'art exécrable des agents de ruine qui veulent notre perte a été de se rappeler et de saisir tout de suite l'importance qu'ont les mots réussis et tout le parti qu'on en peut tirer grâce à un habile maquignonnage

Nulle part ailleurs plus qu'en France on n'a la sainte peur des mots. Avec un mot bien inventé et traîtreusement placé, au bon endroit ainsi qu'à la minute précise, on fait reculer le plus intrépide. Et, entre les mots susceptibles d'agir avec force sur nous, ceux qui ont pour intention spéciale et pour but d'éveiller le sentiment du ridicule et l'épouvante de l'ennui, sont toujours assurés d'obtenir leur plein effet. Être ridicule, ou ennuyeux... quelle horreur! Être l'un ou l'autre, ou les deux à la fois, ces simples suppositions nous glacent. Tel qui risquerait les pires dangers n'ose braver celui de passer pour importun. La réputation de fâcheux, de "raseur", est la seule à laquelle aucun homme ne sache consentir. Chose pitoyable... qu'il suffise au premier imbécile venu de se passer la main sur la joue d'une certaine façon ou de laisser tomber ces mots si délicats: la barbe! pour clouer sur place immédiatement son interlocuteur en train d'être courageux et l'empêcher de faire son devoir! C'est le privilège en même temps que la faiblesse des natures les plus fines, les plus élevées, les plus tendres, de subir à l'extrême cette terreur d'ennuyer. Le moindre signe les arrête. Un geste outré de lassitude, des épaules harassées, des yeux au ciel ont plus vite et plus aisément raison d'eux que la riposte ou l'invective... Avec le simulacre de bâiller on met en fuite un apôtre.

*   *   *

Ayant la clef de cette intimidation, les fauteurs de trouble et de mésentente en jouent à coup sûr. Grâce à cette formule redoutable du "bourrage de crâne" ils créent à plaisir la gêne et l'embarras précurseurs de désordres plus graves. C'est à eux que revient le déshonneur d'avoir produit ce genre particulier de respect humain qui obstrue l'effort et brise l'élan, qui fait rougir d'un sentiment louable et rend honteux d'une vertu.

Il nous est facile, en effet, de voir qu'observant une régularité de méthode très significative, ces éternels mécontents du bien ne lancent jamais leurs sarcasmes et leurs reproches qu'à l'adresse de ceux qui parlent de courage, de patience, de raison, de sagesse et de fermeté. Voilà les seuls coupables, les seuls intempérants qui méritent d'être signalés à la condamnation publique! S'agit-il d'apaiser la douleur, d'essayer de guérir un mal, de démontrer la nécessité, d'indiquer le but, de faire entendre la voix qui rassure et ranime... on bourre. Bourrage! Bourrage! Mais par contre, s'il plaît au *bourré*, plus impressionnable que la sensitive, d'entamer vingt fois par jour son rabâchage de pessimisme et sa complainte d'amertume... ne lui dites pas que c'est lui qui bourre et d'une façon bien plus néfaste et bien plus assommante... Car il prétend s'arroger le droit de juger, de blâmer, de dénigrer, de calomnier, d'accuser, de tout dire à tort et à travers, et d'être justement, à cause de cela, écouté comme un dieu. Ses paroles à lui sont sacrées dès lors qu'elles ont pour mission d'abattre et d'amener la chute. Non, en effet, il ne bourre pas.

Que fait-il donc?

Il vide, et non seulement il vide les crânes mais aussi les os, les veines, les cœurs. Il pompe les moelles de l'énergie et suce les forces vitales. Là où les bons Samaritains de la guerre essaient de redonner du sang à l'organisme de leur frère et d'en opérer au besoin la transfusion en offrant le leur, les Compagnons de la défaillance viennent traîtreusement couper à la dérobée les artères du camarade pour goûter la joie satanique de voir ce sang régénérateur se perdre et couler sans profit. Ces hommes là, dans leur hypocrisie monstrueuse, ressemblent aux macabres rôdeurs qui achèvent et dévalisent sur les champs de bataille les blessés à bout de souffle ou évanouis; ils sont les Thénardier du patriotisme. Comme on fait d'une poche, ils retournent les consciences pour en secouer au vent les richesses qu'on y avait mises.

Que de diversités présentent leurs manèges! Tortionnaires sournois, ceux-ci raclent, ceux-là dépiautent. Il y a les dissolvants et les stupéfiants. Les uns vous empoisonnent ainsi qu'avec une poudre

versée dans un verre, ou vous étourdissent comme avec un cigare par
des raisonnements vénéneux qui vous abrutissent, vous font dormir
et vous plongent dans le coma de la lâcheté. On n'est plus capable
alors que de descendre—comme jadis les énervés de Jumièges—au
fil des événements et de se laisser emporter par les courants mortels
puisqu'on a perdu le pouvoir de les remonter. Les autres, plus
actifs et plus offensifs dans leurs criminelle entreprise, méritent
d'être assimilés aux anarchistes du fait. Armés "de ces bâtons que
l'on met dans les roues" et de tous les outils du cambriolage intellectuel, ils imitent, dans le domaine des idées et des sentiments,
les malfaiteurs qui dévissent l'écrou, percent le réservoir, retirent la
traverse et déplacent le rail pour que le train culbute en pleine
vitesse. En bons désorganisateurs, ils n'organisent que la catas-
trophe. Ainsi, quelle que soit leur manière, ils n'ont tous que ce
même but infâme: *le sabotage moral.* Faute de posséder les moyens
d'endommager l'appareil, ils tâchent de fausser du moins l'esprit
de celui qui le monte. Ne pouvant prendre son fusil des mains du
soldat qui le tient bien, ils essaient de lui retirer son courage, de lui
faire jeter ses autres munitions, celles de sa patience et de son
énergie, et de percer ses cartouches pour que la poudre s'en échappe.
En agitant ici, pour nous, à l'arrière, leur mot-épouvantail de
"bourrage de crâne", les apaches du vide n'ont pas d'autre souci,
en effet, que d'atteindre par ricochet le soldat, de créer entre lui et
nous une espèce de malaise, d'antagonisme scélérat. C'est au nom
des soldats dont ils se constituent sans qualité les représentants
qu'ils osent nous défendre de leur rendre hommage.

Nous avisons-nous d'admirer ces frères magnifiques?—Inutile,
disent les chiourmes, cela *les* ennuie!...

Plaignons-nous leur souffrance et cherchons-nous à la calmer?—
Assez! cela *les* froisse...

Voulons-nous leur crier notre amour?—Gardez-le... *Ils* s'en
moquent! ...

Alors, quoi?—Taisez-vous!

Oui, c'est bien cela! Le silence! Voilà ce que voudraient les
siffleurs du doute et de l'abandon... C'est à quoi rampe et tâche
d'aboutir leur politique de serpent... *Ne plus parler du seul et grand
devoir pour qu'on arrive à n'y plus penser.*

Nous ne tomberons pas dans ce piège impie. Le mutisme n'a
jamais été une condition essentielle de chaleur, de force et de foi.
Toujours on a voulu parler de ce qu'on aime et à ceux que l'on aime.

Pour exprimer les sursauts les plus nobles de la conscience, on ne dit pas qu'elle se tait, mais qu'elle parle; et c'est elle, la parole, que l'on attribue aux morts comme suprême grâce quand on est obligé de leur accorder une part de survivance et une action souveraine dans nos destinées. Continuons donc tous, en dépit des railleurs impuissants, de tenir avec sérénité le seul langage que nous commande aujourd'hui le devoir, et, quand nos soldats à l'avant n'ont peur de rien, n'ayons pas peur, ici, d'un mot.

Text 3: H. Bérenger, *Le Matin*, 6 June 1917

L'HEURE DÉCISIVE
AU TOURNANT DES DÉMOCRATIES
Défaitisme ou organisation?

Le vote de la Chambre des députés vient de poser dans toute sa clarté tragique le problème nouveau de la guerre.

Nous sommes arrivés à un tournant des démocraties en guerre où elles peuvent sombrer dans le défaitisme ou s'élever jusqu'à l'organisation.

Il a d'abord semblé que la révolution russe et l'adhésion des États-Unis raccourciraient la guerre. Du fond de leurs tranchées de trois ans, les soldats de la liberté poussèrent le cri de la délivrance.

Puis l'horizon s'est recouvert. Des nuages, levés de la mer et de la steppe, ont glacé les esprits et reculé les mirages. On s'est dit: "C'est bien long, l'effort américain! Et où donc s'évanouit l'effort russe?"

Jamais, convenons-en, pareille sueur d'angoisse n'avait encore coulé sur les fronts mouillés de nos athlètes. Jamais l'esprit de lassitude n'aura reçu de pareils gages pour perdre, par une seule défaillance, un trésor d'héroïsmes.

Jamais non plus l'esprit démocratique n'aura engagé dans l'univers de plus hautes responsabilités. Jamais il n'aura risqué un plus décisif corps à corps avec les puissances d'autocratie.

Peuple de France, et vous, peuples frères d'Angleterre et d'Italie, noble et antique trinité des civilisations d'Occident, j'en appelle à vos origines, j'en appelle à vos révolutions, j'en appelle à vos résurrections, j'en appelle à tout l'idéal humain dont vous avez la charge. Allez-vous tomber sur les genoux dans le dernier quart d'heure de la bataille? Allez-vous déshonorer, d'une seule déchéance, tout votre honneur et celui de l'humanité?

Eh bien, non! Je réponds d'avance avec vous: L'OCCIDENT NE S'AGENOUILLERA PAS. LES DÉMOCRATIES NE SE DÉSHONORERONT PAS. L'ORGANISATION AURA RAISON DU DÉFAITISME.

* * * * *

Parlons net. Les démocracies ont aujourd'hui à combattre un ennemi plus dangereux que le kaiser, et *cet ennemi est en elles*. On l'affuble, depuis quelque temps, d'un nom nouveau: Le "Défaitisme". Mais c'est une vieille connaissance. Elle s'appelle l'Anarchie.

L'anarchie est aux démocraties ce que la mort est à la vie: un ferment de dissolution qui décompose les formes organisées et les livre, pourries et défaites, à tous les envahissements du dehors.

Il n'y a jamais eu de meilleur auxiliaire de l'étranger que l'anarchie. C'est par l'anarchie que les républiques grecques ont péri devant Rome et les républiques italiennes devant l'Autriche. C'est aussi par l'anarchie que la république polonaise disparut au XVIIIe siècle. C'est par l'anarchie qu'aujourd'hui encore Guillaume espère asservir Orient et Occident.

La démocratie vise à l'égalité de tous par la liberté de chacun. Comme cela n'est pas dans la nature, c'est une entreprise difficile, une véritable œuvre d'art, qui, comme tous les chefs-d'œuvre, réclame du temps, de l'ordre, un consentement commun de discipline, l'organisation d'une force qui se fasse respecter au dedans et se défende au dehors.

L'anarchie, elle, veut bien de l'égalité et de la liberté, mais elle ne veut ni de la discipline, ni de la force, ni du patriotisme. Elle aboutit ainsi fatalement au désordre, au *défaitisme*.

Dans les démocraties fortement nationales et organisées, comme nos démocraties d'Occident, le défaitisme ne naît pas spontanément. Mails il peut devenir une maladie contagieuse, vers la fin d'une longue guerre, si chaque citoyen ne prend, contre le germe et ceux qui l'apportent, toutes les précautions d'antisepsie nécessaires.

* * * * *

D'où nous vient aujourd'hui le défaitisme? Pas de l'Amérique, assurément, mais de la seule Russie.

Et qui nous l'apporte?

La seule Internationale.

Ceci mérite qu'on y réfléchisse doublement.

Nous avons salué avec sympathie la révolution russe, parce que nous nous sommes plu à la comparer à la Révolution française, et qu'en effet elle lui ressemblait par certains traits, comme une benjamine éloignée et douloureuse.

Cependant, la Révolution française n'était pas née de l'invasion étrangère, mais de la révolte intérieure!

La Révolution française est partie de la liberté pour aboutir à la victoire. Elle était fille de la grandeur de nos siècles passés. Elle a mérité d'être la mère glorieuse de nos siècles futurs.

Les autres démocraties d'Occident sont toutes issues d'une filiation semblable de liberté contre l'étranger. C'est l'Angleterre avec Cromwell; c'est l'Amérique avec Washington; c'est l'Italie avec Garibaldi. Dans toutes, le patriotisme en armes ne s'est pas séparé de l'indépendance en action. Dans toutes, la démocratie s'est disciplinée pour la nation par la victoire.

Dernière venue parmi les révolutions, la russe se présente à nous sous une figure un peu plus énigmatique. Démocratie ou anarchie? Patriotisme ou défaitisme? On ne sait encore.

Il pèse sur ces mystères un reste de fatalisme asiatique. Ce n'est plus le cri enflammé des volontaires de la *Marseillaise.* C'est, par moments, la mélopée résignée des mystiques du Nirvâna, père authentique du *Nitchevo* ...

Le plus grave tort de cette apparence d'Internationale que nous rapportaient l'autre jour de Petrograd deux imprudents pèlerins de Stockholm, c'est qu'elle manque de pureté.

Qu'est-ce qu'une Internationale qui commence par reconnaître le kaiser en ouvrant la conversation avec ses Boches du 4 août 1914, les Scheidemann et les Sudekum du chiffon de papier et de "nécessité n'a pas de loi"?

Qu'est-ce qu'une Internationale qui accepte de causer avec l'envahisseur quand l'envahisseur fusille encore, assassine encore, viole encore, déporte encore, maintient sa prétention au massacre et au vol?

Ce n'est pas plus l'Internationale véritable que l'anarchie n'est le socialisme!

Ce n'est qu'une caricature d'Internationale, pauvre défroque de déshonneur et de trahison qu'on nous offre à troquer contre la robe splendide et couverte du sang des martyrs de la démocratie universelle.

Héritières du droit antique, porteuses d'un plus illustre droit, comment nos démocraties d'Occident s'abaisseraient-elles à un renoncement aussi vil?

La France, l'Angleterre, l'Italie, l'Amérique et, espérons-le encore, la Russie encore à leur exemple, mais non elles au sien, se souviendront que si le linceul du désert est tissé de grains de sable, la pierre du Parthénon a tout de même été sculptée par un peuple de héros.

Les peuples de héros ne défailliront pas! Ils poursuivront jusqu'au châtiment les deux dynasties maudites des Habsbourg et des Hohenzollern. Ils exigeront du pangermanisme assassin toutes les réparations, toutes les restitutions, toutes les garanties. Ils démontreront pour l'éternité que démocratie n'est pas synonyme de désorganisation, et que seuls sont dignes de se proclamer démocraties, et de le rester, les peuples capables d'écraser à la fois l'anarchie au dedans et l'autocratie au dehors.

Text 4: L. Daudet, *L'Action Française,* 16 Oct. 1916

Le Scandale des "Lombard-Laborde"
Qu'attend-on pour les récupérer?

J'ai lu dans l'*Officiel* le compte-rendu *in extenso* de la séance de vendredi à la Chambre, la discussion des effectifs, le discours fort intéressant de M. Mourier, les interventions de MM. Poirier de Narçay et Galli à propos des juifs russes réfractaires, QUI CONTINUENT À INFESTER CERTAINS QUARTIERS DE PARIS, ALORS QUE DES CONTINGENTS RUSSES SONT INCORPORÉS DANS L'ARMÉE FRANCAISE! C'est extravagant. Ce qui ne l'est pas moins, c'est … qu'il n'ait été fait la moindre allusion, au cours de cette séance, à la récupération des apaches de presse et des apaches tout court qu'ont maintenus dans l'exemption ou réformés à tour de bras, depuis le début de la guerre, ces criminels de droit commun qui s'appellent le docteur Lombard, le docteur Laborde et le "docteur Georges" ou Garfunkel. Vigo, directeur du Torchon—lui qui ignore les éléments de l'orthographe!—et ses acolytes sont cependant connus et signalés à la Chambre, où ils arpentaient fièrement, jusqu'à ces derniers temps, les couloirs et le salon de la Paix. Ces gaillards, dont quelques-uns, Vigo en tête, utilisent le profitable pseudonyme afin de dérouter l'État civil, ces gaillards ont visiblement l'âge et les moyens physiques de l'incorporation.

Il n'est pas un député qui ne sache que Lombard était l'ami et le collaborateur de Vigo, qu'il a trifouillé au Torchon, qu'il a lancé dans le Torchon l'idée d'une fête à Rouget de Lisle, que le Torchon a protesté comme un beau diable—au nom de l'union sacrée!—contre l'arrestation de Lombard et de ses complices. Les textes sont là. Nous les avons reproduits maintes fois. Il n'est pas un député qui ne sache que le Torchon à Vigo était et est demeuré une usine de permis de séjour, de passeports maquillés, de réformes frauduleuses, dont ont bénéficié de nombreux lascars, en même temps qu'un succédané de la *Gazette des Ardennes* à Paris. Au moment même où j'écris, le Torchon procède à un bizarre rabattage des exemptés et réformés, inquiets de la possibilité d'un nouveau conseil de révision, et a institué une "permanence" à cet effet. Il y aurait lieu de rechercher ce qui se trame derrière cette nouvelle manigance. Il y aurait lieu surtout d'empoigner d'une main ferme Vigo et certains de ses collaborateurs, d'examiner avec soin, pièces en mains, leur situation militaire, de relever les noms des médecins qui les ont, depuis le début de la guerre, maintenus dans l'exemption ou réformés, et CELA A LA LUMIÈRE DU PROCÈS LOMBARD, LABORDE ET CIE. Je répète qu'on arriverait ainsi à un résultat intéressant.

Par une manœuvre aisément compréhensible, renouvelée des voleurs à l'esbrouffe, ces lombardards, ces labordés et ces garfunkelisés sont précisément ceux qui crient le plus fort à l'embusquage ... qui reprochent le plus amèrement à celui-ci ou à celui-là, qui a passé l'âge, de ne pas avoir rejoint les drapeaux, qui insultent des combattants de première ligne comme Maurice Pujo ou le fils de Barrès. Cet alibi ignoble est couramment employé à l'heure actuelle par une demi-douzaine de torchonnets qui gravitent autour du Torchon et qui obéissent à un mot d'ordre. Il s'agit de chercher à déconsidérer ou à décourager les écrivains patriotes et d'allumer des querelles civiles, susceptibles de dégénérer en troubles et en agitations. S'il n'y avait pas eu la censure et la fermeté de M. Jules Gautier, les choses eussent pris une autre direction, plus ouvertement boche, sans doute; mais la vigilance de la censure a rendu impraticable maint projet criminel, et c'est pourquoi l'on se rabat aujourd'hui, dans ce monde spécial, sur les jets de boue et chienneries en question.

Il est néanmoins paradoxal que des repris de justice comme Vigo—qui n'a pas atteint la quarantaine et qui se donne comme un costaud, comme un excellent tireur de browning, selon les traditions du milieu—demeurent à l'abri de tout appel et qu'il en soit de même pour les individus, encore plus jeunes que lui, qui gravitent autour de ce chef de bande. A quoi correspondent ces étranges faveurs? Comment demeurent-elles encore possibles, au vingt-septième mois de la guerre, parmi l'hécatombe de tant de braves gens, utiles à leur pays, de toutes professions et de tous les niveaux de la société? Il y a là une énigme extraordinaire. Ce qui n'est pas moins extra-ordinaire, c'est que cette énigme n'ait pas encore tenté, comme dit le baron Pié, la curiosité du législateur, et qu'on n'ait pas encore regardé d'un peu près les livrets militaires de ces messieurs plus que suspects et qui mènent si grand tapage dans leurs divers papiers hygiéniques, à une heure où le papier est si cher. Il y a eu, depuis le début de la guerre, chez nous, des cas singuliers. Je n'en connais point de plus singuliers que ceux-là. Nous verrons bien si cette situation invraisemblable pourra se prolonger impunément jusqu'à la fin des hostilités, si la pègre de l'Antifrance—constituée comme telle avant la guerre—si la pègre à la solde de l'Allemagne demeurera tranquillement tabou, sur son tas de crottin, sous l'œil bienveillant du gendarme.

Je connais un certain nombre de bons citoyens qui commencent à la trouver mauvaise. On nous serine quotidiennement avec cette question des embusqués, qui trouve un terrain favorable dans l'*invidia* démocratique. Qu'on commence donc par débusquer la crapule!

Text 5: G. Clairet, *Le Bonnet Rouge*, 29 June, 1917

Offensive Réactionnaire

Les républicains,—les vrais, les rouges, ceux qui ne veulent ni d'une République césarienne, ni d'une République cléricale, ni d'une République militaire,—payent aujourd'hui la faute qu'ils ont commise le jour où ils ont pris leurs adversaires pour des hommes de parole.

Le pas de clerc est impardonnable, autant qu'inexplicable.

Les républicains ne peuvent pas se plaindre d'avoir été trompés: leurs ennemis sont déloyaux, certes, mais si obstinément déloyaux que cette déloyauté systématique, opiniâtre et régulière devient presque de la loyauté, tant elle est prévue.

[Censored passage]

Les royalistes, sous la Révolution, passèrent à l'étranger et prirent du service dans les rangs ennemis, n'hésitant point à frapper la France pour être plus sûrs de ne pas manquer la République.

Autre guerre: la guerre de 1870. Cette guerre, au cours de laquelle les patriotes professionnels qui sont aujourd'hui sénateurs restèrent bravement à l'arrière; les royalistes, cette fois, n'eurent pas à se donner la peine d'aller chercher l'étranger hors de France pour le prier de rapporter le roi dans leurs fourgons; l'étranger était venu tout seul; mais tandis que les républicains, groupés autour de Gambetta, s'employaient à repousser l'envahisseur, à lui arracher des lambeaux de territoire qu'il convoitait et sur lesquels il avait mis la main, les royalistes et leurs amis, les cléricaux, parcouraient les campagnes de l'arrière, semaient l'épouvante au cœur des paysans et réussissaient à faire élire cette Assemblée de Bordeaux, qui fut la plus belle collection de réacteurs qui ait jamais été exposée.

Les républicains auraient dû être assagis par ces deux expériences, et par quelques autres.

La guerre de 1914 les trouva pourtant aussi naïfs. Le fléau s'était à peine abattu sur notre malheureux pays, que la réaction invitait les républicains à mettre bas les armes.

"Réconciliation générale! Union Sacrée!"

Vous connaissez les formules. Les républicains "marchèrent". Ils consentirent à voir les garanties constitutionnelles suspendues; ils ne protestèrent pas quand le Parlement républicain fut dépouillé de ses droits et de ses attributions.

[Censored passage]

On n'eut pas à attendre longtemps les résultats de cette "fraternisation", comme on dit au pays d'où M. Albert Thomas nous revient.

Républicains et réacteurs échangeaient des fleurs, mais les hommes de l'Église et du Roy cachaient des poignards et des aspics dans leurs bouquets.

La presse républicaine ne songeait qu'à entretenir l'ardeur patriotique des citoyens-soldats. La presse monarchiste et cléricale s'employait habilement à réveiller les passions politiques et religieuses des curés et de leurs amis.

Les partis républicains se disloquaient; leurs troupes se dispersaient; radicaux, socialistes, ne voulaient plus connaître qu'un nom: Français; les rares groupes qui survivaient à l'union sacrée se consacraient exclusivement à des œuvres de solidarité.

Le *Bonnet Rouge* a dit, à plusieurs reprises, ce qu'avait été la vie des grandes organisations républicaines pendant la guerre; tout ce qu'elles firent, ce fut de secourir les réfugiés, de recueillir les blessés, d'aider les réformés.

Les ligues réactionnaires, au contraire, profitaient de l'abstention politique de leurs adversaires pour se développer et se fortifier, recruter des adhérents et ramasser de l'argent.

Est-il nécessaire de rappeler les multiples conférences et les intrigues incessantes des césariens de la Ligue des Patriotes?

Les souscriptions et les campagnes de la Ligue royaliste d'*Action Française*?

Les souscriptions et la propagande des moines assomptionnistes de la *Croix* et de la *Bonne Presse?*

Nous recueillons aujourd'hui les fruits de cette politique de dupes. Ils sont plutôt amers.

Toutes les forces de la réaction lancent un assaut furieux contre les républicains désorganisés, en attendant de s'en prendre à la République elle-même.

Comme toujours, c'est la calomnie que la réaction emploie le plus volontiers.

Un fleuve de boue traîne ses flots nauséabonds dans la presse de Paris.

[Censored passage]

Mais les républicains ont enfin compris.

Et je crois que leur réveil, cette fois, sera terrible.

Il le faut.

S'il ne s'agissait que de défendre des personnes, ou même des partis, l'effort serait déjà nécessaire.

Mais il l'est d'autant plus que ce qui est menacé, quand on menace des partis républicains, c'est l'existence même du régime et l'honneur du pays.

Appendix III

NEWSPAPERS AND THEIR CIRCULATION

This appendix lists the periodical sources quoted, and gives their circulation where this is known.

The figures (in thousands) are taken from P. Albert, G. Feyel, and J.-F. Picard, *Documents pour l'histoire de la presse nationale au XIXᵉ et XXᵉ siècles*, Paris, 1977, pp. 60-2.

	1 July 1917	1 Oct. 1917	1 Nov. 1917	1 Aug. 1918
L'Action Française	42.5	48	156	78
La Bataille[1]	13	10	11	8.9
Le Bonnet Rouge[2]	24			
L'Écho de Paris	668	488	433	421
L'Éveil	5.7	17	20	15
L'Événement	11.5	7	9	6.8
L'Homme Enchaîné[3]	44	37	45	65
L'Humanité	85	60	66	60
Le Journal	1208	795	885	766
La Lanterne	4.2	3.2	5.8	7
La Libre Parole	19	22	20	19
Le Matin	1490	1034	999	1051
L'Œuvre	125	105	108	105
Paris-Midi	29	18	19	23
Le Pays[4]	78	64	64	44
Le Petit Journal	721	524	515	452
Le Populaire		10.5	11	25
Le Rappel	13	13	13	13

[1] Called *La Bataille Syndicaliste* until 3 Nov. 1915.

[2] Suppressed on 12 July 1917.

[3] Clemenceau gave this title to *L'Homme Libre* between 8 Oct. 1914 and 17 Nov. 1917.

[4] Founded on 1 June 1917.

	1 July 1917	1 Oct. 1917	1 Nov. 1917	1 Aug. 1918
Le Temps	62	58	58	61
La Tranchée Républicaine	16			
La Vérité				20
La Victoire[5]	91	75	67	72

L'Action Socialiste (founded on 27 Sept. 1916)
Le Canard Enchaîné (founded on 4 Sept. 1915)[6]
La Feuille
La Gazette des Ardennes (published at Charleville)
L'Illustration
Le Mercure de France
Les Nations
La Revue des Deux Mondes
La Semaine Littéraire
La Voix Nationale (appeared from 5 Feb. to 22 June 1918)

A description of the French press in 1914-18 is given in C. Bellanger et al., *Histoire générale de la presse française*, vol. iii, Paris, 1972, part 3, chapter 4. See also *Grande Guerre. Nomenclature des journaux, revues et périodiques français paraissant en France et en langue française à l'étranger*, Paris, L'Argus de la Presse, 1917.

Some collections of wartime articles published in book form are included in my Bibliography for ease of consultation. See under J. Bainville, M. Barrès, G. Clemenceau, G. Hervé, H. Lavedan and Ch. Maurras.

The Russian sources quoted are: *Pravda, Rech'*, and *Sovremennyĭ Mir*, published in Petrograd; *Nashe Slovo, Novosti, Rossiya i Svoboda*, and *Zhizn'*, published in Paris; *Sotsial-Demokrat*, published in Geneva.

[5] Hervé changed the name of *La Guerre Sociale* to *La Victoire* on 1 Jan. 1916.
[6] See C. Estier, *La Gauche hebdomadaire 1914-1962*, Paris, 1962, pp. 16-23.

BIBLIOGRAPHY OF WORKS CITED[1]

Akademiya Nauk SSSR. Slovar' literaturnogo yazika, 17 vols. Moscow-Leningrad, 1950-65.

ALBERT, P., FEYEL, G., and PICARD, J.-F. *Documents pour l'histoire de la presse nationale aux XIXe et XXe siècles*, Paris, 1977.

ALEXINSKY, G. *La Russie moderne*, Paris, 1912 (revised edn., 1915).

La Russie et la guerre, Paris, 1915 (2nd edn., revised, 1915).

La Russie et l'Europe, Paris, 1917.

"Le 'défaitisme'. L'origine d'un néologisme", *La Renaissance politique, littéraire, artistique*, 5 Aug. 1922.

Du Tsarisme au communisme. La révolution russe: ses causes et ses effets, Paris, 1923.

Souvenirs d'un condamné à mort, Paris, 1923.

Un Quart de siècle de régime communiste, Clermont-Ferrand, 1941.

La Russie révolutionnaire, des émeutes de la Russie agraire à l'organisation stalinienne, Paris, 1947.

"'Défaitisme'. Naissance et vie d'un néologisme". *Vie et Langage*, Dec. 1957, 538-47.

ALEXINSKY, G. et al. *Voǐna. Sbornik stateǐ*, Paris, 1915.

BAINVILLE, J. *Journal inédit (1914)*, Paris, 1953.

(ed.) *La Presse et la guerre. L'Action Française. Choix d'articles*, Paris, 1915.

Comment est née la révolution russe, Paris, 1917.

Histoire de France, Paris, 1924.

BALLY, Ch. *Linguistique générale et linguistique française*, Paris, 1932 (4th edn., revised, Berne, 1965).

BARBUSSE, H. *Carnet de guerre (1915)*, Paris, 1965.

Le Feu. Journal d'une escouade, Paris, 1916 (1965 edn.).

Paroles d'un combattant. Articles et discours (1917-1920), Paris, s.a.

---

[1] Periodical sources are listed separately in Appendix III.

BARRÈS, M. *L'Âme française et la guerre*, 11 vols., Paris, 1915-20 (articles contributed to *L'Écho de Paris*).

Les Diverses Familles spirituelles de la France, Paris, 1917.

En regardant au fond des crevasses, Paris, 1917.

Mes Cahiers, vol. xi (June 1914-Dec. 1918), Paris, 1938.

Chronique de la Grande Guerre (1914-1920), ed. G. Dupré, Paris, 1968 (articles contributed to *L'Écho de Paris*).

BARRÈS, M. and MAURRAS, Ch. *La République ou le roi. Correspondance inédite (1888-1923)*, Paris, 1970.

BECKER, J.-J. *Le Carnet B. Les pouvoirs publics et l'antimilitarisme avant la guerre de 1914*, Paris, 1973.

BELLANGER, C. et al. *Histoire générale de la presse française*, vol. iii, Paris, 1972.

BENVENISTE, E. "*Civilisation*. Contribution à l'histoire du mot", in *Problèmes de linguistique générale*, Paris, 1966, pp. 336-45.

Bloch-Wartburg = BLOCH, O. and WARTBURG, W. von. *Dictionnaire étymologique de la langue française*, 6th edn., Paris, 1975.

Bol'shaya sovetskaya entsiklopediya, 1st edn., 65 vols. and supplement, Moscow, 1926-47.

BONNAFFÉ, E. *Dictionnaire étymologique et historique des anglicismes et des anglo-américanismes*, Paris, 1920.

BONNEFOUS, G. *Histoire politique de la Troisième République*, vol. ii, *La Grande Guerre (1914-1918)*, Paris, 1957 (2nd edn., revised, 1967).

BOURGET, P. *Le Sens de la mort*, Paris, 1915.

BRASILLACH, R. *Une Génération dans l'orage. Mémoires: notre avant-guerre. Journal d'un homme occupé*, Paris, 1968.

BROGAN, D. W. *The Development of Modern France (1870-1939)*, London, 1940.

BRUNOT, F. *Histoire de la langue française des origines à 1900*, vol. ix. 2, Paris, 1943.

Les Mots témoins de l'histoire, Paris, 1928.

Cahiers de Lexicologie, xiii-xv (1968-9): *Formation et aspects du vocabulaire politique français, xvi*^{e}*-xx*^{e} *siècles*.

CAHM, E. *Péguy et le nationalisme français, de l'affaire Dreyfus à la Grande Guerre*, Paris, 1972.

CAILLAUX, J. *Mes Prisons*, 2nd edn., Paris, 1920.

CLEMENCEAU, G. *La France devant l'Allemagne*, Paris, 1916 (articles contributed to *L'Homme Libre* and *L'Homme Enchaîné*).

Discours de guerre, Paris, 1934 (revised edn., 1968).

DARMESTETER, A. *De la Création actuelle de mots nouveaux dans la langue française et des lois qui la régissent,* Paris, 1877.

DAUDET, L. *L'Avant-Guerre,* Paris, 1913.
  La Guerre totale, Paris, 1918.
  Le Poignard dans le dos. Notes sur l'affaire Malvy, Paris, 1918.
  L'Hécatombe. Récits et souvenirs politiques (1914-1918), Paris, 1923.
  La Pluie de sang. Nouveaux souvenirs (1914-1918), Paris, 1932 (contains dated material).

DAUZAT, A. *L'Argot de la guerre,* Paris, 1918 (revised edn., 1919).
  Le Génie de la langue française, Paris, 1947.
  Précis d'histoire de la langue et du vocabulaire français, Paris, 1949.
  Dauzat = Dictionnaire étymologique de la langue française, 10th edn., Paris, 1954.

Dauzat-Dubois-Mitterand = DAUZAT, A., DUBOIS, J., and MITTERAND, H. *Nouveau Dictionnaire étymologique et historique,* Larousse, 1964 (2nd edn., 1971).

DÉCHELETTE, F. *L'Argot des poilus. Dictionnaire humoristique et philologique du langage des soldats de la Grande Guerre de 1914,* Paris, 1918.

DEROY, L. *L'Emprunt linguistique,* Paris, 1956.

Dictionnaire biographique du mouvement ouvrier français, troisième partie: 1871-1914, vols. x-xv, Paris, 1973-7.

Dictionnaire des parlementaires français, 8 vols., Paris, 1960-77.

DORGELÈS, R. *Les Croix de bois,* Paris, 1919 (Livre de Poche edn., 1964).

DUBOIS, J. "Problèmes de méthode en lexicologie. Les notions d'unité sémantique complexe et de neutralisation dans le lexique", *Cahiers de Lexicologie,* ii (1960), 62-6.
  Étude sur la dérivation suffixale en français moderne et contemporain, Paris, 1962.
  Le Vocabulaire politique et social en France de 1869 à 1872, Paris, 1962.

DUBOIS, J. and DUBOIS, C. *Introduction à la lexicographie:le dictionnaire,* Paris, 1971.

DUMONT, Ch. *Patrie et internationalisme,* Bourges, 1894.

Entsiklopedicheskiĭ Slovar' Russkogo Bibliograficheskogo Instituta Granat, 7th edn., vol. ii and Supplement, Moscow, 1910 and 1936.

ESNAULT, G. *Le Poilu tel qu'il se parle. Dictionnaire des termes récents et neufs employés aux armées en 1914-1918 étudiés dans leur étymologie, leur développement et leur usage*, Paris, 1919.

Dictionnaire des Argots, Larousse, 1965.

ESTIER, C. *La Gauche hebdomadaire 1914-1962,* Paris, 1962.

FAYOLLE, Marshal M.-E. *Cahiers secrets de la Grande Guerre,* Paris, 1964.

FERRY, A. *Les Carnets secrets (1914-1918)*, Paris, 1957.

F.E.W. = WARTBURG, W. von. *Französisches etymologisches Wörterbuch. Eine Darstellung des falloromanischen Sprachschatzes,* Basel, 1922-

FIELD, F. *Three French Writers and the Great War. Barbusse. Drieu La Rochelle. Bernanos. Studies in the Rise of Communism and Fascism*, Cambridge, 1975.

FIELD, T. J. "The Concept of La Patrie in French Writing 1898-1914". Unpublished doctoral thesis submitted to the University of Wales (Aberystwyth), 1972.

FLETCHER, D. "The Emergence of *Patriotisme*", *Semasia,* 4 (1977), 1-14.

GAILLARD, G. "Langue et guerre", *Revue de philologie française,* XXX. 1 (1917), 19-32.

GIDE, A. *Journal (1889-1939)*, Paris, 1939.

GOULEMOT, J. M. "Emplois du mot *Révolution* dans les traductions françaises du XVIIIᵉ siècle des Discours de Nicolas Machiavel", *Cahiers de Lexicologie*, xiii (1968), 75-82.

GOYAU, G. *L'Idée de patrie et l'humanitarisme,* Paris, 1902.

Grande Guerre.Nomenclature des journaux, revues et périodiques français paraissant en France et en langue française à l'étranger, Paris, L'Argus de la Presse, 1917.

GREIMAS, A. J. and MONNOT, R. "Datations nouvelles. Notes lexicologiques", *Le Français Moderne,* xxiii (1955), 137-44.

GRIFFITHS, R. *Marshal Pétain,* London, 1970.

GUILBERT, L. *La Formation du vocabulaire de l'aviation,* Paris, 1965.

La Créativité lexicale, Paris, 1975.

GUILLEMINAULT, G. *La France de la Madelon, 1914-18. Le roman vrai de l'Arrière*, Paris, 1965.

GUIRAUD, P. *La Sémantique,* Paris, 1955.

HANSI (WARTZ, J. J.) and TONNELAT, E. *A travers les lignes ennemies. Trois années d'offensive contre le moral allemand,* Paris, 1922.

HERVÉ, G. *Mes Crimes, ou onze ans de prison pour délits de presse,* Paris, 1912.

La Grande Guerre au jour le jour. Recueil in extenso des articles publiés dans "la Guerre Sociale" et "la Victoire" depuis juillet 1914, 5 vols., Paris, 1917-21.

HERVÉ, G. and HARTMANN, L. *Le Général et le lieutenant. Correspondance entre G. Hervé et L. Hartmann,* Geneva, 1917.

HOPE, T. E. "Loan-words as Cultural and Lexical Symbols", *Archivum Linguisticum,* xiv (1962), 111-21, and xv (1963), 29-42.

"The Process of Neologism Reconsidered with Reference to Lexical Borrowings in Romance", *Transactions of the Philological Society,* 1964, 46-84.

Lexical Borrowing in the Romance Languages. A Critical Study of Italianisms in French and Gallicisms in Italian from 1100-1900, 2 vols., Oxford, 1971.

HORNE, A. *The Price of Glory. Verdun 1916,* London, 1962.

IDT, G. "'L'Intellectuel' avant l'affaire Dreyfus". *Cahiers de Lexicologie,* xv (1969), 35-46.

JOHNSTON, W. M. "The Origin of the Term 'Intellectuals' in French Novels and Essays of the 1890's", *Journal of European Studies,* iv (1974), 43-56.

KATKOV, G. *Russia 1917. The February Revolution,* London, 1967 (Fontana edn., 1969).

KIPARSKY, V. *Russische historische Grammatik,* vol. iii, Heidelberg, 1975.

KIZEVETTER, A. *Istoricheskie otkliki,* Moscow, 1915.

KRIEGEL, A. *Aux Origines du communisme français (1914-1920),* 2 vols., Paris, 1964.

KRIEGEL, A. and BECKER, J.-J. *1914. La guerre et le mouvement ouvrier français,* Paris, 1964.

KUPFERMAN, A. "Le Rôle de Léon Daudet et de l'Action Française dans ia contre-offensive morale: 1915-1918", *Études Maurrassiennes,* vol. ii, Aix-en-Provence, 1973, pp. 121-44.

"Les Débuts de l'offensive morale allemande contre la France (déc. 1914 - déc. 1915)", *Revue Historique,* 505 (1973), 91-114.

"L'Opinion française et le défaitisme pendant la Grande Guerre", *Relations Internationales,* 1974 (2), 91-100.

"Les Campagnes défaitistes en France et en Italie: 1914-1917", in *La France et l'Italie pendant la première guerre mondiale. Actes du colloque tenu à l'Université des Sciences Sociales de Grenoble en septembre 1973,* Grenoble, 1976, pp. 246-59.

Langages, 23: *Le Discours politique* (1971).

Langue Française, 9: *Linguistique et société* (1971).

Larousse = LAROUSSE, P. *Grand Dictionnaire universel du XIXᵉ siècle,* 15 vols., Paris, 1866-76, Supplements 1877 and 1890.

Larousse Mensuel illustré, Paris, 1907-57.

LASKINE, E. *L'Internationale et le pangermanisme,* Paris, 1916.

LASSWELL, H. D. *Propaganda Technique in the World War,* London-New York, 1927.

LAVEDAN, H. *Les Grandes Heures (1914-1919),* 6 vols., Paris, 1915-21 (articles contributed to *L'Illustration*).

LAURE, General E. *Pétain,* Paris, 1941.

LENIN, V. I. *Polnoe Sobranie Sochineniĭ,* 5th edn., vols. 26-35, Moscow, 1961-2.

Lexis. Dictionnaire de la langue française, Larousse, 1975.

Littré = LITTRÉ, E. *Dictionnaire de la langue française,* 4 vols., Paris, 1863-73, Supplement 1877.

LYONS, J. *Semantics,* 2 vols., Cambridge, 1977.

MACKENZIE, F. *Les Relations de l'Angleterre et de la France d'après le vocabulaire,* 2 vols., Paris, 1939.

MAILHOS, G. "Le Mot *Révolution* dans l'*Essai sur les mœurs* et la correspondance de Voltaire", *Cahiers de Lexicologie,* xiii (1968), 84-93.

MALVY, L.-J. *Mon Crime,* Paris, 1921.

MARCELLESI, J.-B. "La Délimitation des unités lexicales dans le vocabulaire politique et social", *Wissenschaftliche Zeitschrift, Martin-Luther Universität Halle-Wittenberg,* xix, 3/4 (1970), 41-8.

MARCHAND, L. *L'Offensive morale des Allemands en France pendant la guerre. L'assaut de l'âme française,* Paris, 1920.

MAROUZEAU, J. *Aspects du français,* Paris, 1950.

MATORÉ, G. "Le néologisme: naissance et diffusion", *Le Français Moderne,* xx (1952), 87-92.

La Méthode en lexicologie. Domaine français, Paris, 1953 (revised edn., 1973).

MAURRAS, Ch. *Quand les Français ne s'aimaient pas. Chronique d'une renaissance, 1895-1905,* Paris, 1916.

Les Conditions de la victoire (*1914-1916*), 4 vols., Paris, 1916-18 (articles contributed to *L'Action Française*).

La Part du combattant, Paris, 1917 (articles contributed to *L'Action Française* from Oct. 1916 to Apr. 1917).

Les Chefs socialistes pendant la guerre, Paris, 1918 (articles contributed to *L'Action Française* from Jan. 1916 to Sept. 1917).

Dictionnaire politique et critique, ed. P. Chardon, 5 vols., Paris, 1932.

MAXE, J. *De Zimmerwald au bolchevisme, ou le triomphe du marxisme pangermaniste*, Paris, 1920.

L'Anthologie des défaitistes, 2 vols., Paris, 1925.

MAZON, A. *Lexique de la guerre et de la révolution en Russie*, Paris, 1920.

MIGLIORINI, B. *The Contribution of the Individual to Language*, Oxford, 1952.

NORTON CRU, J. *Témoins. Essai d'analyse et de critique des souvenirs de combattants édités en français de 1915 à 1928*, Paris, 1929.

Nouveau Larousse universel, Paris, 1948.

NYROP, Kr. *Grammaire historique de la langue française*, vol. iii, Copenhagen, 1908.

PALÉOLOGUE, M. *La Russie des Tsars pendant la Grande Guerre*, 3 vols., Paris, 1922.

PÉTAIN, Marshal Ph. *La Crise morale et militaire de 1917*, Paris, 1966.

Petit Robert = ROBERT, P. *Dictionnaire alphabétique et analogique de la langue française*, Paris, 1967.

PIERREFEU, J. de. *G.Q.G. Secteur 1. Trois ans au Grand Quartier Général par le rédacteur du "communiqué"*, 2 vols., Paris, 1920.

POINCARÉ, R. *Au Service de la France*, vol. ix, *L'Année trouble 1917*; vol. x, *Victoire et armistice 1918*, Paris, 1932 and 1933.

PROUST, M. *Le Temps retrouvé*, Paris, 1927 (Pléiade edn., 1968).

PROVOST, G. "Approche du discours politique: *socialisme* et *socialiste* chez Jaurès", *Langages*, 13: *L'Analyse du discours* (1969), 51-68.

QUEMADA, B. *Matériaux pour l'histoire du vocabulaire français. Datations et documents lexicographiques,* deuxième série *1-* . Paris, 1970-

RÉMOND, R. *La Droite en France de la première restauration à la V*ᵉ *République*, vol. i: 1815-1940, 3rd edn., Paris, 1968.

L'Anticléricalisme en France de 1815 à nos jours, Paris, 1976.

RHEIMS, M. *Dictionnaire des mots sauvages*, Paris, 1969.

RIFFATERRE, M. "La Durée de la valeur stylistique du néologisme", *Romanic Review*, xiv (1953), 282-9.

Robert = ROBERT, P. *Dictionnaire alphabétique et analogique de la langue française. Les mots et les associations d'idées*, 6 vols., Paris, 1951-64, Supplement 1972.

ROLLAND, R. *Journal des années de guerre 1914-1919. Notes et documents pour servir à l'histoire morale de l'Europe de ce temps*, Paris, 1952.

L'Esprit libre. Au-dessus de la mêlée; les précurseurs, Paris, 1953.

ROUX, Marquis M. de. *Le Défaitisme et les manœuvres pro-allemandes*, Paris, 1918.

SAINÉAN, L. *L'Argot des Tranchées*, Paris, 1915.

SANCERME, Ch. *Les Serviteurs de l'ennemi*, Paris, 1917.

Les Batailles de l'arrière. Cinq mois sur la brèche, Paris, 1918.

SCHERER, A. and GRUNEWALD, J. (eds.) *L'Allemagne et les problèmes de la paix. Documents extraits des archives de l'Office allemand des Affaires Étrangères*, 4 vols., Paris, 1962-78.

SLATER, C. "Note critique sur l'origine de *défaitisme* et *défaitiste*", *Mots (Mots, Ordinateurs, Textes, Sociétés)*, i (1980), 213-17.

[SNELL, V.] "*Le Jardin de Marrès*, par Bérénice", Paris, 1916.

SPENCE, N. C. W. "Linguistic Fields, Conceptual Systems and the *Weltbild*", *Transactions of the Philological Society*, 1961, 85-106.

STEVENSON, C. L. *Ethics and Language*, New Haven-London, 1944.

T.L.F. = *Trésor de la langue française: dictionnaire de la langue du XIX*ᵉ *et du XX*ᵉ *siècle, 1789-1960*, I- , Paris, 1971- .

TOUCHARD, J. *Histoire des idées politiques*, 2 vols., 3rd edn., Paris, 1967.

La Gauche en France depuis 1900, Paris, 1977.

TOURNIER, M. "Le Centre de recherche de lexicologie politique de l'E.N.S. de Saint-Cloud", *Langue Française*, 2: *Le Lexique* (1969), 82-86.

"Éléments pour l'étude quantitative d'une journée de 48", *Cahiers de Lexicologie*, xiv (1969), 77-114.

Travaux de lexicométrie et de lexicologie politique. Bulletin du laboratoire d'étude des textes politiques français, i-iii (1976-8), continued as *Mots* (*Mots, Ordinateurs, Textes, Sociétés*), i- (1980-).

VALOIS, G. (GRESSENT, A. G.) *Le Cheval de Troie*, Paris, 1918.

WAGNER, R.-L. *Les Vocabulaires français*, vol. i: *Définitions. Les Dictionnaires*; vol. ii: *Tâches de la lexicologie synchronique*, Paris, 1967 and 1970.

WALDRON, R. A. *Sense and Sense Development*, London, 1967.

WARTBURG, W. von. See *F.E.W.*

WEBER, E. J. *Action Française. Royalism and Reaction in Twentieth-century France*, Stanford, 1962.

WELDON, T. D. *States and Morals*, London, 1946 (1962 reissue).

WELLS, H. G. *The War that will end War*, London, 1914.

WILLIAMS, J. *Mutiny 1917*, London, 1962.

ZEMAN, Z. A. B. (ed.) *Germany and the Revolution in Russia 1915-1918. Documents from the Archives of the German Foreign Ministry*, London, 1958.

INDEX

INDEX

Kerensky, A. F. 59
Kienthal conference 58
kient(h)alien 17, 60, 61
kient(h)alisme 72
kient(h)aliste 60 n.
Kizevetter, A. A. 46
Kompères et Komplices 29-31
Kub, bouillon 29-30
Kupferman, A. 2 n., 43 n., 100 n.

Laborde 183-5
  labordé 184
La Chesnais, P.-G. 46 n., 91
La Fayette, marquis de 127
Langevin, E 145
Larousse Mensuel 18, 24 n., 45, 60 n.,
  81 n., 91 n., 95 n., 98, 108, 111-12,
  137 n.
Laskine, E. 54-5, 57 n.
Laure, général 63 n.
lave-, see under proper name
Lavedan, H. 13, 40, 68 n., **176-80**,
  189
Lenin, V.I. 45, 47, 49-50, 53, **57-62**,
  76, 84 n., 85, 93, 112, 158, 165-6
léninisme 82
léniniste 65, 83, 103
Leriche, V. 150
Lévy, L. 152
Leymarie
  lave-Leymarie 90 n.
libertaire 60, 80
Libertaire (Le) 166
Libre Parole (La) 170
Ligue des Patriotes, see *patriote*
Lloyd George, D. 90, 95, 138
Lombard, Dr 73, 183-5
  lombardard 184
Longuet, J. 27-8, 76-7, 115, 132, 137-8
Lorulot, A. 124 n.
Loyson, P. H. 127, 152
Lunacharsky, A. 151
Lyons, J. 117 n.,
Lyubimov, A. 49

Mackenzie, F. 90 n.
Mac-Mahon, maréchal 141
"*Made in Germany*" 31, 58 n., 159
Maggi (international dairy company)
  28, 29-30, 70, 175
Maginot, A. 74 n.
majoritaire 150
Malvy, L.-J. 13, 62, **87-9**, 90 n., 92,
  95 n., 102-3, 167, 168 n.

malvysme 90 n., 93; see also *caillau-
  malvyste*
lave-Malvy 90 n.
Marcellesi, J.-B. 156 n.
Marchand, L. 28, 34, 35 n., 38, **72-3**,
  98, 99, 102, 116, 132, **149**, 164
Marseillaise (la) 39, 182
Martov, Y. O. 47
Matin (Le) 66, 68-9, 107, 188
Matoré, G. 6 n., 110 n.
Maurras, Ch. 8, 10 n., 13, 14, 16,
  17-18, 30, 33, **36 n.**, 38, 39,
  60, 71, 72 n., **73 n.**, 78, 88 n.,
  89, 108, **120-1**, 122, 128, 130-1,
  136, 137-8, 143, 150, 159, 161 n.,
  162, 170, 173, 189
Maxe, J. 54 n., 71 n.,
maximaliste **51 n.**, 53, 59-60
Mazon, A. 46
Mercure de France (Le) 91, 166, 189
militarisme 61, 121, **134-8**, 150, 152,
  158 n., 159, 172
  antimilitarisme 3, **60 n.**, 99, 136
  surmilitarisme 137
militariste 127, 131, **134-8**, 147, 150,
  153, 158, 161 n.
  antimilitariste 25, 63, 77 n., **99**,
  121, 133, 135, 152
Milyukov, P. N. 158
minoritaire 54, 173, 174
mobilisation civile 169
monarchie 121
monarchique 117
monarchisme 119-21
  néo-monarchisme 159
monarchiste 118, **119-21**, 137-8, 156,
  186
  néo-monarchiste 120
Monier 90 n.
Monnot, R. 140
Monzie, A. de 14-15
Mourier, L. 183
Mutinies 1917 **62-8**, 71, 74, 79, 87 n.,
  105, 107, 169

Nashe Slovo (Our Word) 47-9, 54
national 128-9
  antinational 99
nationalard 129
nationalisme 3, 34, 117, **128-34**, 138,
  157, 159-61, 170
nationaliste 3-4, 82, 100, 104, 117-8,
  120, **128-34**, 137, 155, 156, 157,
  159, 160-1, 174, 175